THE AUNT EDWINA SERIES – BOOK 4

Aunt Edwina
Would Be Shocked

A family history novel

Lynne Christensen

Aunt Edwina Would Be Shocked
Copyright © 2024 by Northleo Writing Inc.

Published by Northleo Writing Inc.
studio@northleowriting.com

Northleo
WRITING INC.

First Edition - 2024

DISCLAIMER
This is a work of fiction. It is written in the form of a fun, charming, and fictitious genealogical adventure. Names, characters, places, organizations, businesses, and incidents are either products of the author's imagination or are used fictitiously. Any resemblance to actual events, locales, businesses, organizations, or persons, living or dead, is entirely coincidental.

For help with your own genealogy and family history research, please seek guidance from a trained expert at a genealogy organization and/or family history organization. Guidance and many helpful websites, articles, and blog postings are available either for free or via payment from a variety of sources. Note that the research strategies and advice in this work of fiction may not suit every person or family's goals.

Hardcover ISBN: 978-1-998051-06-9

Paperback ISBN: 978-1-998051-07-6

eBook ISBN: 978-1-998051-05-2

Dedication

———

To the Italian from New York:

Always a true friend.

I miss you.

The Aunt Edwina Series – Reading Order

Book 1: Aunt Edwina's Fabulous Wishes

Book 2: Aunt Edwina's Wonderful Legacy

Book 3: An Aunt Edwina Christmas

Book 4: Aunt Edwina Would Be Shocked

Each book can be read as a standalone novel, however, do note that many characters recur throughout the series.

Main Characters (People)

———

Abbyleigh Printhorpe: Fortune teller and coffee foam artist at GGRS.

Bernard 'Bertie' Preswick, Fourteenth Duke of Conroy: Julie Fincher's aristocratic art patron. Incredibly wealthy owner of Scotford Castle estate near Oakhurst, Kent and a country house in Brambleford, near Medchester, Kent. Reliable friend of all family history adventurers who need help getting out of incredibly outrageous scrapes.

Candace Blightly: Daughter of Doctor Tessa Blightly. Currently serves as her mother's mobile research assistant.

Constable Bud Snowdrop: Police constable trying to make his mark but forever blotting his copybook.

Detective Thomas Brondyn: No nonsense senior detective who has Constable Snowdrop's number.

Donald Jerome Fincher: Julie Fincher's father. Retired furniture shop manager.

Earl Bovinks: London auction house host with a penchant for secretive furniture.

Ewan Kilburn: Owner/operator of Kilburn's Outstanding Antiques in Plumsden, Kent. Kind, handsome Scotsman who serves as treasurer of the Plumsden Family History Society. Uncle to one piano-playing nephew and one highland-dancing niece.

Finn Severs: Bertie's ex-security service chauffeur trained in evasive driving techniques, bodyguard protection and rescuing his employer's friends.

Frederick 'Fred' Aloysius St. John Todling: Plumsden-based intellectual property solicitor who moonlights as a bookshop minder. Verbose with legalese and opinions. Owns potbellied pig named Barnaby and more.

Gertrude 'Gertie' Porringer a.k.a. 'The Apricot Powerhouse': Boisterous female priest and slightly older cousin to Julie Fincher. Always available for a detailed pedigree chart review and exuberant karaoke.

Greg Farmingham: Non-speaking special needs boy who is fascinated with dinosaurs. Mrs. Farmingham's grandson.

Jacques Lesabrioux: Stoic General Manager of the Greymore Hall estate. Has strong penchant for getting guest services just right.

Jason Raymond: Cybercrime expert and father to Melanie.

Julie Fincher: Twenty-something bohemian style painter. Recent new owner of Greymore Hall and founder of Greymore Genealogy Research Site ('GGRS'). Daughter of Donald Jerome

Fincher. Favorite of Lady Edwina Greymore. Lives in converted barn on Scotford Castle estate near Oakhurst, Kent.

Karl Sommers: Earl Bovinks' expert furniture craftsman.

Lorelei Stoneton: Proprietor of Treemoreland Farm Antiques in Waverly-on-Sea, East Sussex. Curious, organized seller of furniture and bric-a-brac from past centuries.

Mac Bridgemont: Scotford Castle concierge and volunteer guide. Rescuer of wayward garden visitors. All around stalwart on the castle grounds.

Major Barry Whitcombe: Retired military man who uses his pork chop sideburns, vast people network and army expertise to reunite families with their history. Hobby is buying vintage uniforms then rehoming them with proper regimental museums. Based in Medchester, Kent.

Maude Livingstone: President of Plumsden Family History Society. Director of Greymore Genealogy Research Site. A spry senior.

Melanie Raymond: Long lost daughter of a dear friend. She holds no grudges.

Mrs. Farmingham: Grandmother to Greg Farmingham. Hostess to strangers visiting from her cellar.

Oswald "Ozzie" Boggs: Unforgettable Greymore Genealogy Research Site visitor who earned quite a reputation for thriftiness.

Prunella Mayerthorpe: Lead archivist on special floor at Plumsden Archives.

Stephanie Stoneton: Daughter of Lorelei Stoneton who aims to be a textile historian.

Tessa Blightly, PhD: Dinosaur expert in need of help with her memoir.

Timmy Hitchins: Owl fanatic, Chairman of 'O-cubed' and dedicated friend of another GGRS guest with unusual teeth.

List of Characters (Furry Friends)

Barnaby: Potbellied pig often on the lam. Owned by Fred Todling.

Holophusicon "Holly": Galumphing English Sheepdog owned by Fred Todling.

Muscles: Mooching brindled pug owned by a film director.

List of Characters
(Ancestors, Infamous and Portraits)

———

Lady Edwina Greymore: Helped raise Julie Fincher after Julie's mother died. Was family matriarch and aristocratic owner of Greymore Hall estate near Oakhurst, Kent. Community philanthropist connected to all the right people. Left a rich legacy to help anyone interested in researching their family history.

Old Duke of Conroy: Bertie's nineteenth century ancestor who went from riches to rags, to riches again, and no one is really quite sure how ... yet.

Chapter 1

_____

Café, Greymore Genealogy Research Site, Oakhurst, Kent. Mid-April. Morning.

Another day, another ancestor. This was how my life as Julie Fincher evolved since I'd founded the Greymore Genealogy Research Site ('GGRS'). GGRS was a large, modern center on the Greymore Hall estate, a vast country location that spanned 350 acres and boasted walking trails, miniature goats and the final resting place for Aunt Edwina way up on a lovely hill overlooking the Kentish Weald. My grandmother—she insisted we call her Aunt Edwina to feel young—rested there beside her longtime love, thanks to the wonderful family history treasure hunt she'd prepared for my cousin Gertie and I. Aunt Edwina left me the bulk of her estate, trusting me to do the right thing. She adored family history as well as genealogy research, along with all the eccentric characters accompanying forays into the past. I jumped in with both feet, using a good portion of my inheritance to found a community research center open to the public. We helped people research their ancestors, delving long ago in the past. Today, however, was pressing the limits of our capacity.

A pleasant looking woman in her thirties stood before us at the information desk. She had a bright, open face, a gregarious smile and good eye contact. Her hair was styled in a short, curly bob, and the most distinctive thing about her was the way she strode across the floor with great purpose. I wondered if it was nature or nurture that gave her such a strong presence in the room.

"Good morning and welcome to the Greymore Genealogy Research Site. I'm Julie. Can I help you?" I asked.

"Do you work with dinosaurs?" she asked with a grin.

GGRS Manager and spry senior Maude Livingstone took one look at me, arched an eyebrow and said, "Don't you dare."

I grinned and abandoned any idea of a joke. "Not usually, no. Even our computers are super up to date." My mind went a thousand miles an hour to think if any dinosaurs still actually roamed the earth. All I came up with were sharks, a certain type of land lizard, and the Loch Ness monster. Not bad for a two second mind scan.

"Oh no, not real ones. It was just a joke," our visitor said.

"I'm sorry?" Her visit now had both Maude and I confused.

"My mother is a dinosaur expert, just discovered a new Triassic period herbivore and is writing up her memoirs. She's unfortunately stuck at home, recuperating from a back injury. We have a somewhat urgent need to search our family history as her manuscript is due at her publisher in three months' time."

"At least you didn't say three days," I replied. "We get quite a few people through our doors who think their entire family tree is available with one click of a mouse." I looked at our newest visitor, intrigued. "And your name is?"

"Oh my, I am so sorry. I'm Candace Blightly and my mother is Tessa."

"As in Doctor Tessa Blightly from the television?" My mouth sagged a little.

Candace nodded. "That's my mother. Unfortunately, she was filming a segment in the Alberta Badlands, in Canada, near Drumheller, when she slipped on a rock and injured her back. Believe me, flying her home on a hospital stretcher was quite the experience." She shrugged. "We joke that she made sure she got a lie-flat seat."

I smiled. "Your mother is a very impressive lady, quite accomplished." Doctor Blightly was a world-renowned paleontologist who discovered Tyrannosaurus Rex's cousin at the beginning of her career, just after she earned her PhD. She was also responsible for debunking a rare fossil at auction, determining that the specimen was: 1) actually much younger than presented; and 2) artificially dyed to appear authentic. Doctor Blightly's fame and fortune soon followed. She was just as well-known for her amazing illustrated textbooks on the Jurassic period, as she was for her very popular children's book about camping with dinosaurs, chocolate pudding and a rickety, old canoe. Creative and talented, there was no end to her ambition, nor limit to her success.

"Yes, they certainly broke the mold with my mother," Candace said. "She feels quite foolish indeed, slipping on a rock while she was there."

"Alberta, isn't that near the West Coast of Canada?" I asked.

"Yes. It's between British Columbia and Saskatchewan. Alberta is a prairie province known for its year-round sunshine and crisp winters. Drumheller is dinosaur dig central in Alberta and has a world class museum proving it."

"Intriguing. So how can we help you today?" I asked.

"We're working on the social history of the area where my great-great-grandparents grew up. They ran a greengrocer shop that eventually expanded into three other villages. Our understanding is that they opened the first shop right here in Oakhurst."

"So you have done some initial research already?"

"My mother's actually downloaded the digitized records, but with her stuck at home she can't get the ones that aren't online yet. I'm acting as her mobile research assistant, but she is really the expert."

"I have an idea. Our center is up-to-date with the latest technology. We could actually do a videoconference call with your mother to get this project started, if she's comfortable with something like that." I gave Candace a kind look, letting her know it was certainly acceptable to turn down my suggestion if it wasn't appropriate.

"You know," Candace said with a grin, "I think she'd really appreciate that. Do you go above and beyond for all your visitors needing help?"

I smiled. "Strict policy: we only help the ones researching dinosaurs and greengrocers."

Her face dropped. Then she grinned at my joke.

I continued. "My late Aunt Edwina led by example. As children, my cousin Gertie and I always saw her helping others. She was an intense believer in correct genealogy proof standards as well as family history research. This is why I'm so fascinated with social histories of the area, and would love to help with your greengrocer line."

"Oh, that would be fantastic," Candace said. "I'd like to peruse your bookshelves a bit first, get a few facts checked, then perhaps we can arrange a call when I'm a bit more organized? Right now I'm looking for a specific tinned goods supplier located in a nineteenth century village just outside London."

"Of course, peruse away," I said.

Candace smiled and I knew we had gained another dedicated researcher here at GGRS. It made me happy to know that our facility was making a real difference connecting the present with the past.

✻✻✻

Moments Later.

Gertie elbowed me and pointed out eccentric researcher Ozzie Boggs, the man who always had a get-rich-quick-scheme on the go plus a penchant for forgetting his front teeth. Dear Ozzie had fallen asleep at computer carrell number four … again.

Never mind.

GGRS helped anyone and everyone interested in researching their family history. Topics ranged from conserving and preserving photographs, census records, parish registers, genealogy software programs, old crafts, village traditions, seafaring ancestors, obscure wills, odd pronunciations, smudged records … the list of possibilities was endless. We now had a thriving volunteer program, a strong name in the community and a bright future.

Thank goodness we also had a part of the grand old estate—built in 1629—dedicated as a wonderful café. Hot and cold beverages, snacks, meals, desserts were all on offer; we served anything to keep our researchers on-site, happy and well-nourished. Not that a gooey cinnamon bun or thickly-iced brownie were super healthy; management excused our delectable desserts by convincing themselves that visitors had a healthy salad to start ... at least some of the time.

Our new Scottish barista brought new meaning to the words 'let me make you a coffee'. Sure, all of the basic things one expected in their cappuccino were there: coffee, milk, a dash of sugar and artisan foam. What made Abbyleigh Printhorpe's hot beverage counter different from the rest was the fortune telling she did on the side. Well, on the top of the cappuccino, to be exact. Every customer was the recipient of a very skillfully drawn image in their beverage. How Abbyleigh did it with just a spoon and a stir stick amazed everyone, including me. And she did it all under a massive curtain of deep-black, false eyelashes, elegant gray hair in a top knot and claret-colored lipstick. Her clothes were hip, almost a 1960's mod look, and she had the go-go boots to match. Everybody liked her, yet I noted one in particular was slightly less warm to the idea of his future being predicted than the others.

That would be none other than our favorite retired military man, Major Barry Whitcomb. Always dressed in a pressed suit and with porkchop sideburns, the Major was one of our regulars. He could always be counted upon to keep the troops in order, producing a military-like efficiency with any family history research project, no matter the time or place. We'd all warmed up to him after he'd gone overboard correcting things to make up for his glaring faux pas of parking an historical tank in Greymore's back meadow. Not only had the Major finessed the turf repair, his other, most intriguing payback was swift and sweet. Under his riding-crop-slapped-against-the-boot coaching style, my cousin Gertie and I had watched hunky Plumsden antiques dealer Ewan Kilburn, pudgy Constable Bud Snowdrop and verbose solicitor Fred Todling careen around an expert-level, outdoor obstacle course. They'd bragged to us ladies about being able to finish in no time flat … then promptly gave up before an ambulance was needed. Maude, Gertie and I also got our cars vacuumed plus a lengthy archival document transcription done as the final part of the men's penance.

Today the Major was faced with a new hurdle in the form of Abbyleigh. She saw him advance in her queue, and noticed when his prim moustache begin to quiver. I'd seen this behavior from him once before; it happened last week when she drew a lion in his cappuccino and predicted he'd have a romantic week ahead.

Her prediction went over like a ton of broken bricks. The Major thought the psychobabble was preposterous. The Major also found himself in the midst of a rather serious crush on Abbyleigh and didn't know how to proceed. The conversation—I'd watched it all because I happened to be right behind him—had ended abruptly, with a puddle of coffee on both the counter and on the floor. A few splashes went onto the Major's razor-sharp tweed trousers as well. But never mind. He was too dazzled by Abbyleigh and her lovely Scottish accent. The spilt coffee wasn't even noticed until I prodded him in the elbow and brought him back to planet earth. He spluttered apologies and scarpered with his chocolate croissant, never mind the napkins and his change.

The Major was in love.

"Do I detect a delectable daydream occurring right in my midst?" I heard off to my right. A light spring breeze had just wafted inside and entered through the side door.

I turned to see Ewan standing there, a bouquet of fresh, fancy red roses in hand.

"Oh, they're lovely," I said, burying my nose in their scent.

"Yes, indeed." Ewan leaned in close. "Er, they're for Abbyleigh. The Major chickened out at the front door and I'm making a secret admirer delivery on his behalf."

I pulled back, cheeks flaming, like they were freshly painted with creosote. "I see."

"Not that it would be a stretch for you to guess they were for you. From me," he said. "Because you deserve roses. Every day. All days …" He trailed off into gibberish and now held the flowers by his side.

"But they're not." I looked at him, slightly curious at why he was so tongue-tied and appearing eager to put the other foot in his mouth.

"I'm not having a good moment here, am I?" Ewan said, quite forlorn.

Poor Ewan. At this moment, if our burgeoning romance was a report card, he'd receive a failing grade and a teacher's comment *try harder*.

"Oh Julie, there you are. Thank goodness." Maude walked up looking quite distraught. "Bertie's on the telephone. Apparently, the filming's been moved up an hour so we're needed on set much earlier and–"

I switched into super-organized mode. No time for a drawn-out conversation about misleading flowers. "Ewan, Abbyleigh's on break and will be back at the café counter in two minutes. Maude, there's a full vanload of us going up to Scotford Castle to help Bertie as actors in his promotional documentary film. We'll need to make sure someone's in charge of locking the GGRS front door."

"Jacques, remember? He's staying back at the ranch." Ewan offered what he hoped was something helpful in the midst of all this chaos.

"Oh good," Maude said. "I'm all at sixes and sevens trying to remember everything Bertie asked us to bring to his place."

By 'his place', Maude was just ever so casually referring to the expansive—and expensive—Scotford Castle estate owned and operated by our good friend, the Fourteenth Duke of Conroy, Bertie Preswick.

Out of the corner of my eye, I saw the Major lurking in the corner. I gestured for him to come over.

"Has Ewan delivered the flowers yet?" the Major hissed.

"No, I haven't," Ewan said. "Look, you can't namby-pamby this. You can command an elite unit in battle, so you can most certainly stand up straight and deliver these to the woman who has captured your heart."

At first, I thought the Major might give Ewan a dressing down, remind him who was the older of the pair, who was in charge ... but the Major knew it was a conflict he simply wouldn't win. He took the flowers from Ewan and froze in place as we all watched Abbyleigh saunter back into the café and don her apron.

She nodded over in our direction. Then she spied the red roses in the Major's grasp.

Abbyleigh smiled ever so sweetly and then called out, "Major, are those for me?"

His face went beetroot red and he nodded.

"I told you there would be romance in your world soon," she trilled in a sweet voice.

"With my deepest affection, you are most kind," the Major choked out. All of us were waiting for him to give her a salute to finish off his stiff presentation.

Ewan took pity on him and went over to smooth the waters.

Lovely. Two romantic bumblers now in motion.

Maude put her arm through mine and turned us back towards the information desk. "Now, Julie, there's just a few more items I need to go over with you."

Chapter 2

GGRS Information Desk. Thirty Minutes Later.

Maude and I were deep in conversation when we heard a ruckus at the front doors. Both of us looked up to see a skinny man, mid-sixties, rush over to the information desk. He was resplendent in camouflage jacket and matching baggy pants.

Maude assumed the obvious. "I believe you'll find the Major in the café, Sir."

"The Major?" our newest visitor asked. "Is that what you call him?" He had a nervous look about him, underscored by slightly bulgy eyes, a disappearing chin and a very fair ring of hair around his scalp. I noticed a pair of field binoculars slung on a strap across his body.

"Yes. Aren't you a military friend of the Major's?" I asked. It was the logical question to ask, considering he was dressed like a battle-field news reporter.

"Heavens no. I'm Timmy Hitchins, Chairman of the local bird watching club. We're Oakhurst's Obstreperous Ornithologists."

The way Timmy said his last name made it sound like "Itchins". Dropping the 'H' made it sound like the man forever needed a good scratch.

Timmy looked around the room, frantic. "The club's known as 'Oh-Cubed' to insiders."

Three words starting with 'O' in a row. 'Oh-Cubed'. Got it.

"That's quite the club name," Maude observed.

We both should have known better. The very first thing Maude taught us was never to make assumptions in genealogy. Assuming Timmy was here for a military meeting with the Major was just as bad as assuming the first 'Anne Jones' one found on a census was an English ancestor's mother. Reading on, it became obvious that the first 'Anne Jones' died 105 years too early and that the real Anne Jones came from Scotland!

"Do you need help with some genealogy research?" I asked him.

"N-no. I'm here for the owl." He stood up straight, and as he did, his binoculars case banged against his left hip, making him wince.

Maude and I replied in stereo. "The owl?"

"I heard it's in a bedroom here at Greymore."

Now everything made sense. I smiled. "My father had an owl fly into his new suite here at Greymore but it's long gone now. We delicately shepherded it back outside where it belonged in the wild."

"Your father told us that at our latest meeting. He also showed us this picture," Timmy said with angst, hauling out his phone and showing us a crisp photo of the owl. Only then did I notice the odd white streaks underneath one wing. In our haste to get the owl removed from my father's suite, we'd obviously overlooked the plumage color factor.

He continued. "It is extremely rare to have non-uniform color as it makes an owl less hidden from potential prey below its flight path. It's wonderful to see the owl so well fed and healthy. The bird's adapted quite well to its plumage defect, I'd say."

We were family historians and genealogists. Today we'd already discussed dinosaurs. Now we were considering non-standard owl plumage.

I have an urgent need to read a parish register!

"Is perhaps, Julie Fincher here?" Timmy asked.

"I'm Julie," I said, "and Maude's the manager of the research site."

"Pleased to meet you both. Would you mind if my friend and I took a quick walk on the grounds to see if we can ascertain the owl's nesting location?"

"Of course, you're more than welcome to," I said. "There's a well-marked public path out back. Is your friend joining you later?"

"He's actually going with you on the filming bus," Timmy said.

I hadn't counted on any of our lot being keen birders, except for my father and he'd never mentioned Timmy to me.

Timmy continued. "You all know him. It's–"

"Ozzie Boggs." The stocky, balding man said his name with glee, walking in with raised hands and—luckily today—all his teeth. This was the man once convinced he'd been wronged out of ownership of one of the largest confectionery companies in the world when his ancestor's will wasn't correctly probated. Sadly, Maude and Gertie's rigorous genealogy proved Ozzie wrong and it was quite a letdown for him. Still, he'd made some good friends, had a great adventure and now appeared to be a keen birder.

Or was he?

"Been away in Costa Rica spotting toucans," Ozzie said.

Come to think of it, yes, Ozzie was sporting a slight sunburn.

"And now you've returned to do more family history?" Maude asked with a teasing smile. She had quite the sense of humor when she was in her element, like the time when she'd noted how Ozzie was selling day-old scones to GGRS visitors.

"I'm interested in my second cousin. He used to own a bakery–"

"Tell me it wasn't on Pudding Lane," Maude shot back. It would be most fitting if Ozzie's ancestors were the ones who started the Great Fire of London in 1666.

"They never made puddings. Just bread, I think," he replied, in all seriousness. "Alright if Timmy and I have a quick whip round then make it back here on time for the bus to the castle?"

Maude and I must have exchanged an overly obvious glance. No one had quite scrubbed their minds of Ozzie throwing a candied octopus at his solicitor Fred Todling after a disastrous attempt to use muddled genealogy to prove his ownership of the confectionery firm near London.

Ozzie caught our visible apprehension. "Don't worry. I already cleared it with Bertie. He's eager to have Timmy play the part of a skinny court jester for the film."

I grinned. After all, Bertie was the one who paid for Ozzie's bail following the candied octopus incident, mainly because he found out that an old school chum was the confectionery firm's CEO and hadn't upheld their fancy London club's code of honor.

"What the Duke wants, the Duke shall have," I said.

In my heart of hearts, I knew this would make for a very interesting experience.

***

Scotford Castle. 1:30 p.m.

Bertie's ancestral home boasted four-foot-thick stone turrets, fabulous architecture and a plethora of rooms that impressed even the more ardent of hide-and-seek players. The estate was 478 acres large and lovingly tended by a bevy of staff and farmer tenants. Bertie was keen on organic farming, and his produce always tasted better than store-bought. He rented out portions of the venue for weddings; its lovely terrace was surrounded by soaring arches overlooking Scotford Lake and brought in much needed income. I was glad he ran his estate like a profitable enterprise; repairs and maintenance on the castle alone cost a fortune. There was only so much old money in the business bank account; new injections of funds on a regular basis were what kept the estate financially viable.

The GGRS electric van effortlessly glided in beside the collection of film crew work vehicles. Portable dressing room trailers were set up at the side of the parking lot, well away from the front pathway. The walk to the castle involved a bridge over a moat, and was a favorite spot for photos. My guess was that actors, aka 'talent', were subtly told to keep hair, makeup and costuming ministrations away from prime background scenery.

None of our team usually performed excessive primping and fussing over ourselves at the mirror. I could count on one hand the number of people who came in wearing full makeup to do their genealogy research. The large majority of family historians simply believed that it came down to practical choice: paint one's face OR get an extra hour per day to research fascinating ancestors.

"I know where my vote goes," I said absentmindedly, putting the van into park.

"Pardon?" Gertie asked. My cousin was a jolly priest in charge of youth ministering for her region of England.

I blinked and grinned. "Sorry, I spoke without thinking. Those dressing rooms made me think of all the goop they're going to put on our faces."

"Never doubt the power of the smokey eye," Gertie said.

"When applied correctly and as necessary, yes." I gave her a stern look. "The last time you wore a smokey eye was on a super-hot day. It all melted and made you look like you'd been in a boxing match."

"But it looked good at the beginning, didn't it?" Gertie asked, somewhat desperate for vindication.

Ewan leaned forward from the bench behind us. "Ladies, may I suggest we leave hair and makeup to the professionals?"

"A very wise suggestion, Ewan. Thank you." I looked over at Gertie. "See? The voice of reason."

"Well, I don't know what you're all going on about. I'm quite looking forward to getting my time in the professional makeup artist's chair," Gertie said.

The Major coughed politely beside Ewan. "Ladies, might I remind you that our ancestors didn't wear all these fancy cosmetics we have nowadays?"

I smiled. "They had other vices. Queen Elizabeth the First covered her face in white paste made partly of lead. Seventeenth century ladies wore face patches in the shapes of stars and moons to cover smallpox scars. Rouge was invented in the Victorian age and–"

"I stand corrected," the Major said. I sensed he was still feeling a bit fish-out-of-waterish after his awkward rose presentation to Abbyleigh back at the GGRS café. Hopefully today would provide a welcome escape to all our worries, both large and small.

A Scotford Castle team member drove up beside us in a golf cart bearing the estate's logo. I got out to greet him and received a firm, dry handshake in response from Mac Bridgemont. I'd met him before as he was a concierge and volunteer guide for Scotford Castle. Bertie often sang his praises, including the time Mac rescued three senior citizens who got lost in the walled garden behind a rather enthusiastic thick patch of foxgloves early one summer. It was a teary-eyed, fuchsia-mauve-and-off-white-petal touristy experience until stalwart Mac showed up with his shock of white hair, kindly blue eyes and reassuring manner.

"Julie, is your team ready for the cameras?" Mac asked in his smooth voice. His deep baritone always made me wonder if he'd had a career in radio. The man could recite a grocery list and people would tune in.

I gave him a smile. "You bet. All present and accounted for."

"Now, if you'll just bear with me as I check off the talent list," he said, holding up a clipboard.

"Makes me feel like a piece of meat," Maude quipped. "Talent list, my foot."

"It's for security and efficiency, both," Mac replied as kindly as he could.

"Snacks are being provided, correct?" Timmy Hitchins asked. "I do hope they're serving pecan tarts and that freshly squeezed orange juice from the estate shop."

Gertie gave me some side-eye then whispered, "He's going to be high maintenance talent with those demands."

"Let's hope it's an aberration," I said.

The rest of the team exited the van and I handed Mac my list. It was an impressive typed page, hot off my office's printer:

The History of Scotford Castle: Late Elizabethan Period to Present
Cast List/GGRS Talent
Julie Fincher: Duchess of Conroy, Eighteenth Century
Donald Jerome Fincher: Furniture Craftsman, Nineteenth Century
Gertie Porringer: Duchess of Conroy, Sixteenth Century
Ewan Kilburn: Gamekeeper
Fred Todling: Judge, Seventeenth Century
Major Barry Whitcombe: Colonel in the Boer War

Ozzie Boggs: Banking Clerk, Nineteenth Century
Timmy Hitchins: Court Jester, Seventeenth Century
Maude Livingstone: Housekeeper

"Right. All this looks in order," Mac said as he compared his list to mine.

Security procedures needed to be followed as there would be a ton of cast and crew roaming inside the castle while filming took place. As the Fourteenth Duke of Conroy, Bertie was custodian of numerous priceless works of art, sculpture, furnishings and records. When one must ensure that treasures were properly passed along to the next generation or government organization, it was imperative to follow security protocols. Bertie did not have any heirs, so with each passing year, it looked like Scotford Castle was going to end up in the hands of administrators who would keep the estate alive and open to the public through one of the worthy not-for-profit organizations tasked with preserving the nation's heritage.

"Everyone, if you'll now follow me, I'll walk you over to the dressing rooms." Mac led us over to the cluster of six white trailers, each with a series of four doors on one side. When Gertie and I entered our dressing room, we were met by a hair stylist and makeup artist, both lovely ladies who were very experienced with their craft. We sat in comfortable chairs in front of mirrors edged by soft lights. A vase of multi-colored Gerbera daisies was at each work station, sitting on a counter that held an assortment of pots, lotions, styling tools, hair accessories and false eyelashes.

"I don't have to wear those, do I?" I asked.

Gertie snorted. "Jules, these lovely ladies are going to make us look like authentic period drama actors, not overdone glitzy club attendees."

"Advice from the woman who once wore bright blue eyeshadow and fire engine red hair to disguise herself," I said.

We soon had the trailer's room filled with laughter. Gertie ended up being right; the makeup and hair styling we underwent was to keep our faces non-shiny and to ensure we looked as if we were from the correct historical time period. The documentary film we'd volunteered for was one of Bertie's latest fundraising schemes. Scotford Castle was a black hole, moneywise, and a true labor of love. Repairs were constantly being done, and long-term capital projects included the roof, flooring, outbuildings and more. Thank goodness Bertie's late father had the foresight to tackle the Victorian-era plumbing and electrical rewiring needs before the entire estate was entrusted to Bertie's capable hands. Our dear friend was in both an enviable yet tenuous position: his family name and centuries of heritage relied upon his strong shoulders to carry the burden of continuity. Bertie did so with gusto and with admirable reverence for the thirteen Dukes before him. However, his enthusiasm was always tempered by the fact that he had to meet a large payroll and upkeep bill each month. He responded with the estate farm shop, encouraging tenants to perform organic farming, opening up parts of the castle to tourism and now, this film.

A film shoot was also a potential black hole for money. Undaunted, Bertie put his best manager in charge of the budget and soon had everything detailed into sensible line items. It was an adequate budget to get a quality film made, but not so ostentatious to pander to on-set, star-like demands such as Timmy's diva catering request.

After makeup, we were told to head up to the castle for costuming. Maude and my father got a ride on Mac's golf cart while the rest of us walked. I couldn't help but smirk at Ewan's new sideburns.

"I know, I know. They weren't my first choice," Ewan said, his false whiskers bobbing up and down with every word he spoke. "Who roped me into this acting gig anyways? Oh right. It was you lot." The antiques shop owner tried in vain to play a curmudgeonly friend.

Gertie and I laughed. "It looks like you have a couple of broom ends glued to your face," I said.

"I realize that. I just can't pull off this look like the Major can," Ewan said.

Our heads all turned to check out the prim and proper military man. The Major played a key role in our past family history adventures, and we could always count on three things: One, his network. Two, his punctuality. Three, his pork chop sideburns. His facial hair was literally the stuff of legend and it suited him to a tee. He walked up the path a couple of strides ahead of us, with great focus and determination. He would be a star on camera, of that I was certain.

Ozzie and Timmy lagged behind, so Ewan and I waited for them to catch up.

"I'm researching another branch of my family tree," Ozzie said.

"Any more confectionery companies?" I asked.

"No, this time I'm learning all about my ancestors who lived in the workhouse. Sad story, really," Ozzie said. "They were down on their luck and ended up there."

"Workhouse families were split up. Men on one side, women on the other," I added. "They even put the young children to work."

"From what I've read so far, it was spartan living conditions," Ozzie said.

"Flea-infested blankets, gruel and hard labor. The workhouse wasn't a place anybody aspired to enter," I said.

We neared the castle entrance. I anticipated that the full group of us would be significantly overwhelming once we got loose on set.

Chapter 3

Front Hall. Scotford Castle. After Costuming.

We mingled inside, admiring the centuries-old décor. I smiled up at the portrait of dear Aunt Edwina, loaned to Bertie for a castle exhibition depicting local aristocrats and other 'worthies' of the area.

Bertie came up to me and smiled. "I say, you are a lovely Duchess. Just perfect, my dear."

"This necklace is super heavy, Bertie. I cannot believe the Duchess wore so many diamonds," I said.

"Ah, but you don't have the full effect yet." He leaned over in my direction. "Follow me, please."

I looked around and saw that everyone was already separated into smaller groups by era, deep in discussion with the director addressing his crowd of somewhat wayward talent. No one would miss me for a moment or two.

"What is it you need, Bertie?" I asked him.

He put a finger to his lips and had me follow him down a wood-paneled corridor that led to a door at the end of the hallway. He scanned his electronic key card, opened the door and welcomed me inside his secret crisis room, aka safe room. It was a masculine office, with deep forest green walls, ringed by polished oak bookcases. A couple more eighteenth century hunting scene paintings hung on the walls under softly-lit brass lamps. A massive gleaming desk was in one end of the room. There were no windows. When one was wealthy, security was unfortunately a prime concern. Bertie had survived an horrific kidnap attempt at the age of seven, and the castle underwent a complete retrofit as a result. As he grew older, the threat waned when the perpetrator was sentenced to prison, but it always stuck with Bertie. It was a large reason why he hired Severs, ex-security-service, to be at his side and function as all around right hand. Chauffeur, security protection, personal assistant and more. Severs was always there, always around ... one just didn't see him all the time. He moved in the shadows, quite like an effective ghost.

There were various bits of ornate furniture around the room, a couple of comfortable, tartan-upholstered wingback chairs plus a card table near the food storage unit. I knew under the desk was his red panic button. A marble bust of his father sat on a pedestal and curtains done in a crimson damask were tied back with silken ropes and tassels over trompe l'oeil windows for effect. Bertie's antique silver snuff boxes were on a special shelving unit and I knew the collection's value was magnificent.

There were ample stocks of emergency food, water, medicine as well as a massive, metal safe at the very back of the room. Bertie once showed me the safe after it was installed because he wanted to show me his precious family tree, the one added to by each generation since the dukedom was coined. Bertie needed to put the receipt for two of my watercolor paintings inside, protected for his banking meeting later that week. I remembered my awe at the safe being a walk-in, full height of eight-feet. It was a room unto its own and contained a bank of four fireproof filing cabinets against one wall plus some open shelving.

Bertie now entered the safe's digital combination, pulled down the arm, and opened up. I was faced with a glittering array of family jewelry. Diamonds, rubies and emeralds, all on beautiful velvet stands. There were heirloom earrings, necklaces, chokers and bracelets plus even a few old shoe buckles adorned with expensive gems.

I took an inward gasp. "Bertie, are these real?"

"Yes, they are the actual family heirlooms. A couple of them go back to the sixteenth century in the Duke of Conroy lineage. I only bring them out for special occasions, and between you and I, usually store them at my bank's vault in London. Today, however, is special and I want you to wear the Duchess of Conroy's real diamonds. Everyone here thinks they're paste, costume jewelry."

"Why risk the real jewels for a television show? No one will know the difference."

"I will. And that's why you are going to wear £5 million worth of jewels this afternoon."

I started to back away. "Oh no, Bertie, I couldn't. What if a diamond falls out? What if the clasp comes undone? What if I forget I'm wearing them and–"

"I'll supervise, don't worry. I'm just trying to create the most realistic film possible. I want to show Scotford Castle at her best."

"By having me wear your family heirloom jewels?"

Bertie put a hand on each of my shoulders and looked at me with a serious face. "Julie, trust me. All right?"

I nodded. When Bertie got into one of his focused moods like this, there really was no arguing with him. He had a better vocabulary, life experience, aristocratic standing and much fatter wallet than most, yet he never lauded it about us. Bertie never let us forget his greatest delight was selling mango chutney from the back of his fancy SUV. He was a good egg and I resigned myself to doing his bidding. Today was, after all, Bertie's party.

He fastened the real diamond necklace around my neck, weighted down even more with a massive teardrop emerald in the center. Knowing that the jewels were real gave them a special feel and weight, something that only centuries-old craftsmanship could provide. Bertie stood beside me as we looked in the mirror. He was the ever-present calm and cool aristocrat: plum cashmere sweater, expensive suede shoes and soft corduroy trousers. His clothes were obviously perfectly tailored and bespoke. One automatically assumed that they came from the finest shops in London. He'd indeed created his perfect castle estate for filming, right down to the details of the jewelry.

"You are appearing on camera too, right?" I asked him.

"Of course. I'm hosting the series and the team from GGRS is acting out the historical scenes I describe in my narration. Scotford

Castle had numerous interesting historical developments over the centuries, you know." He gave me a kind look.

"I think my favorite had to be the one where the messenger for King George the Third took respite here after delivering the ill-fated letter from the businessman who decided to cross the monarch. I always wondered if that's where the term 'don't shoot the messenger' originated," I said.

"It actually goes farther back than messengers arriving on horseback with bad news. Town criers were supposed to be untouchable and it's even referenced in a Shakespearean play. I like to think that the messenger who slept here one night was a part of that folklore," Bertie said. "But I digress. We have a scene to rehearse." He locked the safe and left the room, gesturing for me to follow him.

I raised my eyebrows and sighed. Acting was so not my thing. Painting? Yes. Acting? Definitely not. All of us at GGRS vowed to help Bertie in order to keep the cost of talent low. There was no way he could afford a cast of A-listers and still make money for Scotford Castle renovations. So, he relied on amateur talent and a lot of good luck to try and pull this off. Most of us had amateur theater experience. Hopefully good direction, sets, costumes, makeup, hair and lighting would prevent us from turning the production into a total comedy show.

With Fred Todling, Ozzie Boggs and Timmy Hitchins on set, it was a big roll of the dice.

I took a deep breath and followed Bertie's lead.

"Our scene is being filmed in my study," he said.

In a hallway leading to the café, we passed a group of cool film people all dressed in black turtlenecks, jeans and understated expensive sneakers. I heard a few of them drop lingo about past shoots. At the moment, they were on break, delicately sipping coffee and perusing a table laden with snacks. A sturdy, brindled pug sat at the base of the table begging for treats with sad, soulful eyes. I raised an eyebrow to Bertie as we walked past.

"Oh, that's Muscles. He belongs to the director and is well-behaved, so long as he's allowed to mooch off the snack table."

"Oh Bertie, you're a little behind the times. Film set food stations are called 'craft services.'"

He shook his head. "Why do people have to go and make things so complicated? I'll stick to my mango chutney business." He was a gentleman and liked Scotford Castle to follow a particular set of traditions that were both respected and adhered to by all staff. When something really radical was proposed, Bertie's forehead would scrunch up and you could just imagine his brain whirring away, trying to figure it all out. He had a smart phone and used the internet, but with aristocrats that went back centuries, heritage and historical ways of doing things ran deep.

We passed Ozzie and Timmy in the hallway, forcing both of us to stop for a second look. Ozzie was dressed up as a threadbare-clothed clerk straight out of a Charles Dickens novel. Timmy had bells on his long, pointed shoes and was dressed in a Harlequin outfit of burgundy, white and carmine, complete with Elizabethan ruffs at the wrists, ankles and neck. I sincerely hoped that he wasn't planning on wearing this outfit out birdwatching because there would be no way he could stay camouflaged wearing that billboard getup. Still, Timmy wore it well and wasn't fazed by the fact that he looked like an overcaffeinated circus clown.

Timmy grinned as he saw Bertie and I approach, giving us a brief bow. "Your Grace, and Your Grace," he said to us with great enthusiasm. Timmy then did a little dance. The bells on his shoes reminded me of Santa Claus' elves in shopping malls. It was out of context here amongst GGRS staff and Scotford Castle.

Bertie was up for it. "And a fine day to you, too. I do like both your costumes," he complimented.

Ozzie stood up a bit straighter. He was wearing a brown waistcoat, a cravat wound around his neck about 500 times and close-fitting brown trousers. I noticed he had a quill in one hand.

"When are you gentlemen filming?" I asked.

"We just have," Ozzie said. He gestured behind him and I saw a photographer surreptitiously hiding around the corner, pointing a camera at us.

I was a bit shocked. "Why on earth would they want to photograph us talking in the hallway?" I asked Bertie.

"Ambience and candid shots, apparently," Bertie said. "I was sworn to secrecy and not allowed to speak of it until somebody noticed. That is apparently how one captures the most authentic shots."

The way he talked, he made it sound like it was all some extremely complicated magic trick.

My throat went a bit dry. It was getting a bit overwhelming.

"We are filming the actual scripted lines in my study," Bertie said, with what he likely hoped was a reassuring voice.

I shrugged. "I'm wearing an eighteenth century gown and looking at two genealogy researchers dressed as a court jester and miserly office clerk. At this point, I don't think anything could be farther off script than this."

I was wrong. Again.

Fred strutted down the hall looking a bit too pleased with himself. He wore a long black gown plus a wig with fake white curls cascading over his shoulders and partly down his back. For once, Fred was at the apex of the legal profession and boy, did he ever revel in his newfound status. Tiny glasses perched on the edge of his nose and he carried a fancy prop: one large, gold-leafed book. Apparently, no matter what Fred was asked to say on camera, he was certainly enjoying every moment.

Our newly minted judge gave a little chuckle. "I say, those paste diamonds do shine up quite well, Julie," Fred said.

"Yes, they do," I said, keeping Bertie's secret. "You look quite happy in your judge's robes."

"I am indeed quite chuffed to be wearing aforesaid chief justice robes entirely and completely in the effort of dispensing effective and canny advice, encouragement and punishment to all those who come before me, doled out in appropriate quantities depending upon the person appearing before me, of course."

Bertie and I just looked at each other.

"Wow, Fred," I said, "are you really on-set in a courtroom here at Scotford Castle?"

He shook his head. "It is a metaphorical illusion, one that merely and largely tempers the mind whilst I go about reciting my assigned dialogue in aid of promoting said wondrous and esteemed estate for its fanciful aristocratic patron."

Fred would find it hard to follow someone else's script because most of the dialogue would be two lines maximum, with heavy indentation. In reality, the way Mr. Thesaurus spoke he needed margins no wider than a rabbit's hair in order to cram all he wanted to say onto a page. That was just Fred. We all were used to his verbosity, like a gentle stream babbling in the background, us being the dipper birds who darted about and focused back on the stream once in a while after we'd tended our mate, nest, young plus checked for predators. It was just impossible to listen to that torrent of words without some sort of mental break.

Bertie gestured that I should keep following him. As we moved, Bertie looked behind him and said, "You make a fine judge, Fred."

Kind words from the aristocrat really did have quite an effect on Fred. He gave a small half bow and continued his original way down the corridor. Thankfully, we were too far away to engage in any more lengthy conversation.

Bertie escorted me to his study where a mass of cameras, tripods and umbrella lights were set up. A continuous soft flash went off as they checked the lighting and reflection in the room. A sound-man had earphones on to check some draft recordings, while the production assistant looked busy, intently focused on a clipboard holding a busy to do list. I was ushered into a fancy chair on a riser opposite Bertie's enormous desk and double credenza set.

"I'll leave you here in the crew's capable hands while I go and get changed," Bertie said.

"Change?" Bertie looked perfectly aristocratic to me.

"Surely, you don't expect me to be on camera like this?" Bertie exclaimed. "I can't compete with your gown and jewels in casual wear," Bertie said. "I won't be a moment." He pressed a button on a nearby wall, one concealed quite well into the surround of the hearth. With an elegant 'ping', an elevator door glided open and Bertie stepped inside. It would have accommodated up to four people, or just Bertie and four large suitcases.

Leave it to the aristocrat to have an elevator or two in his castle.

"Miss, are you ready for your close up?" a film crew director asked me as he stood at the edge of the scene near the cameraman.

"Um, yes." I was distinctly out of place amongst all these lights, cables and cameras. It was a foreign world because I usually worked quietly behind the scenes. My triumphs were found in amongst dusty old records, crinkled forgotten pages and quiet whispers in a low-lit archives facility or record office. Being thrust front and center under hot lights and gooped-on makeup was definitely not my scene.

But it was for a good cause, as sales of the film to a streaming service would raise important funds for the restoration of Scotford Castle. I was of the full, utmost opinion that nationally significant heritage locations and buildings had to be maintained, and I had the full support of GGRS behind me. It would be a travesty to lose our history, and that's why I stood here today in uncomfortable clothes with a plastic smile on my face. It wasn't just for Bertie. No, it was for England. And Great Britain, And the United Kingdom. And …

I was jolted back to reality with some still-shot camera flashes, followed by my being filmed practicing a few lines of dialogue. All of these people were focused on me, managing all sorts of odd equipment, including a soundman holding a pole with a fuzzy end, a makeup lady who was forever dabbing people's foreheads with blotting paper, plus a director who mouthed lines at me when I forgot. I was a complete amateur, yet valiantly on set with the rest of GGRS to bolster Scotford Castle's renovation fund.

A few minutes later, a sound distracted me. I dripped with diamonds and the roof dripped with … a water leak? This didn't look good at all. I pointed upwards, completely ruining the scene and the director sighed.

"Cut!" he yelled. "Whatever is the matter now?" he asked, a frown on his face, likely because we were on the seventh take.

"The roof is leaking and it's coming down on top of Bertie's plaster cherub wall décor," I said with a great deal of urgency in my voice.

Just as everyone started to panic, the elevator dinged again and the door glided open for the second time today. We saw Bertie standing on the plush carpet, resplendent in a tuxedo, ruby-stone class ring and gold cufflinks. Of course his cummerbund was perfectly matched to the family Scottish Tartan. It was subtle but elegant.

That's how the aristocrats rolled in this country. Wealthy but under-stated. Elegant yet not overt. Living in fancy homes with leaky roofs.

Bertie once told me he dearly wished to get more marketing value out of repairing the boiler, installing air conditioning and replacing the carpet. It was an unfortunate reality that those things didn't offer any glamorous cachet to the tourist trade. No, what really drove in the crowds were celebrities, film locations, history of battles and costumes, as well as amply stocked tea rooms and gift shops. I didn't blame them; I could not recall ever seeking out a manor house based upon its new hot water tank nor wear-resis-tant commercial grade carpet. It was just a quiet punishment that owners of these grand estates had to endure, hoping the ticket sales would at least keep their heritage business at the break-even point as the year's tourist season progressed.

Bertie saw my face, and instantly got a look of concern upon his own. "Whatever is the matter, Julie?" he asked.

"Your roof. It's leaking again, I'm afraid. I'm really worried about those plaster cherubs."

Bertie's face turned into simultaneous shock and concern. "Those are from the Georgian era. We need to corral that water right away."

He pressed another quiet button on the wall, spoke into the inter-com, and a few moments later his butler and two workmen arrived, buckets and sponges in hand. They set about fixing it while the film crew clustered over to the side taking a break.

"You should turn off the electricity," I suggested.

"Already in hand," Bertie said. "Severs takes good care of those types of things and it was his first inclination when he heard that they were near the Old Masters paintings."

Of course. The Old Masters.

Multimillion dollar paintings weren't a problem in most homes.

I looked at Bertie. "I think they called my scene a wrap, so all that's left is your historical summary overview with you at your desk."

"I'm also supposed to describe what you're wearing on camera and tell the audience how my ancestor danced the night away in her fabulous jewels and gowns."

I put a hand to my throat and pretended to swoon. "You'll have the audience breathless, Bertie."

He frowned. "Not as much as I will be when I get the repair bill for this roof leak. I fix one thing, pay the invoice and then there's something else that goes wrong. I just can't win."

I patted his arm with a reassuring hand. "Bertie, into every world a little rain must fall. Your friends are here and will get you through this. How about we go and check out how the others are doing? I'm sure Timmy's court jester outfit will put a smile back on your face."

❊❊❊

On-Set. That Afternoon.

Surprisingly, Fred took offense to playing a judge overseeing a sewer commission case, hence requiring some last-minute script rewrites. Timmy tripped over his long shoes and face planted into a large potted fern in the conservatory. Ozzie had immense problems holding the quill in the correct position and ended up splattering ink all over his clothes, yielding a rapid trip back to the dressing room for repair. The Major acted a real treat and of course Maude was perfect as housekeeper. Gertie was an overly enthusiastic Duchess of Conroy from the sixteenth century and Ewan somehow managed to carry out a pretty convincing gamekeeper scene. A lot of my really good friends were here and it was fun delving into a world we didn't often see. Family history types were not known for showmanship and flamboyance. Instead, we took great delight in quietly finding obscure documents and long-lost relatives. What we did today, however, was support Bertie and make Scotford's history much more alive.

I always found it amusing how Bertie acted just like one of us. There was always something about him that whispered he traveled in a different lane than the rest of us, yet he never put on a toffee-nosed show. It wasn't that at all. Rather, it was in the fact he actually knew that 'being on tenterhooks' harkened back to the actual frame of small pins that was used to dry dyed woolen cloth. Bertie instinctively knew that a 'red letter day' referred to how ancient church books listed every day of the year, where monks, priests or scribes outlined the special days in red ink. It was even linked back to illuminated manuscripts and he could go on for an hour about those as well. Bertie was special, just like every individual at GGRS.

I fervently hoped I could soon shed these fancy jewels plus gown and get back into my regular clothes.

The crew fervently hoped that Bertie would be kind enough to show them his car collection.

"You look absolutely stunning," Ewan said as he rounded the corner. He looked at me with a warm smile on his face, definitely more used to seeing me in a blouse and pressed slacks as opposed to this high society outfit.

"Thank you, Mr. Gamekeeper," I said, noting the three fake grouse he held as props.

He shrugged. "From my scene."

"Film. Where the make-believe becomes real," I replied.

❋❋❋

Later That Afternoon.

Once we were all out of costume, Bertie did the honors and took us to his twenty-five-car garage. It really would be better named as 'car warehouse'. Inside was a vast collection of vehicles shined up to utmost perfection, ranging from the fanciest antique sedans with silver hood ornaments down to exotic sports cars with doors opening on hinges at outrageous angles. Of course, the smooth concrete floor was absolutely immaculate, with not a spot of oil nor transmission fluid in sight. All of the tires gleamed to perfection.

"Do you ever drive any of these or are they just collection pieces?" Gertie asked. "Surely a vehicle is meant to be driven."

"Of course we do. We use them on rotation to ensure that all the parts stay lubricated and we can catch any necessary minor repairs before they become major ones," Bertie said.

Ozzie whistled low through his teeth. "I hope you have good security here."

"I leave that up to Severs. He's got things well in hand," Bertie said. "Do take a look around, and once we're finished here, I have a lovely dinner awaiting all of us in the grand dining room."

Murmurs of appreciation spread through the crowd. While some of the men and Gertie started into a conversation about horse-power, which then digressed into design and model preference, the rest of us headed back to the front hall with its black-and-white checkerboard floor pattern. I was more interested in the artwork and remembered the paintings on the wall we ogled when here for Bertie's summer solstice party. I looked closer and the artists' skills were second to none. Any museum curator or art collector on the planet would drool to have these paintings in their collection, but they were not for sale. The estate's fabulous paintings were just as much of a part of Scotford Castle as were its turrets and mango chutney venture. Frankly, to me, there was nothing wrong with that at all. And, following such an interesting day, I truly believed that all of Bertie's guests felt the same.

Chapter 4

——

Grand Dining Room.

We ate in a secret place. It was secret because the public wasn't allowed to see this room, let alone step inside. This special sanctuary was where Bertie privately entertained royalty, politicians and celebrities. The film crew had already been sent home for the day and this evening was a thank you to all of the volunteer talent who donated their time to the Scotford Castle cause.

The polished walnut table could sit forty-eight people. If one didn't have a party that large, sections of the table could be removed and both ends squeezed together to shorten it. I wouldn't like to be in charge of that heavy maneuver. It must be a massive job to manage this level of seating plan, and that's not even taking into consideration all the politics and aristocratic hierarchies involved. I could not even begin to imagine what castle staff went through trying to figure out who sat where based upon family-bestowed title, recent achievements on the battlefield, compared accomplishments and celebrity status. It was a headache-inducing job that I wouldn't take in a million years.

The room was lavish and masculine, absolutely covered in well-polished wood paneling. There were umpteen sideboards up and down the long room and six waiters stood at attention around the perimeter. Silver domed covers were on every dish and we all sat under the gentle glow of fancy chandeliers bearing a gazillion pieces of crystal. We all knew, of course, that each piece of crystal was polished by hand and the chandelier was lowered for cleaning by a mechanized chain operated by a button on the wall. There were a few pieces of armor hung high up on the wall and brass plaques underneath them at eye level denoted them as being worn during the seventeenth century English Civil War. Bertie's late father's hobby was painting historical battlefield watercolors; they were elegantly framed and hung in between the plaques. A shadowbox collection of military hats from Bertie's grandfather's time in the army had pride of place above the head of the table. Bertie's family went back numerous Dukes over the centuries; his heritage was something to celebrate and share with the world. I was glad that the public could enjoy Scotford Castle, yet I was also reassured seeing Bertie had carved out a private living space of his own. It was import-ant to enjoy one's family heritage and make sure it was respected.

"Fred, who is looking after Barnaby and Holly?" Bertie asked with a grin, enquiring of the talkative solicitor's potbellied pig and English Sheepdog.

Fred chortled. "Constable Snowdrop. And what a splendiferous evening I have planned for that trio, indeed. Walkies followed by Holly's favorite television program and then a light snack before

---

they are bedded down for the night in cozy duvet wonderland that facilitates only the highest levels of REM sleep."

Okay, we just have to ask.

"Fred," I started, "your English Sheepdog has a favorite television program?"

"Of course. Holly primarily enjoys New Zealand travel documentaries. I found a new television streaming service that has thirty eight new episodes and she's glued to the screen."

"And what does Barnaby think of that?" Bertie asked.

"I have to admit my pedigreed porcine is not as attracted to these far-flung destination screen celebrations. Barnaby is content munching on his broccoli jam sandwiches and snoozes away at my feet. It's all quite enthusiastically pastoral if I were to describe it via an exceedingly fine point to our esteemed assemblage here tonight."

"The only question is will the village of Oakhurst be safe without Constable Snowdrop's watchful eye?" Gertie teased.

For a moment, Fred thought that Gertie was serious. I could see it flash across his face, the pure fear that he had seconded Oakhurst Village's only law enforcement personnel away from serious duty. The fact of the matter was that Constable Snowdrop's current most important duty was ensuring the clock on the village green always stayed within five minutes accuracy of the actual time. The village crime rate was about zero, making for a pretty quiet job as a policeman.

Luckily, Fred then got the joke. For a learned man sometimes he was a little bit naïve, like the time he mistakenly showed up wearing a toga for a formal dress event here at Scotford Castle. All his friends gathered together to rescue him from a lifetime of regrets and embarrassment. It was just what us family history and genealogy researchers did to help each other out.

Bertie stood up at the head of the table and cleared his throat. It was his quiet signal for everyone to stop chatting and listen to what he was about to say. After a few more hurried murmurs, the room fell silent and we fixed our eyes upon our host.

"I would like to say a formal thank you and raise a glass to all of my friends who have willingly participated in the rather outlandish costuming, wigs and makeup here today. Scotford Castle, as you know, is extremely dear to my heart and I am trying everything I know how to preserve and maintain her for the future. She's an expensive lady to run and always has her eye on the most expensive roofing material, wiring and plumbing. She doesn't sleep when something is wrong and her creaks and groans absolutely insist that I take care of her posthaste. She is my most devoted companion, yet my most expensive hobby. Tonight, my dear friends, thank you for supporting this beautiful lady we know and love as Scotford Castle."

Bertie raised his glass of champagne and toasted us. We returned his toast with jolly calls of 'Hear, Hear,' and 'To Scotford Castle'.

Ozzie was the only one who had failed to change out of his costume. He insisted on staying in character for the dinner event, despite the pleas of the wardrobe department. We all knew that when Ozzie got something in his head, it was just best to let it run until he was satisfied. Our eyes shifted to him as he gently banged a spoon against the heirloom, family-crest engraved, cut crystal goblet.

I wasn't the only one to cringe.

Each one of those glasses was likely worth the price of a weekend getaway—for seven people—all food, beverages and offsite excursions included.

"Ahem," Ozzie said, standing up from his chair. "I have a proposition for you, Duke Bertie."

Never mind he kerflummoxed the title ... we were all used to Ozzie by now.

"Yes, Ozzie?" was our kind, affable host's response.

We all sat in great anticipation. Personally, I wasn't sure if Ozzie wanted to try on one of Bertie's grandfather's army hats or make an offer to buy a suit of armor from him. With Ozzie, one just never knew.

"Timmy and I were wondering if we could go metal detecting in your back fields," Ozzie said.

All eyes went back to Bertie. It was like watching a croquet match in quintuple time.

"Metal detecting? Whatever on earth for?" Bertie asked.

Ozzie gave a small, surreptitious smile, one that said he was up to something, likely using skewed genealogy research. "We have our reasons."

Timmy butted in rather unexpectedly. He'd changed into evening wear and had donned a 1970s tuxedo that smelled of mothballs. I still hadn't gotten over the wide, margarine-colored bowtie and matching cummerbund. At least he was trying to do the right thing. Seeing him standing supporting Ozzie's request reminded one of a lobbyist for an ill-fated cavalry campaign in some distant part of the old British Empire.

"It's like this, you see, dear chap," Timmy said. "Ozzie and I have researched the grounds and believe an ancient Roman Mint was once located here."

"And you're hoping to find a coin hoard?" Bertie asked with palpable disbelief. He gestured for the pair to sit down so they could continue the conversation between elegant cream-colored candlesticks as opposed to talking over them.

"Well, yes," Ozzie said, "the research all checks out."

Ah. A sore spot. He'd promised us proper research when he was doing his surreptitious confectionery company takeover that we were unfortunately roped into by hook and crook.

"Honest, it does," he said. He glared at Fred for support.

"Indeed. My client has done it correctly this time and I have triple checked with the managers of the Roman antiquities department at several prominent institutions. There was, for all intents and purposes, an ancient Roman mint on Scotford Castle's lands," Fred confirmed.

"How would you know where to start?" I asked. "This estate has nearly 500 acres of land."

"We have some likely looking places," Ozzie said.

Silence around the table. People tried to mentally balance the disbelief with the audacity of the request.

Bertie to the rescue, yet again. He leaned to the side as the waiter put a bowl of warm lobster bisque down in front of him. It was such a contrast: a rich, elegant meal with a member of the nobility versus the image of Ozzie and Timmy trampling over hill and dale, clanking their equipment like gold rush prospectors. Bertie had this well in hand. "Gentlemen, I propose an equitable solution. I will allow it, so long as it's done professionally and also that we split the proceeds fifty/fifty."

"And the appropriate authorities are contacted and allowed access to preserve any historical finds," I added.

"Of course," Bertie said. "The work must follow the legalities of treasure trove discoveries on private lands." He looked over at Ozzie with a firm gleam in his eye. I'd seen it before when Bertie was urging colleagues to see his way. "Gentlemen?"

Ozzie looked at Timmy and they nodded at each other. Ozzie then got up, went over to Bertie's seat—it was a bit of a hike, mind you—and shook the Duke's hand. Bertie smiled with his usual patience and Ozzie then trundled himself back to his seat. By the look on Ozzie's face, one assumed he'd just negotiated a world peace treaty with incredibly impressive odds in his favor.

We'd have to keep a close eye on Ozzie and his ornithologist friend.

"We'll start tomorrow, then?" Timmy asked, hopeful.

"Filming is done, so why not," Bertie said. "Just stay out of the back pasture with the bull."

"No worries," Timmy said. "I know my way around livestock."

"Oh, you have a farming background?" Ewan asked.

"No, but I've spent years volunteering at the bird rescue center," Timmy confirmed with confidence and a knowing smile.

How wild birds were related to testosterone-laden bulls was beyond all of us.

"Isn't this soup divine?" Fred stated, trying to divert the topic.

"Bisque, Fred, bisque. And yes, it's lovely," Maude said. She'd kept awfully quiet during this recent exchange and I knew why. After the last incident with Ozzie, she was keeping her distance. I'd noted her and Gertie having intense discussions while Ozzie pled his case. Good for them. At least only a few of us got schnookered into his latest scheme.

As for myself, I actually looked forward to seeing Ozzie and Timmy rummaging around the back fields trying to bring another get-rich-quick scheme to fruition. I'm sure they expected to find an absolute treasury of Roman coins, all solid gold of course, with a value that would easily make them kings of their own castle in short order. It wasn't the way how most family history forays or antiquity finds went, however I wasn't one to spoil their fantasy.

"I do have one more announcement for everyone here tonight," Bertie said. "You may have noticed a photographer prowling around the premises?"

"He did make himself a frequent fixture in many of the rooms where filming occurred," my father said.

"Very observant," Bertie said. "He was not there to disturb, but rather to observe and document the proceedings. You see,

Scotford Castle is also producing a coffee-table book for sale to the public. I thought people would enjoy the behind-the-scenes work about our film." He sat back and looked awfully proud of this promotional idea.

"I love the idea, Bertie," I said. "People always want to go further than what's on screen and opening up Scotford a little bit more to show perhaps even some bloopers would be a great idea."

The instant terror streaking across Fred's face was obvious.

I looked at the solicitor. "What did you do?"

"I was doing some warm up exercises, you know, preparing vocal cords as they do in the theater," Fred said.

"You mean your ballet narration performances?" Ewan said with a grin.

"Ah, my friend, do know that my famed ballet performances take nerves of steel plus the ability to project my well-trained, three-octave-range voice out across–"

"Umpteen sets of parents who would clap no matter what happened?" Ewan continued.

The entire table of us laughed. There was no way Fred was going to convince us that his community ballet attempt was anything close to a Shakespearean play.

"Perhaps I do not tread the fabled boards of some illustrious grand hall in the center of London, offering my stage talents to the likes of royalty and senior government officials. Nevertheless, I do take all my performances quite seriously. When I was warming up, I sang a 1960s pop song and had the moves to match."

Now Fred's reticence made sense.

"And the photographer took a photo of you?" I asked.

I looked over at Gertie. She and I exchanged a knowing glance.

"Tell me you were in costume, please?" Gertie asked, "And how many muscles did you pull?"

Fred hung his head like a truant schoolboy. "Full wig and robes for my judge's performance on screen. However, I must admit I did not exhibit the required decorum for the high office as I was performing my warm-up routine in front of the mirror."

An endless array of possibilities raced through our minds.

"Never mind, Fred, we do have complete editorial control on this one," Bertie assured him.

"Thank heavens," Fred said. "I would certainly not wish my clients to see me making a mockery of the very institution from which I earn my utterly esteemed and most privileged living."

This, from the man who made oodles of money representing a television star Persian cat with an odd question mark pattern of fur on its head.

"Did anyone video it? It has excellent social media potential, a great way to get pre-film release publicity for Scotford Castle," Gertie said.

Bertie looked interested, but rather unsure of how to proceed. He liked new methods of marketing but really had no clue about social media so was pretty scared about dipping his toe in without some professional guidance.

Fred looked like he wanted to disappear under the table.

"Talk to your marketing people, Bertie," I advised. "This lot has some great ideas but the execution leaves something of a quandary."

He looked relieved, although I didn't see how hard it would be for the owner of the fabled castle to politely refuse the effervescent video antics of a slightly out-of-touch solicitor.

"How big is this place?" Ozzie blurted out. A small dribble of bisque trickled down his chin. Timmy pointed it out and Ozzie wiped it away with a pristine napkin that had somehow acquired a few other stains during the meal.

Bertie gave Ozzie the smile he reserved for people who were painful to deal with yet couldn't be shown the door. "Scotford Castle has over 215 rooms, 40 of which are in the separate guest wing converted to a hotel. Each of you is provided with your own guest room this evening as a thank you for your contributions to the filming work done today. In the morning, we'll look at some initial footage while we enjoy a large buffet breakfast in the tapestry room."

"You have a room just for carpets?" Timmy asked.

Very gauche.

Again, Bertie took it all in stride. "Well Timmy, not 'carpets', per se. They are wall tapestries purchased by my ancestors as wall hangings. You see, castles built of stone have very cool temperatures inside and the tapestries were used as wall hangings to insulate the rooms. It kept the residents much warmer."

"Kind of like stuffing in old rags to fill gaps in a wall?" Timmy said with a hopeful expression on his face. One had to hand it to him, the ornithologist was rather tunnel-visioned and I supposed that going from owls to carpets was a bit of a stretch.

"I suppose that could be a somewhat relevant analogy," Bertie replied.

The mixture of people at this table truly was amazing, but that's what I loved about family history so much. It was different backgrounds, experiences, and walks of life that made it all so fascinating. One wouldn't have the social history if there weren't different experiences and different livelihoods in our community. The most important thing was that people could sit down at a table, break bread together and learn from each other. It made the family history and genealogy worlds go round and I was simply delighted to be included.

My thoughts were interrupted by a rather delectable smell wafting in from the opposite end of the room. The waiters were back in single file, each carrying a main course dish that would be served individually to each guest, using a spoon and fork to portion out an exact amount. By the time we were ready to waddle out of here later this evening, I was sure we would have eaten enough food to last us three whole days. I looked forward to a cozy night's sleep in the castle; it truly was a special experience. Being hosted by a Duke at his centuries-old family home was a surreal experience. Bertie was spot on to document everything and leave proper records for future generations. Never mind that he had no sons or daughters of his own; at least it would all be preserved for whatever national charity was eventually granted custody. Bertie told me this was his ultimate plan, but I always wondered about the winsome expression on his face when he talked about a lack of descendants. It was a bit of a sore spot and I could tell there was a story behind his thoughts.

Perhaps he'd share it with us one day.

Chapter 5

————

Hotel Annex Wing, Scotford Castle. 10:02 p.m.

It was a gloriously luxurious guest wing, a place that most people would consider fit for royalty. We weren't talking gold-plated toilets, but it was close. Bertie really had gone all out trying to make it super-star accommodation. Our family history group wasn't used to living with towels folded into the shapes of swans and mints on pillows. Rather, we were fascinated over how much of Bertie's family history and genealogy lined the walls of the hotel space. I'd lost track of the number of replica land deeds, marriage certificates and seventeenth century castle repair bills that hung in discrete frames. He had a dozen swatches of fabrics from eighteenth century bedroom furnishings framed behind UV-resistant glass, as well as a shadowbox holding the original salt and pepper shakers used for a royal visit sometime in the nineteenth century. Overall, it was an amazing walk down memory lane, almost as if one could hear Bertie's ancestors musing over their guests as one ambled down the ornate, wood-paneled hallways.

The room numbers were all done in bold, brass door signs fixed on top of a mahogany rectangular base. There were electronic key cards, a spy hole on each guest room door and a no-barrier entry over all thresholds. Each room had an ensuite plus tea/coffee station. The curtains opened onto either a) the interior courtyard of the castle where one might be lucky enough to catch a glimpse of the Duke of Conroy going about his daily duties; or b) the opposite side to his vast estate showcasing the pastoral farmland that surrounded the estate. My room faced out to his fields, and off in the distance I saw two men, their headphone-clad heads bobbing up and down as they slowly walked the perimeter of the field. It was rather late for them to start the metal detecting today, mere hours after being granted permission, but that was just the Ozzie Boggs way of doing things.

"Is there anything else I can get you, miss?" I heard behind me. I swiveled around to see one of the Scotford Castle bell staff standing at attention holding my freshly polished ankle boots I had worn on the trip here. Once again, Scotford Castle exceeded expectations.

"No, thank you, I'm very well taken care of here," I said.

"Very good, miss. Please do not hesitate to call if you require any assistance." The bellman left, silently closing the door behind him.

I took another look out of the window and as night fell, saw Ozzie and Timmy still walking the perimeter of the nearest field, stopping and starting every once in a while. I was sure they would be out tomorrow morning at five o'clock before breakfast to find that Roman Mint. At least it would keep them out of trouble.

My phone rang and yielded a familiar voice on the line.

"Julie, it's Ewan. Have you seen those two jokers out in Bertie's back field?"

I sighed. "Ozzie and Timmy are providing a little late night entertainment for you, too?"

"They earn big points for ingenuity," he said, with a laugh.

"I suppose. The chances of them finding any great treasure hoard is about as likely as Bertie's ancestral ghosts appearing before us in their kilts tonight."

"Now that I would love to see," he said.

"How did your filming go today? I didn't get a chance to ask you at dinner," I said.

"Quite well, thanks. I have never been so prodded and preened in all my life, but we managed to get the scenes done. And you?"

"I was gussied up in quite the costume. Well, you saw–"

"Quite beautiful, indeed," he said.

"Oh, the workmanship on the gown was exquisite and–"

"I meant the person, not the jewelry," Ewan said in a tender voice.

It dawned on me. Ewan was very close, in a nearby room of his own, and we were having a nighttime conversation by telephone. My heart raced and I was certain it wasn't from the caffeine in the tiny mint chocolate on my pillow. My breathing accelerated, a romantic fluttering and tingling sensation inside all at once. I was flattered.

"Oh. Thank you, that is kind," I replied.

"Perhaps we can spend some time together tomorrow?" he asked, hopeful.

"I'd enjoy that, Ewan. Sleep well." As I hung up the phone, my mouth curved up in a smile, a special one reserved for the antiques dealer who now claimed his own special place within my heart.

***

2:00 a.m.

I didn't set my cellular phone's alarm, because I knew I could trust Bertie's hotel staff to wake me up at the right time. It was so much more pleasant to talk to a human being when groggily rousing oneself from beneath the covers as opposed to being subjected to the piercing screech of some insistent electronic contraption.

Yet it persisted.

Again, again and yet again.

As I looked at the phone, I saw it was many hours before I was supposed to get up. Plus, the phone didn't even show the alarm going off.

Then I smelled something odd, something really out of place.

Next, I saw the source of the smell through a crack in the curtains where I'd forgotten to pull them tight. Tiny wisps of grey smoke filtered up past my window, headed up towards the sky.

FIRE!

The evacuation signal came from a disc-shaped alarm placed high up on the wall. In between piercing screeches, it played a calm announcement telling us to leave the building at once.

'Fire' was a word that sent sheer terror through the mind of any historic building manager. To think a fire was here at Scotford Castle constituted both the horrific as well as the unbelievable. Throughout the centuries, there was not a single time where Scotford Castle had fallen victim to flames. Oliver Cromwell, nearly, but never flames. I held out faint hope that it was something gone awry in the kitchen; perhaps something was left in the oven too long. As I got up to look out my window, I knew that wasn't the case. The smoke was just too strong. It billowed out from the rear of the castle and signified something very, very wrong.

Bertie.

The antiques.

His library.

The family records.

Precious photos.

Irreplaceable history.

A rash of thoughts tumbled through my head as I threw on a plush hotel robe, shoved my feet into slippers, grabbed my purse and headed over to the door. I checked the door for heat, felt none, and then cautiously opened it.

Ewan and a member of staff stood right there, about to pound on my door. My boyfriend had a worried look on his face. "We need to get everybody outside. Now," he instructed, showing me Maude and Gertie right close behind him.

We proceeded to bang on guest room doors, waking the GGRS team from a well-earned rest after a long day on set. Luckily the hotel was only hosting us tonight—er, this morning—due to the filming. The crew stayed off site at a local hotel.

Everyone was clad in bathrobes and had either a purse or ruck-sack slung over their shoulder. The alarm continued to blare up and down the hall. 'Evacuate premises immediately. Follow the exit signs. Evacuate premises immediately. Follow the exit signs,' a proper British woman's voice insisted in a calm tone. I decided it was a special person who was hired to record this voice. I was certain I'd never forget it.

Thirty seconds later we had everybody out, milling in the hall. Ewan led the group to the emergency exit and outside.

"Where are ... oh, good." I saw our two metal detector-ists in our line of people and breathed a sigh of relief. They were similarly clad in nightwear but had also grabbed their metal detectors on the way out. I only hoped they considered their identification and wallets more important than their trea-sure-seeking devices.

"Does anyone know what happened?" Gertie asked.

"I hoped it was a meal gone bad in the kitchen, but obviously not," I said.

"It's wisest to keep clear," the Major said. He still, somehow, looked in command even whilst clad in a hotel bathrobe.

"It's coming from the back part of the building," Maude said. "I think we're safe on the opposite side."

"I agree," Ewan said, taking charge. "Let's head to the front of the castle."

"We need to find Bertie and help him rescue what we can before the fire brigade arrives." I said. "Think of the United Kingdom's heritage going up in flames."

"I cannot stand idle while that's happening. None of us can," Maude said, starting a brisk walk. We all followed her. She was sensible and wouldn't do anything rash.

We hurried to the front of the castle, an odd group of guests at o'dark thirty in the morning. Our feet flip-flopped as hotel-provided slippers slapped against the soles of our feet. Thank goodness there were no mirrors anywhere because we would have been horrified to be this out-of-decorum.

But decorum didn't matter in a fire.

It didn't matter that Maude's hair curlers were in and covered by a mauve net. It wasn't the time to laugh at Fred's bumblebee cartoon pajamas nor to check if Ozzie remembered to put in his false teeth. No one cared that the Major's sideburns weren't perfectly groomed, nor did they mind that Ewan had a great streak of soot across his face from accidentally brushing against the side of the castle where some cooling ash had coated it. We were all in this together. Friends. Helping each other.

People rescued, we now turned to rescuing heritage treasures.

We met Bertie at the front of the castle. He wore a frantic look that temporarily shifted into relief when he saw all of us there. My heart ached for him. Bertie's entire life—ancestry included—was starting to assemble on his front lawn. My mouth hung open as I looked at this pseudo-rummage sale of priceless treasures scattered everywhere. His staff were already busy rescuing artwork, books, tapestries, place settings, sculptures, woodcarvings and so much more. The front courtyard soon displayed a mishmash of blankets, plant nursery sheeting and plastic tarps. Basically they used anything they could quickly get their hands on to protect the treasures from damp. The books were definitely at risk of damage. Piles and piles of precious things were laid out on picnic tables, benches and a couple of massive tree stumps, leftovers from the horrific storm England experienced a few decades back. It was both frightening and devastating. After all Bertie's decades spent preserving his family heirlooms, it came down to this. Scotford Castle's treasures were at the mercy of his staff, guests, estate tenants plus volunteers we saw hustling up the drive, no doubt attracted by the plumes of flames and smoke. No one wanted to see Scotford Castle on fire. Bertie was a kind landlord and had done so much for his local area, the county as well as the heritage of England itself.

It was time to repay him and we all pitched in without being asked.

Bertie sized us up. "Oh, thank goodness you're all here," he said, doing a rapid headcount of the GGRS team. "I do not know how the fire started. Right now, we're just trying to salvage whatever we can before the fire gets too close. The fire department is nearly here and staff are busy with their internal fire mitigation techniques at the source out back of the castle."

"It looks pretty serious, Bertie. How can we help?" I asked.

We quickly stepped out of the way to avoid a ten foot by twenty foot painting being carried out by two waiters. I recognized them both from serving at our dinner earlier, but at the moment they were only dressed in pajamas, not in their black-and-white uniforms.

Gertie focused on me. "The library. All those precious books, and the paintings in the front hall."

I nodded. "Right. Gertie, you and I will get the paintings. Everyone else into the library to the right just off the main entrance. Take out as many books as you can, and use those two wheelbarrows over there," I called out.

Bertie handed out face masks from the castle's recent pandemic stock. Ewan and the Major commandeered the wheelbarrows and everybody else trooped in behind them. They soon had an assembly line going filling up the wheelbarrows and carting them outside, full of books. Someone had found additional hotel linens for the front lawn where they could put the books down with at least some protection from damp. It was not a time to be perfect, and rigorous preservation techniques were tossed way out the window. It was either haphazard rescue or risk the books being burned to ashes. This was just us, volunteering to try and help save anything we could in a very short period of time.

Gertie and I dashed inside the front hall and took the paintings off the walls, tripping the security alarms that Bertie had carefully installed to protect his art collection. Alarms didn't matter right now. Both my cousin and I were carrying multimillion dollar paintings out of the castle to be set up on a park bench. Never in a thousand years did any of us expect to be getting this up close and personal with such valuable items, in such a desperate situation.

On our way out, we passed the Major trundling out a wheelbarrow full of gilded page topography books. Ewan was hot on his heels with a wheelbarrow full of books about Bertie's family's interest in railway development. More of the Duke's life flashed before his eyes, certainly an assault on his senses. All the treasures Bertie had so diligently protected for so many years, in his private spaces, were now carted outside like sacks of potatoes, hurriedly stacked in heaps as the trundlers went back inside for another load.

Fred gave us cause for amusement, stumbling along right after Ewan, his arms laden with overflow books, an archer's quiver full of arrows slung over his shoulder and an ancient knight's shiny armor helmet on his head ... backwards. Bertie rushed over to help the wayward solicitor before he ran headfirst into a tree.

Gertie and I decided to put the paintings down inside a machine shed off to the side, a place where Bertie kept his antique tractors dry, one that doubled as a ticket sales building. We found a spot beside some ancestral portraits I recognized from the front staircase, and I was completely sure that their stern faces looked even more unforgiving today underneath their fancy hats, feathers and tortoiseshell hair combs.

Bertie's face was filled with worry. We heard the flames crackling in the turret farthest away from us. I remembered seeing the film crew go in there to do some filming with Bertie yesterday, but hadn't gone to visit that part of the castle myself. Right now, all we could focus on was saving his precious heritage, and that was an extremely tall order. The wail of sirens came upon us and the fire brigade roared up the front drive. The firefighters took matters in hand within moments of arrival and set to work extinguishing the horrific blaze. Water soon entered the castle, sprayed gallons per second, soaking everything in sight.

We'd taken out everything that we could rescue.

Now, all we could do was watch.

We heard a structural beam groan, creak and then collapse. Followed by another. Then yet another. Then came a huge, prolonged crash of metal.

"That's likely the sword room," Bertie said. "My family's weaponry collection goes back to the War of the Roses."

❀❀❀

Moments Later.

"At least it's not raining, old chap," the Major said as he walked by carting another barrow full of books to the front lawn. His words were somewhat ironic as a third fire hose started up on the opposite side of the castle and began gushing a torrent of water down onto the smoldering roof.

"I'm so sorry, Bertie," I said, putting a gentle hand on his arm.

"As a young boy, I used to play badminton in the long portrait gallery. My ancestors always looked so disapproving as they stared down upon my cousins and I, racketing back and forth," Bertie said with great sorrow.

Bertie looked at me, at the raggedy bunch of people around him ... then the aristocrat pulled himself together. He had an innate sense of leadership built into him through the generations. "Right. We've done all we can here. Staff have some seats arranged in the stables, so let's decamp over there."

"Your strength is admirable, Bertie," I said to him.

He stood up straighter. "Not much else I can do under the circumstances, is there?"

I was speechless. He'd lost so much. An immense feeling of guilt must run through his mind, as custodian of centuries of history.

He gave me a somber look. "Julie, my ancestors lost their lives in the English Civil War, the Battle of Waterloo as well as World Wars One and Two. My loss today isn't even close to their sacrifice. We will rebuild and that is simply how it must be."

❊❊❊

Stables. 6:23 a.m.

Bertie still kept three matched pairs of fancy, high-stepping hackney horses to pull the antique carriages around the safe estate paths. They were a bonafide hit with the tourists, and also a popular wedding event request. He had two pairs of liver chestnut horses—darker, burnished bay—each with four short white socks. The other pair was black, and these horses were used for funeral processions. Many in the Kentish weald still observed long-held traditions, and the Victorian-era hearses were pulled by black horses with tall black ostrich plumes at the apex of their bridles. They provided an elegant, yet somber, way to lay a deceased family member to rest. In past decades, this forty-stall stables was full of horses, but now, with only six Hackneys plus two draft horses, it was rather empty. This was in our favor today as it made for ample places to store the precious treasures coming out of the castle. The stables were warm, dry and had a sturdy roof so this was somewhere we could protect ancient things. An assembly line started moving things off the front lawn and into smaller vehicles for transport to the stables. It made for a rather odd appearance, all these people in their nightclothes carting off expensive books and artwork crammed into nooks and crannies of their cars, SUVs and even a tenant's floral delivery van. It would make any conservator's hackles rise, seeing all of these wonderful objects and antiques being carted away without protective covers or bumper pads. No corner protectors, no acid-free tissue paper, no safety boxes. Yet, it was just what had to be done.

We kept working. As I made umpteen trips back and forth to the front lawn, I noticed the sound of flames was dissipating. It was unfortunately replaced with the acrid smell of rubble still burning with hot embers. The fire was quick and hot, giving the fire investigators some good clues as to its origin. Bertie always adhered to fire regulations, ran fire drills with his staff, and ensured he had an on-site crew who knew how to deal with an emergency. This fire incident just did not make sense to anyone in the community. Answers were needed.

I looked up at the clock in the middle of the stone arch covering the front drive near the castle. It was once attached to a gatehouse next to the drive, but apparently the gatehouse was smashed when a prior Duke held a circus on the front lawn and two of the elephants got loose. All that was left now was the arch with its clock, and it revealed we had worked through the wee hours of the morning. I heard the last water hose get turned off and the sound of rushing water replaced by the tromping of firemen's boots. A beautiful sunrise was on the horizon and gave us some solace from the horrors of the evening before.

I made my last trip back to the stables, my bedroom slippers now nearly completely worn through. Everybody else was in the same boat: exhausted, sooty and upset for Bertie. A bright beacon of hope was seeing a line of four disaster response company vehicles wind their way up the drive, en route to save as many of the castle's precious treasures as they could. A couple of news trucks followed, the occupants no doubt wanting a statement on camera from the Duke of Conroy about this horrific event.

Someone from the village deli was kind enough to rustle together some sandwiches and they were now being unloaded from the shop's delivery van. I doubt anyone had asked for this nor put in an order. It was just what friends did to help each other in times of need. In the stables, the grooms had set up additional makeshift seating using straw bales. We sat two to a square bale, munching our sandwiches as the horses ate their hay and oats behind us inside their stalls.

Bertie stood, ashen faced and tired. He raised his glass of water, looking out at the crowd. A restoration crew member came over and asked for approval to erect a few tents on the lawn to protect certain items. Once that distraction was dealt with, Bertie tried again:

"Everyone, may I have your attention please? I would just like to say I am both humbled and grateful for all your assistance over these past few hours. This has been a devastating fire for Scotford Castle and while there are still lots of unanswered questions, I am so glad that we were able to save many of the historic antiques and treasures. Without your help, many would have been reduced to cinders. Thank you so much."

He quickly sat down, overwhelmed and unable to say more. Bertie was usually such a polished speaker but today's events were just too much for him to bear.

Somebody had to say something to ease this man's pain. To my surprise, it was Ewan. He stood and returned the toast with his own glass of water. "Bertie, when you offered us a relaxing night on the country estate, this isn't exactly what I had in mind."

The crowd laughed. It felt good to smile after such a difficult past few hours.

"Well, many country estates offer an evening by the fire," Timmy offered.

More subtle laughs.

"But," Ewan continued, "everyone here is so sorry that you have endured such a tragic loss. Rest assured, we are here to help with the cleanup and anything else you need from your community."

There were tears in Bertie's eyes and he raised his glass to Ewan. "Thank you. Thank you everyone."

The deli sandwiches we ate early in the morning were extra tasty. Why? They were prepared by community-minded friends and colleagues showing their true appreciation for the history of a long-established, worthy family and a well-recognized landmark. The haphazard meal we shared while clad in our soot-covered bathrobes was all about people showing community spirit.

Chapter 6

Head Groom's Office. Next Day.

Bertie set up a temporary office in his employee's space. The fire investigation team was on-site, closely followed by the insurance claim adjuster. As insurance claimant, Bertie wasn't currently allowed anywhere near the proceedings. It was fair, but still heartbreaking to see the king of the castle banned from his own home.

Nevertheless, he put on a brave face as he spoke to me from behind a desk covered in feed invoices, carriage repair quotes and a stray grain or two of oats.

"You said you needed help so I'm here," I said.

"When the time is right, I'd like to hold a fun event for everyone who helped save the contents of Scotford Castle," Bertie said.

"That's very generous of you. I'm sure everyone will appreciate that kind gesture. I'll help you any way I can, but don't you think it's a bit too early–"

"Er, that's not why I asked you here today."

"Oh, right. My rental?" I lived in a converted barn on Bertie's estate. He was likely doing an inventory of surrounding properties to take stock of anything possibly damaged by flying embers.

"No, not that either," he said.

I was baffled as I looked at the aristocrat surrounded by things normally handled by his staff.

I heard a clang and glanced out the window. There, with incredibly bad timing, were Ozzie and Timmy preparing for a metal detecting walk in the parking lot.

Seriously.

Bertie saw my face fall. "Let them be. At least it will be entertaining to watch them dig up tin cans, old nails and rusty frying pans."

"I highly doubt there is a Roman Mint coin hoard out in your back fields."

"Never say never, and fifty percent of an amazing find would do wonders to help restore this place," he said.

"But surely the insurance–"

Bertie shook his head. "Only if they rule the fire accidental."

I was shocked. "But how could it be otherwise?"

"Scotford was under strict requirements to maintain proper fire suppression equipment, techniques and protocol training. If they find one iota of a mistake, they will deny the claim."

"And leave the castle in partial ruins? They can't do that," I said, quite indignant.

"I've seen it before. Happened to a good chum of mine up in Lancashire. Which brings me to why you are here."

I folded my hands together over top of the desk. "Anything, Bertie. Really. Just ask."

"I am not allowed back in my private office, you see, per my legal team's advice. And inside the safe room are some intensely private family papers that simply cannot be made public."

"You're worried they've been exposed in the fire? Wasn't the safe fireproof?"

"It is. But I believe I have been robbed."

"Looted during or after the fire?"

He nodded. "Severs told me he didn't feel well and believes someone slipped him something. With him out of the security picture, it was a lot easier to take advantage of me at my lowest moment."

"Oh dear."

"I'm missing a fancy silver tea service, a few gold bars and paintings, including the portrait of Aunt Edwina you so kindly loaned to me for our recent art exhibition. Severs did a quick inventory before the insurance people forced us out."

"Why take Aunt Edwina but leave the other expensive antiques and art?" I asked.

"Severs believes someone or something interrupted the thieves. Perhaps it was the fire itself."

"Are you certain? Because all of your things are well, everywhere." I gestured out into the stables, and the hodge podge stacks of antiques, books and paintings was quite evident. It made my heart ache just looking at it. I had to admit Bertie was in much better spirits than I had expected. He was holding it together a lot better than I would, had this horrific fire happened at Greymore Hall.

"Exactly what are you looking for?" I asked him, my question quite innocent and only posed in the spirit of trying to help.

"Well, along with the normal stock certificates, investment paperwork, the estate title deeds, financial records and key jewelry pieces in the safe, there is a deeply personal family secret that cannot ever see the light of day," he said. "It's in one of the filing cabinets inside the walk-in safe."

This was one of those moments that genealogists faced all the time. The question of whether to tell or not to tell. Learning new facts and then deciding whether to reveal it or conceal it from clients. However, I didn't work for Bertie. He was simply a good friend of mine, but he placed me in an awkward position.

I gave him a straight, honest stare. "And rather awkwardly, I must ask, how am I supposed to know what to look for if I do not know what it is?"

"It's a set of about ten pages, slipped inside a dark navy blue colored envelope. The envelope is sealed and has a gold label on the front marked 'private and confidential'. It's at the back of the top drawer of a filing cabinet inside the walk-in safe." He handed me the digital combination scribbled on a feed invoice plus a key card. "Here's my electronic key card for the door to the safe room. Only Severs and I have key cards, and they are usually kept in a box accessed by fingerprint scans from one of us," he said.

"I see."

"I took the advice of my father. He was still alive when it happened," Bertie said.

"What happened?" I asked without thinking. "Sorry. It's none of my business. I will see what I can find, hopefully avoiding any obstreperous insurance and fire inspectors."

"I would not ask unless it was critical." Bertie's eyes stared deep into mine, in a plaintive, sad-puppy-dog-eyes type of way.

"Of course, Bertie. Let me see what I can do." I scampered out of the groom's office as best I could without knocking over any of the piles of priceless antiques stacked everywhere. Somehow, he had now accumulated a 1970s glassware collection plus an entire set of black and white glitzy debutante ball photos. Goodness only knows who the pretty young women were, but they, too, were obviously part of Bertie's vast ancestral world here at Scotford Castle.

❊❊❊

I walked my way over to the castle entrance, stepping over bits of charred wood and ashes as I went. For safety reasons, all staff were banished to the exterior of the castle and every single one of them was there working double time, busy with brushes and brooms, sweeping up the damp debris that now littered the castle and grounds. I nodded at Severs who was trying his best to keep an eye on all the various collections out front. He gave me a quiet nod as I put a finger to my lips and walked inside the front doors.

It was once a grand front hall, but now the beautiful carved cherrywood paneling was in ashes. Either the fire made its way to the front—and it was one heck of a long way—or there were two separate fires. The floors were tile or stone and had held together, but everything was coated in a layer of grey, dark grey and black. The smell of wet ash and soot assaulted my nasal passages the moment I stepped foot over the threshold; the smell was far stronger here than inside the stables. My eyes smarted at the bits of tiny debris that still floated through the air. The fire hoses had been in here with vigor and everything was soaked. I looked up at the beautiful stained glass windows and saw that all but one of the fourteen had survived. Each one of them showed a famous Duke receiving his title from his own father, and these scenes recorded multiple centuries. There were horses, fair maidens and beautiful landscapes, warmed by a kind sun coming over green hillsides. They harkened back to a time when succession was paramount and solidly based upon parental lineage. The seventh Duke's stained glass was shattered, the various colored shards strewn like jagged pieces of candy underneath the broken window. I walked further inside the castle, past the singed stanchions in place to guide visitors on the public tour of the castle. The looped velvet ropes had burned up in the fire; all that remained were brass poles looking for something to connect. I walked further still, hoping I didn't run into anybody. I knew that the structure was deemed safe to enter; they had already cleared out any beams due to collapse along with any unsafe walls. My concern now was not being discovered by anybody during my secret quest.

I used Bertie's electronic key card and entered the safe room. Bertie always kept it locked, even if he was only leaving the room for five minutes. He just did not risk a potential loss. I held my breath, unsure as to what I would find. But no breath holding was necessary, because the room was in pristine condition, unaffected by the fires. There was, however, one thing out of order and it had nothing to do with fire damage. The safe's door was wide open, leaving no doubt whatsoever that Bertie's most precious inner sanctum was breached. He had been robbed and whatever that deep family secret he was hiding was now at risk.

I put on a pair of vinyl gloves I'd taken from the stables' first aid kit and headed for the filing cabinet that supposedly contained the navy blue envelope. The top drawer to a filing cabinet was already open, hauled out on its tracks, the once neatly organized manila folders now disheveled. Years ago, I watched Bertie slip my receipt into a tidy folder marked 'receipts'. Scotford was an immense estate with a lot of accounts receivable and accounts payable; back-of-the-envelope accounting certainly would not do here. Something was indeed very wrong here because all of Bertie's careful sorting was completely disheveled.

I walked closer, and started to rifle through the folders. I started at the back and went through every single file and hangar on the rack inside the filing cabinet.

No navy envelope.

I even tried the rest of the drawers, then the rest of the filing cabinets. Nothing.

Bertie's secret was loose and we had no idea with whom. All I knew at this moment was that Bertie's secret was stolen and placed into nefarious hands. It was frightening.

"Miss Fincher?" I heard behind me.

I turned to see Severs, and realized he must have trailed me inside, ever the diligent right-hand man.

I spoke in a low whisper. "His Grace asked me to come in and look for an envelope in his safe. I cannot find it."

I never called Bertie 'His Grace'.

It just bubbled out of me at this awkward, sensitive moment. It was said out of deep respect for my friend.

Severs' eyebrows quivered ever so slightly—he was trained not to show emotion—and he responded in a steady voice. "Then I suggest we allow the authorities in here immediately with their fingerprint crew. This room was not breached by the fire, that is quite clear to me."

"But all of Bertie's things, his precious things. His Grace's privacy was invaded." I looked at Severs for help.

Severs issued me a serious glance. "I've already reached out to my contacts and started work on this, coordinating with the police, of course. We must consider the power of social media and the internet. The information could already have been shared with goodness knows whom."

"You think we're too late?"

He nodded. "Unless there is a ransom demand pending."

"We all pitched in to save the heirlooms, the antiques, the paintings and tapestries ..."

"Yes, and everyone did a valiant job. But there must have been someone who slipped into the group of community members, someone with more nefarious thoughts on his or her mind."

"What do I tell Bertie?"

My question hung in the air for a moment or two while Severs considered his answer.

"Tell His Grace the truth. His secret is no longer concealed."

***

Head Groom's Office. Ten Minutes Later.

Severs, Bertie and I pondered our next steps. How the frivolity and filming of yesterday seemed so far away now. I longed to rewind back to when we were giggling over Fred's periwig and Ozzie's office clerk uniform. It was a million years away from what we faced today. The gloom of reality now hung over us. I really didn't want to know Bertie's deep, dark secret.

"You are quite certain no one can hear us?" Bertie asked Severs.

"Positive. We're alone behind these thick walls. I have already done a sweep for listening devices," Severs replied.

"You have got to be kidding me," I said. "This isn't a spy nest."

"You would be surprised at the length some competitors will go to," Bertie said.

"For your mango chutney recipe? That seems a bit far-fetched to me," I said.

"No, competing for tourist dollars. Everybody wants to know the others' plans, and if there is no cooperative agreement in place, such as Holgarth Hall has with the local gardens, then it is every threadbare aristocrat for himself. All of these big old manor houses have roofs to repair and none of them come cheap. That's why I've always kept my personal finances completely separate from those of Scotford Castle business."

"In other words, your fine treasures on display don't pay for the roof leak nor the new linens for the dining room table," I said.

"Precisely," Bertie replied.

As if on cue, a couple of roofing tiles slid out from the pile of debris to the right of the castle and clattered down to the cobblestones.

"Getting back to the matter at hand," Bertie started, "there is a reason why I needed to meet with both of you. I want you to hear this from me before whomever stole my paperwork leaks it to the press."

"You aren't in any danger, are you?" I asked.

"No, no, nothing like that. It's just very complicated and some would say even rather shameful," Bertie said. "But that was her choice, that is how she wanted it."

I frowned. "She? Who is she and what did she want?"

Bertie sat up straight and clasped his fingers together under his chin. "I have an illegitimate daughter. She is now twenty years old, has no contact with me and lives in America, the East Coast, to be specific." Bertie paused there as if to gauge our reactions.

It shocked me, because he'd never breathed a word of his daughter the entire time I'd known him. I looked over at Severs for his reaction, and he sat there stoic, like the rock Bertie expected him to be. I guessed Severs only wanted to be given his employer's next assignment.

Bertie continued. "I paid for her entire upbringing, school, university, her first car, house … all in exchange for no contact and no scandal. Everything went through the family's solicitor's office, all very formalized."

I was stunned into silence by this information.

"Believe me, it was not my choice. It was her mother's," Bertie said.

"Because an illegitimate daughter was not useful for the line of succession?" I asked.

"Actually, my parents didn't know at the start. I was at university and met my daughter's mother there," Bertie said.

"Do you even know her name?" I asked.

"Melanie. My daughter's name is Melanie," Bertie said. His voice was subdued and ashamed.

"I take it that the papers in the envelope were all about her existence, the support payments you made, how to reach her mother's solicitor etc.?" Severs asked.

Bertie nodded. "Precisely. And if the tabloids ever get hold of the fact that Melanie exists and we've completely cut off contact, I am deathly afraid it will impact tourism revenues here at Scotford Castle. After fourteen generations, I could not bear to see the Scotford estate fail on my watch."

Severs and I shared a glance. It was indeed quite the conundrum.

I cleared my throat. "Why did your girlfriend not want you involved?"

"Oh, another ridiculous story. I was so keen to escape my privileged upbringing, and just enjoyed being a normal person for once while I was away at university. I kept my impending dukedom concealed from my then-girlfriend, Lucy. When she found out, she was already pregnant and made the decision right then and there. She's American and did not want her child stifled over here in behind all of our 'stuffy aristocratic traditions' as she called them."

"That is odd, because a lot of people would adore having an English title," I said. "In the early twentieth century, it was all the rage for wealthy Americans to send over their heiress daughters to marry a titled man who was in desperate need of a large infusion of capital to maintain his estate."

"Not Lucy. She was adamant. She then threw it back on me, saying how I had concealed my background from her in order to try out a normal life on a temporary jaunt. She had huge trust issues and I can't say I blamed her," Bertie said.

"So what happened?" I asked.

"She went back to Boston after finishing third year university. By choice, she had our daughter in America. We had a poignant, final goodbye when I flew over to meet them both, Melanie being only an infant at the time. By then, my own parents knew, my father intervened and our family's legal team worked out the rest. I wasn't allowed to say anything, but the theft of the papers changes everything. I have already telephoned my solicitor and let him know. I would hate to be accused of intentionally breaching the confidentiality agreement."

"Will your daughter inherit?" Severs asked.

"No," Bertie said, "the dukedom requires that only legitimate heirs can inherit or my line goes dead. I intend to donate Scotford Castle to the nation or a trust to keep it going as a tourist destination long after I am gone. It no longer matters that I am heirless."

"It's sad you broke up with Lucy," I said.

"Lucy said the concealed identity wasn't a strong enough foundation for marriage. And she was right. I was not comfortable with who I was back then. The title, all the wealth, the expectations, the people and the estate one is responsible for as Lord of the Manor. It weighs a lot on a young man's shoulders."

We all contemplated his perspective for a moment.

Bertie sighed. "After Lucy, finding a woman whom I truly loved proved an impossible challenge. I was forced to do the tour of all the young heiresses in England. No sparks ignited. I was sent abroad again at age thirty and still found no one in the aristocratic circles on the continent. And then my father died, Scotford needed a lot of renovations, and time just got away from me."

"I would think producing an heir would be top of mind for a Duke, for any aristocrat for that matter," I said.

"Perhaps. But Scotford was in a bad way. Tapestries needed emergency restorative embroidering, the portrait gallery had fifteen paintings that needed cleaning, the stables' brick flooring was crumbling and, well, that's how it was."

It was shades of what had happened when pipes burst over top of the guest room where Ewan was sleeping during the last holiday season. The poor man was soaked with water right after a warm, cozy Christmas dinner at Greymore Hall.

Today, Bertie revealed a lot more of himself. As I looked at his sagging shoulders and the worry lines across his face, I saw a man beaten by circumstance. Not only was his elegant home devastated by fire, he then had to suffer the indignity of his most precious secret being put out into the open. It was even scarier because we did not know who had the information nor what they planned to do with it.

"I am really sorry, Bertie. You've had an awful lot to deal with in the last day or so. Is there anything we can do?" I asked.

"Be there for me once I have a gameplan together. You've already sat here and listened to my woes. I think the best thing to do now is for you to go back to GGRS and get something positive done with your researchers. I would like some quiet time to think about what to do next," Bertie said.

"I shall continue revising our security system upgrade and over-seeing cleanup, if that is acceptable, Your Grace?" Severs suggested, giving an expectant look to Bertie.

"Fine, thank you," Bertie said.

Severs left without a noise. I knew the man could move as quietly as a ghost if needed. It was all just part of his training.

"He feels awful," I said.

"The fire and robbery were not Severs' fault. Although right now I am convinced this was an inside job. There were a lot of people here filming over the past few weeks." Bertie said.

"And what are you going to do?" I asked Bertie.

"Deal with more police, insurance and fire investigators." He glanced out the window and saw his once elegant grounds changed into holding bays for castle debris and various antiques storage. The conservation crews were hard at work conserving the most damaged materials. They had already started to dry out various books inside numerous tents with thin washing lines set up to air out individual pages.

Bertie sighed. "What a week. I feel like a monk whose abbey was just raided by King Henry the Eighth."

Chapter 7

—

GGRS, Greymore Hall. Next Morning.

Candace Blightly, the dinosaur expert's daughter, was back to do more research. She came over to the information desk and gave us another winning smile. "It looks like your team has loads of fun together. I saw the well-stocked café and the electric van out front. Do you take research field trips too?"

"Yes, to various archives and other research sites. The most recent excursion was rather sad, however, as we were staying overnight at Scotford Castle when she caught fire," I explained.

"Oh dear. Scotford Castle is one of the gems of the area. How bad is the damage?"

"Extensive, but the community pitched in to help save a lot of the antiques, heirlooms, artwork and papers. It's a massive cleanup job for the professional crews right now. Bertie, that is the Duke of Conroy, has paid for conservation staff but we're also looking for volunteers."

Candace smiled. "Tell you what, let's get my mother's memoir project back on track and then I'll come over and help out for a few hours."

"That would be lovely. Very generous of you." Inside I was smiling because I knew that if someone was willing to volunteer to help with the conservation work, they would likely get hooked and come back day after day. There was something so special about being able to interact with centuries-old documents and antiques. The connection one felt to the past could never be undone. Touching the objects that one's ancestors and prior residents of the community had actually worked with offered a unique, special bond that would always hold firm.

❈❈❈

Front Lawn, Scotford Castle. That Afternoon.

Bertie approached me with a sheaf of papers in his hand and looked very concerned. "Hello Julie."

"Dear Bertie. How are things here?" I cast an eye over the now much more organized priceless antiques and heirlooms scattered across his front lawn. Staff were going through and making a formal inventory. It was obviously a significant task.

"About as well as one could expect, considering the tragic circumstances. I am trying to match the existing castle inventory with the individual provenance records. Both books were stored at the bank in the safety deposit box, so no worries there. The real problem is locating a few items that were improperly recorded in the seventeenth century."

"So who does one blame for that? King Charles the Second?" I asked.

Bertie gave a soft laugh. I was trying to cheer him up and it was the quickest comeback I could think of under the circumstances. Then he got more serious. "It is not so much casting blame with anyone, but rather proving to the insurance man how much everything was worth. You see, there is a theory racing around that I purposely set fire to the castle in order to collect on the insurance policy."

"Oh right, after centuries of your family living here, you're just going to burn everything down, pocket the cash and scarper off to some far flung Caribbean Island? I don't think so," I said in a firm voice. "Would you like me to talk to your insurance representative?"

He gave me a kind look. "That is very kind of you, but no. The estate, as you know, is so vast and to replace these items is absolutely mind-boggling expensive. That is why the adjusters are being so picky."

"But surely there can't be any question of them denying a claim? You are a member of the aristocracy, Bertie."

He gave a deep sigh. "Apparently, my title gives them even more reason to be concerned, considering the number of great houses falling into disrepair over lack of funds in the past few decades. They want to see audited financial statements from Scotford Castle just to ensure that she was financially viable before the fire."

"Doesn't it just come down to what the fire inspector says?"

Surely that is the only way to make things truly fair.

"It's in the fine print of the insurance contract. If there is any shadow of a doubt, they have the right to do further digging.

And yes, that includes financial records of the property in question. As Scotford Castle is a separate legal entity running on its own, then those are the financial statements they have a right to see."

"Well, I hope none of this red tape is slowing down the conservation, preservation and rebuilding efforts," I said.

"Of course not. We're full steam ahead to make sure everything possible is conserved and preserved. The impacts of both smoke and water damage will be mitigated with each and every item. I owe it to my ancestors and to the local community." Bertie stood a little straighter when he mentioned his ancestral heritage. It was something every aristocrat had to take seriously.

Quite honestly, my opinion was that every single person had a responsibility to take their ancestry seriously. Everyone belonged to some sort of community. Decades, even centuries ago, everybody contributed something. Just because one did not wear a crown or drive a gold-plated car didn't mean that they weren't important. Sometimes the best social histories came from those a lot further down the ladder, the ones who worked the lands, the shops and the seas. Nothing beat getting dirt under one's fingernails once in a while; it made everything much more real.

"A couple of paintings are causing me unending grief. I have a couple of Old Masters from the seventeenth century but the insurance adjuster says the provenance is not good enough. I have a handwritten note from the butler here at the time, yet they want it proven another way."

"Well, unless they decide to offer you a time travel machine, I have to suggest that's really not possible," I said.

"I tend to agree," Bertie said.

"I would be happy to take a look at them if my art history background can be of help. Maybe I have seen them in a textbook somewhere and that would help convince your insurance man."

There was a contemplative silence between us old friends, comfortable with each other, and using teamwork to resolve a challenging problem.

"That's where he comes into the picture," Bertie said, gesturing off to our right. We both turned to see Ewan striding across the lawn to meet us.

After shaking Bertie's hand and giving me a kiss on the cheek, Ewan got right down to business. "I posted a list of your stolen goods to my antiques network. This includes museums, dealers, archives and family history societies. It is a very strong network and everyone keeps an eye out for everyone else, as no one wants to deal in stolen goods. For someone to actually steal from a site of national importance is absolutely abominable."

"Oh, thank you so much for helping, Ewan," I said. "That's very positive, isn't it, Bertie?" I hoped my voice sounded jolly and uplifting to the man who had suffered so much over the last few days.

"Wonderful. Thank you, Ewan," Bertie said.

"I'm sorry to say, I've seen underhanded selling before, even stealing to order after previewing a house clearance sale. I'd like to check a few more things on your inventory list, mainly because I already had an inquiry from a dealer in Devon about a familiar-looking silver snuff box," Ewan said.

"Severs can assist you," Bertie said, gesturing over towards the stables where his security chief stood.

"Thanks."

Bertie called out after Ewan. "Mind the ash. It's not one hundred percent cleaned up."

Ewan left us and began walking closer to the castle. Bertie and I were now alone again.

I knew exactly how much all of this pained Bertie. Scotford Castle was normally kept in a pristine state with absolutely no specks of dust allowed. To have the whole thing partly-gutted by fire, now sodden with damp ashes everywhere, was just not in Bertie's nature. Nor was it in his staff's normal job description to do this much cleanup work. A tall chef I'd seen last week in his kitchen whites was now relegated to sweeping the front steps and a burly gardener was neatly arranging books. I cast a glance over to the front entrance and saw five disaster response vans parked there. Bertie would be working out of his groom's office for quite some time yet. This project, including conserving and preserving all the precious antiques and heirlooms, was going to take months.

"What about ticket revenues from tourism?" I asked. "How big of a blow will this be to the estate?"

Bertie took a deep intake of air and then let it out in a big rush. "It's going to be devastating, I just don't know by how much yet. I've been sitting in that stables office trying to rack my brains, thinking of any other way we can generate some cash for the estate."

"You have your weddings with horse-drawn carriage trade, the estate shop, the produce from your estate. And at least part of the hotel wasn't damaged," I said in a somewhat hopeful voice.

"No one wants to fall asleep to the acrid smell of burnt gilt frames," he said. "What it will come down to is how we can still provide a world-class experience for our guests while allowing the restoration work to proceed."

"You could have some community days. Invite the public in for a day on the estate, and let people see how the castle is being restored. A lot of people actually find a look behind the scenes quite interesting. Those who are into handicrafts and construction would be far more interested in seeing behind a brick wall. They'd be fascinated learning about all the little things workmen over the centuries have dropped under the floorboards, plus how craftspeople restore a castle to its former glory. It's a far more interesting experience than just looking at fancy jewels and dog-eared photos inside a glass case."

Bertie rocked back on his heels ever so slightly. "You know, you might be onto something there, Julie. Let me think on that for a bit. Embrace the fire. Hmm. Turn it into a learning experience."

"And your other big problem? The missing family papers?"

He shook his head. "That secret cannot get out. The tabloids would have a field day and it might even start all this unnecessary legal wrangling over the estate. My daughter is a straight 'A' student at a big university in Boston. She's well-adjusted, has a great future ahead of her as a pediatrician and she's happy. She doesn't need any of my baggage."

"Melanie sounds like a lovely person. I'm surprised you've given up on ever being a part of her life," I said.

"Her mother wanted Melanie to be raised in a normal household without any airs or grandeur. Work hard for her life and earn her way up through society. That's exactly what happened, so kudos to her mother."

"But she's your daughter, Bertie," I said in a soft voice. "You have rights, too." Inside I was appalled at how cold this illegitimate child was made to feel about her father.

"Melanie has a wonderful mother and a caring stepfather she's known since she was one and a half. I made sure she wants for nothing financially and that I get her school reports every term. She's got a large trust that her mother doles out in appropriate quantities for school, her first car, clothing allowance, her first house, holidays. It's all paid for, just not getting to her all in one lump sum to party away. Not that she would, of course. She's very responsible."

Bertie sensed I was uncomfortable with the decision. "My daughter thinks she was a result of a one night stand and that her mother never even got my name. It was easiest all around, especially at the time."

I gave him a serious glance. "Your wealth may buy you silence, Bertie, but it won't secure you a settled heart."

Chapter 8

GGRS. Late Afternoon.

"Right. That's the lot of them," Ewan said as he unloaded the last pile of books from the GGRS electric van. We'd set up a convoy system to shuttle a few vehicle loads of books to temporary accommodation in some rooms at Greymore Hall. Bertie was ever so gracious with his thanks and I told him it wasn't necessary. Good neighbors who respected the community and those who lived nearby always shared a duty to help each other. I had other feelings about not-so-good neighbors, including the noisy, dirty and uncaring ones who lived like they were the only people on the planet and ignored everybody else's privacy, space, ambience or peace and quiet.

I looked at all the gold-tooled, leather-bound books in the room. "At least Bertie assigned us the ones that weren't smoke damaged. These ones came out of the castle in the first few wheelbarrow trips, and they're in a lot better shape than the ones from the back of the castle that are all now with the conservationists."

"We're doing all we can to help, Julie," Ewan said. "Fancy going up to visit Aunt Edwina and Elliot?"

"Honestly? I don't know if I'm up for the walk. I'm bone tired." I said.

"I've already resolved that potential issue. Come with me, my dear," he said in a grandiose tone. I slipped my hand into his and he led me to the front doors of Greymore Hall. At the bottom of the steps sat a pristine white, electric golf cart, emblazoned with Greymore's logo. In the back was a large picnic basket.

Ewan squeezed my hand. "We'll both sit in the front and I'll drive. Blankets are on the back seat along with dinner inside the picnic basket. Sound good?"

"Sounds divine. Exactly what we needed."

"I worry about you, you know. You try to be all things to all people, help everybody. Sometimes you just need to take a break and do something good for yourself," he said.

"Oh, it's just such a big undertaking and I want everything in GGRS to turn out right. We have a lot of people to help, a lot more adventures to take."

"Just take me along with you," Ewan said with a tender smile.

❀❀❀

Under the Hollow Oak Tree. Twenty Minutes Later.

Our picnic spot overlooked the Kentish weald in all its grandeur. Ewan and I were at a very special place indeed; Aunt Edwina and her first love Elliot, an RAF pilot who was shot down in World War Two, were remembered up here with proper memorial stones.

Ewan thought of everything. A waterproof sheet for underneath our picnic blanket, travel cutlery and glasses, fresh salads, cheeses and peach cobbler. Sparkling raspberry water for fizz. As we sat together, munching quietly and looking out over the undulating hills framed by an apricot sunset, I was filled to the brim with appreciation for everything I had in my life.

My family. The people. This land. Our community. Greymore Hall and everything Aunt Edwina taught me.

I bit into a particularly yummy tomato—sweet, crisp and tasting like it was grown in a sun-drenched organic garden—and then closed my eyes to enjoy the moment. It was pure and utter bliss. The last rays of sun from this warm day radiated down upon us and the carpet of new green out in the fields gave us all hope that new life was starting to sprout. Kent didn't let us down; for centuries it was a yeoman's and agricultural laborer's paradise, providing bountiful soil, strong crop yields and steady employment for good workers. The market economy had already started back in the fifteenth century when agricultural laborers charged more for their services for summer harvest work versus winter chores. Enterprising young men and women could climb the social ladder, sometimes becoming landowners themselves through hard work, determination and a bit of good fortune. As for me, my good fortune was already bestowed upon me. I had family, friends and purpose. My past was connected to the present ... and also to my future. Frankly, all of this was such a great gift and I didn't know how to begin saying thank you for this life of mine. It had its ups and downs, certainly, but I wouldn't trade it for the world.

"More sparkling water?" Ewan asked, shaking me out of my reverie.

"Er, no thank you. I'm good."

"Satiated?" He gave me a kind look. Ewan gave me lots of those.

"Satisfied with the day. We helped a dear friend and now I have some quiet, alone time with my favorite guy. It's wonderful."

Ewan put his arm around me and pulled me close. Together we watched the sun go down and when there was nothing left but twilight, he gallantly packed up our picnic accoutrements and drove us home. He stopped the golf cart a little way before the manor house. Ewan leaned over and gave me a sweet kiss. I put a soft hand to his cheek, feeling the stubble grown in during the day. Our eyes met, and as I stared deep into his, I saw our future ... together.

✳✳✳

Scotford Castle. Next Day. Noon.

Even through Bertie's expensive binoculars, they looked like a pair of uncoordinated elves traipsing across the land. As the two men neared, one stocky and plump, the other taller and gangly, anyone could see they were incredibly serious about their new hobby. However, watching them clamber over bare fields, resplendent with a few soggy patches left over from the overnight rain shower, made one wonder about these head-to-toe muddy creatures who would soon be upon us.

I glanced over at Bertie. "They look like swamp creatures, something coming out of the lagoon or compost pit. I thought metal detecting was a rather conservative hobby."

"That was my understanding as well. I tried it for a couple of hours at a charity event on the beach one day, and apart from getting saltwater on my leather brogues, I can't say I came out of it looking like I needed a bath."

"I say we hose them off. Are the firefighters still around?" I shot him a winning smile.

"How droll. The fire engines are long gone. The police report was written up by Constable Snowdrop. I told him there was zero chance of things being merely misplaced, considering who has access to my safe," Bertie said.

"Indeed."

"We're down to police working on the robbery, haggling with the insurance people and awaiting the fire investigator's report," Bertie said.

"And did they give you any sense of what their conclusions were?" I asked.

"No. Everyone's tightlipped about the whole affair. It doesn't help that the fire investigator's sister owns a shop in Plumsden that sells a chutney product in competition with mine."

Ah, yes. Bertie and his mango chutney venture. He was ever so pleased with it because it was the first thing he had done on his own without relying upon his vast inheritance or title. His hand-signed labels had now yielded to preprinted labels with a facsimile of his signature. The demand generated by this Duke's in-person sales tours had simply gotten too high for him to sit there signing labels for hours at a time. After a long conversation last winter, I'd finally persuaded him to give up the time-consuming signature task.

Bertie's comment about the chutney competitor had me curious. "How does your chutney stack up against hers?"

He scoffed, like only a toffee-nosed aristocrat could. "Her product is far too sweet. I had a mystery shopper go in and purchase a couple of jars. I had some on my toast at the next luncheon. It was far too sugary and overcooked. There was absolutely no crunch to the vegetables either. Customers like texture, not limp goo."

Spoken like a true chutney connoisseur.

I had no idea there was so much to vegetables, spices and vinegar.

"Well, it's not like people want to spread raw zucchini or tomato across their sandwich. Isn't it supposed to be a slightly mashed down, vinegary condiment?" I asked.

"Yes, but hers was beyond belief. There was absolutely no tanginess, no substance to it at all. Very subpar," he said.

"And the fire inspector is holding your chutney's superiority against you?" I asked in disbelief.

"Of course he'll never admit it, but I think he's got his nose out of joint thinking that I use my vast wealth to make a better chutney than his sister."

"Bertie, listen to yourself. Your castle has just suffered a major fire, yet here we are having an animated conversation about chutney."

"It's important!" he yelped.

Aristocrats weren't supposed to yelp.

"And yet once again you perfectly and handily prolong the public perception of the clueless aristocrat." I gave him a grin then gestured over at Ozzie and Timmy who were now only about 200 yards away and barely out of earshot. "Those two look rather suspicious, don't you think?"

"They look like rag and bone men from the 1940s," Bertie said, referring to the grown up street urchins of the era who used a horse and cart to collect recycling and scraps for down purposing.

"They're even more raggedy than that."

Bertie gave me a serious look, but there was the tug of a grin at the side of his mouth.

"Don't trust them an inch. Do a lot more listening than talking," I advised.

Ozzie and Timmy were now upon us. "Hello Duke," they said in unison.

They were extremely muddy and damp. The state of their clothes was likely attributable to the one wet patch I knew existed at the south end of the field, something Bertie and I noted the last time we took his carriage and fancy, high-stepping hackney horses for a tour around the Scotford estate. Bertie's tenant farmers did a lovely job and all his fields were kept in pristine order. It was both an expectation and an unwritten rule to qualify for living within the confines of this ancient, fabled estate. Bertie did a fabulous job and I admired him for stepping up with such fierce devotion and fortitude. I supposed I was the same way; Aunt Edwina left me an enormous legacy and I intended to see that through as best I could.

Ozzie and Timmy looked out of place. Exceedingly so. Both were splattered with mud, appearing as though they'd wrestled with a recalcitrant puddle. Each of them carried a state-of-the-art metal detector with them, casually swinging their instrument with each step they took. They were done searching the ground for treasure today, and Ozzie had a shoulder bag slung cross body over his chest and hip. The bag looked quite heavy. I was skeptical about its contents, and rightly so. With Ozzie, it could be anything from false teeth to leftover smoked mackerel sandwiches. He needed to live with a warning sign around his neck, one of those bright, big orange construction signs. A couple of traffic cones in his wake would also be wise.

"Ozzie and Timmy. Any success with our intrepid field exploration?" Bertie called out.

"Nada. Just a few bits of rubbish," Ozzie said. His statement appeared to confirm our doubts regarding any potential success of this treasure-hunting venture.

That was until Timmy unzipped the bag Ozzie wore and pulled out the so-called 'rubbish' they'd traipsed back from the field. It was rubbish all right, but not the kind one would expect to find at a modern day campsite. This particular rubbish from Bertie's property appeared to be centuries old. Specifically, we saw shards of real pottery and tiles showing hues of aquamarine blue, ruby red and deep green.

"Where did you find these?" Bertie asked, astonished.

"Underneath these," Ozzie said, digging further into the bag and hauling out a rusty horseshoe, a shiny metal vase with chipped gold paint, a tiny silver teacup and saucer plus five bent blacksmith nails. "The horseshoe nails triggered the metal detectors, so we started digging. We found the horseshoe first, then the vase and teacup with pottery shards and tiles underneath."

"I think the teacup was an offering to the Pagan Gods," Timmy said with great confidence.

"That should be worth a bob or two," Ozzie added. "And look at these pottery shards. We're close to finding a big hoard. I can just feel it in my bones," he said with glee.

"It might be from some sort of Roman settlement," I suggested. "Those tiles could be from a fancy mosaic floor inside a villa."

"I'm impressed," Bertie said. "A couple of my ancestors perpetuated the rumor about a Roman settlement, but their efforts to prove it were greatly unsuccessful."

"All it takes is modern technology," Ozzie offered in his characteristically brash, undiplomatic manner, this time a bit more officious than usual.

"A metal detector doesn't guarantee you'll find anything," I said.

Bertie was still fawning over the pieces these two unlikely treasure seekers found. "I don't believe it, I really don't believe it."

Timmy decided to add in his two pence. "Maybe it just took a different perspective. I was attracted to a piece of undulating land, and some of that is due to my ornithology background. You know, knowing the propensity of certain birds to land on rises to avoid predators."

Timmy's theory sounded as likely as us being whisked away to the moon inside a spaceship filled with green aliens.

Bertie, ever the diplomat, nodded his head. "Perhaps. Now how about we go into the safe part of the castle and I offer you some refreshment?"

"We'd love to," Ozzie said. "I'm parched."

It was a sorry, muddy troop of two that lagged behind us as we headed up to the castle. Bertie expertly guided us through the ash-laden front hall and then off to a parlor. It was one of the rooms largely untouched by fire, except for some soot damage on the molding plus on the floor-to-ceiling hearth against the far wall. It was signed off as structurally safe, denoted by the temporary engineering signage posted beside the door.

Bertie pulled on the cord at the edge of the room, requesting one of his household staff to come and attend to us. It always made me smile, watching these ancient traditions upheld by the modern aristocrats of today. Silk-tasseled attention getters were not yet replaced by electronic intercom systems here. Old habits died hard, and traditions never did. Not even a significant fire would shut down the ancient workings here at Scotford Castle.

I noted how Ozzie looked smug, like he'd just scored coveted tickets to a football match final. It was as if, for once, he'd done better than his ancestors. After his failed escapades at the confectionery firm, it was nice to see him get a win. The man needed something to smile about after all his hard work. Deep down, Ozzie Boggs was a nice person; he just was as bristly as a porcupine when one first met him.

"No, not there!" Bertie yelped, as Ozzie tried to lay his metal detector on top of a lone, fancy, lacquered side table, one of the few remaining pieces in the room.

"Ooops. Sorry," Ozzie said, yanking back the detector to swing again by his side. "Is that an expensive one?" he asked via a rather crass question.

"That table? It belonged to a Duke of Conroy a couple of centuries ago," Bertie explained. "It's worth the price of a small flat ... in Kensington Gardens."

"Oh my." That impressed Ozzie. Even he knew how posh that London neighborhood was.

A staff member walked in and Bertie leaned over to explain what refreshments he would like brought into the room for his guests. The staff member left without a sound and Bertie turned back to us. "There, all settled. Our fearless historical discoverers can expect a hearty snack."

"I think the best thing to do is find a safe place to lay out all the pottery shards and see what we really have. Perhaps they all reassemble back into one pot," Timmy said.

"Did you find anything else in the area?" I asked.

"Nothing yet, but where there's smoke, there's fire, I believe," Ozzie said, obviously without thinking.

Bertie and I exchanged a horrified glance.

Ozzie didn't seem to notice and bulldozed his way onto the next conversation topic. "I say," he commented, swinging his metal detector by his side as he walked, "this is a neat old hearth. My aunt has one just like it, especially with the darker colors of brick here ..." He raised his metal detector up to use as a pointer.

I grimaced, knowing full well that one should never wave about pole-like objects in an historic manor house filled with valuable antiques.

When Ozzie accidentally whacked the brick with his metal detector, it was akin to a single strand of wool in a sweater being pulled, the one that unravels an entire garment. A hairline fracture started in the brick where Ozzie made contact with his metal detector. We watched as the vertical crack slow-motioned upwards through the next ten rows of bricks, making an eerie, dry, breaking sound as it traveled. Something shuddered and dust started to emanate from the tall hearth.

More shuddering.

More dust.

This wasn't good.

We were all mesmerized, looking at the hearth seemingly coming to life. This was an old, historic room, largely stripped of many treasures due to the recent fire, yet it still offered a magnificent presence with its gilded wood chair rail, rich red carpet and cream painted walls. The only things left were the fancy side table as well as an eight-foot banquet table with a white tablecloth and a few chairs in the middle of the room. It was likely the best Bertie could do in the circumstances to ensure the crews were fed. I could tell he was torn between what was happening on the wall and the priceless antique nearby.

Bertie seized control of the situation and yelled, "Get to the center of the room!" As he yelled, he picked up the side table and moved it towards the other side of the room.

Just in time.

The entire hearth started collapsing into itself, creating a huge pile of broken bricks and dust. We moved to safety, then stood incredulous at what we'd just witnessed.

Ozzie had an awfully guilty look on his face. "Oh dear, I'm ever so sorry. I had no idea that a little tap from metal detector would do something like that. My apologies."

A whack is not a tap.

"We were told this room was structurally sound. To think if we'd been standing closer." Bertie sounded forlorn.

"Well, we weren't standing there, so no harm done," I said, putting a gentle hand on Bertie's arm. "You got us to safety."

Bertie was just as surprised as the rest of us. "That was a solid brick hearth. The fire must've weakened the mortar, or something structurally behind the hearth was affected by the fire. Perhaps a supporting wall was damaged. This castle is centuries old and we never really know what's behind the walls."

Now that there was nothing left of the hearth, we were tempted to look closer. The dust had settled, and we could see strong supporting wooden beams on either side keeping the other parts of the walls in place.

"Bertie, I think you need to see this," I said, nearing the gaping hole behind the pile of broken bricks.

"What is it?" he asked.

"I think we owe Ozzie a thank you for revealing something of intense genealogical interest. I'm now looking at a coffin plus a wooden chest with a big hasp. I think Scotford Castle has just revealed one of her deepest secrets," I said. "What a fabulous find."

Chapter 9

Front Entrance. Half An Hour Later.

Bertie, Ozzie, Timmy and I were all perplexed. We now stood outside the front of the castle as a structural engineer from the onsite restoration team checked the safety of the newly not-so-secret room behind the crumbled remains of the hearth.

"I'm afraid I don't have any expertise with castle construction," Timmy said in all seriousness. "Now, if we'd found an owl skeleton in the room, then I might be of use to you."

I decided to follow the old adage, 'if you can't say anything nice, then don't say anything at all'.

"What do you think that room is for?" I asked Bertie.

"I have an inkling, but I dare not say until we can get a closer look," Bertie said. He gazed at the front entrance and saw a couple of restoration crew members waving us over. "Looks like we'll have our chance now."

The three of us followed him in an excited group. We were going to enter the secret room, and see what we could find. Back inside, Bertie led us around the big piles of shattered bricks, following a tiny path that the crew had now cleared for us. We walked into a room that was about ten feet by twenty feet. Prior to this, it was concealed, hidden behind the hearth and the wood paneling. Scotford Castle was so huge that there was absolutely no way Bertie could figure out every secret hideaway.

"You never would have found this collection without the fire," I said.

Bertie was busy determining if there were any distinguishing marks on the coffin. "You're right, Julie. We have to look for the silver lining in this cloud of smoke and ash."

"Do you know what it is?" Ozzie asked.

"Meaning do I know who is buried within the confines of said coffin?" Bertie asked in a stilted voice. "The silver plaque is clear, come over and see for yourself." Bertie bent down and blew on the top of the coffin to dislodge a heavy layer of dust. I supposed he'd seen a glint of silver underneath it and that's what led him to the upper end of the coffin where it widened. The coffin was built strong enough to survive the wall collapsing around and onto it.

We all gathered close and leaned down to see, 'Duke of Conroy, 1811' inscribed on the silver plate screwed onto the top of the coffin.

"I would've thought all the Dukes would be in a family crypt or a mausoleum," I said.

Bertie grinned. "They are. All except this one. This particular Duke of Conroy from the nineteenth century would want things done in the most eccentric manner possible. He's lovingly known as the 'Old Duke'."

I could tell that Bertie's story was going to be a doozy.

Our favorite aristocrat began to explain. "The coffin and the wooden chest we see here today have long been rumored to exist. When the Old Duke passed away in 1811, there was no funeral and no details about what happened to his remains."

Ozzie and Timmy looked at each other, aware that they were now part of some deep dark secret that merged eccentricity with death. Often the stomping grounds of a genealogist, it either resulted in sheer hilarity following an ancestor search, or gloom and doom when someone proved how foolish an ancestor really was. For Bertie's sake, I hoped it was the former. I had already heard various stories and rumors from my time spent living in the converted barn here on the estate.

Ozzie tugged on my sleeve like a child desperate for a chocolate bar. "Who's that Duke? Is it somebody infamous?"

I turned to Bertie. "You're going to have to tell us all. They've already seen everything that the papers are eventually going to report."

"Very well then." Bertie ushered all of us towards a corner of the small room. "As you wish. Now, what I'm about to tell you stays in this room until we have some sort of public relations messaging figured out. And that doesn't mean you down at the pub tomorrow night with a few choice words, Ozzie. Please. Remember who bailed you out of jail when you destroyed part of that confectionery store." Bertie gave Ozzie a stern look.

Ozzie made the sign of the zipper going across his lips. Timmy repeated the gesture. However, without a legal document from solicitor Fred Todling, we only had our gentlemen's agreement. For now, it would have to do.

"Why on earth would the Old Duke want to be buried all by himself in a secret room inside the castle?" Timmy asked. When Timmy thought, he screwed his face up into a sea of wrinkles, making it hard to see his eyes. He appeared genuinely mystified at this whole discovery.

"Perhaps because of the Old Duke's scientific interest," Bertie said. "The man was very secretive and the rumor was he donated his body to science, against his advisors' opinions. He also believed in alchemy, plus lost the family fortune. Somehow, he then saved the castle and regained his wealth, but no one knows how. Rumor has it towards the end of his life he lived at Scotford with a monkey and a lion."

"Well, I don't know how you lot feel about it, but when I'm gone, have at 'er," Ozzie said. "If somebody can learn something from the shell I've lived inside all these years, then fill your boots."

His rather crass statement wasn't exactly what Bertie was looking for to help improve the ambience in the secret room. "It just wasn't done amongst the aristocrats back in the day," Bertie said. "It's like the Old Duke was a rotten branch of the family tree that didn't belong on the ancestral rolls. Dukes are supposed to be dignified, formal, issuing goodwill to all humans and what have you. They're not to be involved in dubious activities and bizarre science."

I'd read about this. Now I had the chance to ask Bertie something I'd been dying to for ages but hadn't dared out of fear of offending my good friend. "What do you mean about his dabbling in alchemy?"

"Well," Bertie started, brushing off some more dust from the coffin lid. "As the story goes, the Duke had a laboratory on-site. He was convinced it would allow him to regain the family fortune lost in some dubious spices trading venture involving an ill-fated ship rotten with woodworm."

"Cool," Ozzie said. "I've read about those alchemists. They were quite something back in the day."

"Turning common metals into valuable gold?" Timmy scoffed. "Piffle. That lot must've had rocks in their heads."

"Not so fast, gentlemen," I said. "Alchemy was a very famous and popular pastime in centuries past. It was the basis of folklore, wishful thinking in numerous homegrown laboratories. Even some of the famous scientists of the day believed. We're talking the respected stalwarts, scientists responsible for founding the modern-day principles of physics, astronomy, mathematics and microscopy."

"So that's what we have here?" Ozzie scoffed. "A dead Duke and some old laboratory beakers?"

"Again, I wouldn't put it exactly like that, Ozzie, but it's a close rendition of the truth," Bertie said.

"Well, I'm not interested in opening up a coffin to stare into the eye sockets of a dead Duke. How about that wooden chest over there? Might be something very interesting inside that," Ozzie said. "Might be filled with real gold."

"Er, indeed." Bertie strode over and fiddled with the hasp, the slot for the key empty. He brushed off more dust and traced the inscription on the brass plate on the trunk: 'Duke of Conroy: Private Science.'

"Private science. A rather momentous ask for the Old Duke who boasted over four hundred estate staff and tenants, one hundred of them living inside the castle itself," Bertie said.

"Surely they were supposed to be discreet," I said.

"Yes, but I think explosions, evil-looking boiling liquids and gassy smells would have pushed the boundaries of modest decorum," Bertie said. "That's why the rumors persist to this very day."

"Some scullery maid likely told a butcher's delivery boy a tale and it just ran from there," I suggested.

"My ancestor was written up on numerous occasions in the newspapers of his time," Bertie said. "He was the unfortunate relation, the man no one wanted to claim as their own."

"Kind of like one of the King Georges?" Timmy asked.

"Truthfully, King George the Third was medically unwell. My ancestor was healthy as a horse, just exceptionally eccentric," Bertie said.

Try saying Bertie's last two words three times fast.

"What did the papers say about him?" I asked.

"Oh, the usual scandal, the wild and wonderful things that went on in his laboratory. The money that was thrown out the proverbial window. The jaw-dropping expenses of aristocratic excess."

"But don't most aristocrats get away with it? They're just known as eccentrics and insulate themselves away behind their stacks of cash?" Ozzie asked.

"Hmmm." Bertie faced information that was relevant to his present situation as well.

"But why was this room walled up in the first place? Who was responsible for it?" I asked. "Why would the Old Duke want to be buried inside his own castle's living quarters?"

"It is bizarre. I've never seen any reference to it in our archives. Now that we know the room is here though, we might hone in on some vague allusion to it in letters or a diary, but there's nothing I could put my finger on at this very moment," Bertie said.

"Do you have ghosts here?" Ozzie asked. His eyes bulged a bit wider at the thought.

"Two," Bertie replied in succinct voice. "A housekeeper from 1890 and a duchess from the sixteenth century. The housekeeper wears a long black dress and glides around checking dust on all the mantlepieces. The duchess is often seen sitting at the harpsichord in the drawing room and actually plays quite well."

"You mean you've actually seen her play?" Ozzie asked.

Bertie nodded rapidly. "Seen and heard. Have you not seen her?" He smiles. "She particularly likes floating in with her harpsichord and serenading the occupants of room number 403."

Ozzie's eyes went wider. "But that was my room!"

"I'm aware of that," Bertie said, perhaps secretly gleeful he'd got his own back at Ozzie for disassembling his castle's brickwork.

"Are there any former Dukes of Conroy who roam the halls, upset with something you've done, like moving their favorite painting?" Ozzie asked.

This was all getting a bit silly.

"Bertie, we need to get that wooden chest open," I urged.

"Perhaps it's like those Egyptian tombs with everything inside so the person can use it in the afterlife," Timmy suggested.

"Wouldn't that be handy," Bertie said. Then he paused. "Well, I never. Look at this." He pointed to a small ledge behind the chest, the one that rested against the wood paneling fronting the main hall. On the ledge sat a very dusty key.

It fit perfectly into the chest's lock. Bertie swung open the lid and it creaked from lack of use. He ensured it stood up on its own by bending the hinges slightly back, away from themselves. He peered inside as we all clustered around him. "Friends, I have absolutely no idea what this is," he said.

I heard somebody clear his throat behind us and turned to see Severs. "Your Grace, perhaps I should fetch some protective gear?" It was Severs' way of politely insisting his boss didn't do anything rash or foolish that would put his person in danger.

"Very wise, thank you," Bertie said. "The voice of reason has spoken."

It was agony waiting for protective glasses and gloves. Once properly attired, Bertie bravely reached down into the depths of the wooden chest and pulled out whatever willingly came to the surface. When he was done, he had two leather pouches tied with a leather string, each one bulging and sounding like it contained rocks. He also pulled out a stack of parchment with fancy scripted writing on it. I wasn't sure exactly what these documents were for, but they looked official and important. Each one of them had a wavy edge at the bottom of the page.

"That's the lot of it," Bertie said. "No secret laboratory in here. Perhaps it is just money and old castle administration documents."

Severs looked relieved that Bertie had stopped rummaging. The tricky part of working with aristocrats was that they had money to do whatever they wanted, but often times not the common sense to head off in the right direction. Severs had such concerns about his charge. Always. I didn't blame him. Bertie was a tough cookie to wrangle.

Bertie undid the leather pouches and we all looked in on a set of shiny ... rocks. All of them were different, vivid colors.

"You'd better be careful those aren't radioactive," Timmy warned. "I saw one like that inside a special case in a museum."

"Severs?" Bertie asked.

"There is a possibility, Your Grace," the ever-polite man replied.

"Oh, you won't have to worry about that. Those all look like standard minerals to me," a voice behind us said. "Mind, if you've got some red cinnabar hiding in there somewhere it contains mercury, so you don't want to get near that."

I turned to see Candace Blightly, the daughter of our dinosaur hunter/memoir writer who had promised to help out with this massive restoration project. Candace looked ready to work, and likely had already gauged this to be a very interesting assignment. I made quick introductions as well as an explanation for what we were doing in the dark little room behind a broken hearth, kitted out with an open wooden chest, bags of rocks and a sealed coffin.

Bertie looked slightly ill as he brushed his hands together to remove rock dust.

Candace peered over his shoulder. "I see iron pyrite, sulphur, quartz and salt. Nothing dangerous." She gave us a reassuring look. "I majored in geology at university. A literal chip off the old block."

"Thank you. Your timing is impeccable," I said.

Candace looked around the room some more. "I've heard of these places. They boarded up certain hearths and windows because of the tax first implemented in 1695?"

"A wonderful guess and largely historically accurate. It's true that many people boarded up hearths and windows starting in 1695 to avoid the tax, but alas it's not the case for this particular room in the castle," Bertie explained. "This hearth was open to the room, plain as the eye could see."

"Why such an odd, little, hidden room? Was it damaged in the fire?" Candace asked.

"No, this is a room we, well Ozzie, just discovered." I gave her a rapid explanation as to why an aristocrat, a family historian and two metal detectorists were standing around in a dusty room devoid of sunlight. We weren't vampires, rather, we were keeners in genealogy and discovering treasures from the past.

"It looks like you discovered the Duke's mineral collection. Since time began, rock hounds wanted specimens every color of the rainbow. In their quest for a wide ranging palette, they failed to focus on the dangers of cinnabar and uranium." She saw the worried glance flicker across my face. "Relax, I don't see anything that even remotely looks like those two culprits here."

"And why would he keep these ones in a separate bag?" Bertie asked, holding up the second leather sack.

"Convenience, maybe?" Candace replied. She took a closer look at a few split rocks that showed a dazzling array of colorful crystals inside a dull grey outer layer. "Hang on a minute, these ones are different. They're called geodes. What used to be white quartz crystals inside turned purple when the water evaporated and left the minerals in the air pockets."

"So this doesn't look like an alchemy laboratory to you?" I asked.

"Nothing of the sort. You need beakers, heat sources, places to harden molten rock. This is just someone's hobby mineral collection."

Ozzie and Timmy had quietly slipped back out to the middle of the room, having spied the arrival of a huge tower of sandwiches awaiting Bertie's guests. I had to give them credit, metal detecting did likely drum up a good appetite.

"I wonder if the rocks are related to the paperwork here?" Bertie asked, showing us a pile of thick, folded, official-looking documents that also came out of the chest.

I opened one of the folded pages and saw big scripted letters at the top, 'Indenture'.

"What's an indenture?" Candace asked.

I took on that one. "I learned that in my Genealogy 101 class. An indenture is a signed contract. What we have here are apprentice-ship indentures, typically a seven-year contract document between a master and a young person, usually a boy. It's meant to solidify the working relationship where the master agrees to take the child on, house, feed and clothe him, plus train him in a trade in exchange for an initial payment from the child's parents, a charity or parish poor relief authority."

Bertie looked chuffed that I'd found something of better histor-ical value than two bags of rocks. Perhaps I was really coming into my own with this family history research gig. Perhaps my career as a painter was only meant to be short and was now getting superseded by genealogy. One thing about life was certain: things changed more often than one would expect. The most successful people were those who took on their latest challenge with dignity, focus and aplomb.

"I wonder if this mineral collection belonged to one of the appren-tices," I said. "Typically, apprentices would be boys starting around fourteen years old and it's just this sort of thing that they would be interested in collecting."

"How could an apprentice afford such a collection?" Bertie asked. "Apprentices weren't paid more than a few shillings a week, if at all."

"It could be a treasured gift from a rich uncle," Candace suggested.

"Or a gift to an illegitimate child," Ozzie added, coming closer with a delicate cucumber sandwich in his hand.

Bertie, Severs and I exchanged a fervent look.

"Er, perhaps. That would be quite the family record, wouldn't it?" Bertie added in an overly forced jolly tone. "How many indentures are there?"

Little did Ozzie know that he had just stepped on a topic that was exceedingly relevant to the current Duke. Right now, it appeared that Severs and I were the only other people in on the secret.

A quick deflection was needed. I made a quick assessment of the remaining paperwork in the wooden chest. Unpacking precious documents here inside a rather dusty room without proper archival supplies was a bit risky.

"It looks like six indentures in total, Ozzie. Folks, I think we need to get Maude and Gertie's input on this paperwork. That means a trip back to GGRS," I said.

Bertie looked awfully relieved at my suggestion. It was a gentle yet effective ruse to distract.

"Right then, onward," I said, giving Bertie a firm nod that only a confident, helpful friend would offer another.

Chapter 10

——

GGRS. Later That Day.

Maude, Gertie, Ewan and I clustered around the map counter at GGRS. Bertie reluctantly wasn't able to join us because of the rotational grazing meeting he had with his tenants' agricultural committee. The castle mystery was, for now, trusted to our capable hands. With Maude and Gertie on the case, we were certain of figuring out most genealogical mysteries ... if true answers existed.

We unfolded all six indentures, each with a wavy line at the bottom of the page. Maude had taken some time to read over the details of each one and would educate us. Today she was wearing a beautiful sky-blue cardigan and matching knee-length skirt, together with ballet flats and a lovely dahlia brooch in silver. She'd brought a lot of wonderful things with her from her former Petmond Grange manor house; of course, the big antique furniture had to stay, but all the little heirlooms, jewelry and side tables she could cram into her suite upstairs were definitely here. Every day she showed us something new, whether it was a beautiful necklace, a hair comb, an interesting snuffbox or a miniature portrait from her ancestors. It was like balm for the soul looking at all of these treasures from the past. She'd already slapped Ewan's hand more than once when he offered to put some of them in his antiques shop. I'd never forget her words: 'I just can't sell my history, Ewan. Wait till I'm in the grave and then you can get busy. Until then, I must insist that you cease badgering me.'

It'd been quite a funny exchange of words, because Maude was the last person on the planet who would be classified as uppity or obstreperous. But put someone in the way of Maude enjoying her own heritage, and that really got her goat. She would be the first in line to defend her family history. Overall, it was a good sentiment to hold and share. It taught people the value of the past, appreciating its impact on tomorrow.

"We have six apprenticeship indentures in total," Maude started. "The trades represented are scrivener, goldsmith, bricklayer, silversmith, bookbinder and cabinet maker. The names of the boys are all here and here is the list of apprentices matched with their trades that I've typed up."

She handed each of us a printed copy of her summary:

John Cooper – Scrivener
Keith Smythe – Goldsmith
Michael Munnie – Bricklayer
Charles Lyons – Silversmith
Daniel Yardley – Bookbinder
Henry Dartnell – Cabinet Maker

Maude continued. "Note that we still have no information as to why the Old Duke employed them as apprentices."

"Look. Munnie and Lyons. The legend of the Old Duke said he lived with a monkey and a lion. This has got to be the root of the family story," I said with glee.

"Well done, cousin!" Gertie chortled. "With six boys all at once, I wonder if the Duke had multiple illegitimate sons with mistresses to match."

I gave a bit of a smirk to Gertie. "The Old Duke was seventy-two years old at the time he signed as sponsor for six boys about fourteen years old. Six mistresses is quite a balancing act for a man in his thirties, let alone fifties."

Maude bristled and got testy with immediate effect. "I'll have you know that sixty is the new forty."

"Not in the early nineteenth century. Life expectancy for both men and women was much lower back then." I gave her a steely stare. Then I shrugged. "All the records support that."

Maude sniffed. "A fair comment."

"I know," Ewan said, finally adding something to our conversation, "perhaps the boys were some of his tenants, and their masters went bankrupt. The Old Duke stepped in to help out as a benevolence for the people who worked his land."

"All six masters, all different trades, going bankrupt in one year? That isn't very likely," Maude said. "Remember, it used to be a crime to go bankrupt. Nobody wanted to end up in the poorhouse otherwise known as the 'workhouse'. That was a one-way trip downhill and many people never made it back out again. It was a stain on the family name that often never was overcome by the next generation."

"What, specifically, did the indentures have to read?" I asked. "I know that they have to list the names of the master, father and son, but is there anything else we need to be looking for?"

Gertie nodded. "There's a number of things that seem quite outlandish today, but on a standard indenture the apprentice would not be allowed to play dice or cards, get married, frequent taverns or, how do we say, engage in any forward or inappropriate relations with the opposite sex. They also had to pledge faithfulness to their master and promise to behave at all times. In return, the master would pledge to house, clothe, feed and train the apprentice for a period of seven years."

"But not all indentures were specifically granted to learn a trade," I said.

"I did read the same thing in one of my books," Ewan said. "There were an awful lot of servants taken on that lived in big households."

"Indeed, it could be an indenture for trade training, but there were many who were apprenticed as laborers or servants in big houses. Some who were sent overseas had indenture papers that paid for their passage and they spent the next seven years working it off. Good masters in the New World—known as North America today—would actually grant their former indentured servants a little parcel of land and some clothes to start out on their own."

"How did one qualify to become an apprentice? Especially without a father?" I asked.

"For the more advanced trades, such as goldsmith or embroiderer, one would have to prove that the family earned a certain income every year which would allow the son to set up a specific trade in a certain town. The more advanced trades also often required that the sons were of English heritage and legitimate. There often wouldn't be indentures for masters to take on their own sons and nephews. Soldiers took on their younger siblings sometimes and orphans could have been sponsored by the Overseers of the Poor."

"Maybe we should look at some workhouse records and see if these six boys were orphans that the Old Duke and Duchess employed?" Ewan suggested.

"We could start there," Maude said, "but I would be more apt to check with Bertie and see if his family papers mention anything about this lot. It's very odd that they were all indentured on the exact same month, day and year. It's strange that he had a job lot, so to speak."

"Why do you keep thinking illegitimate?" I asked.

"Why not?" Gertie asked. "It makes good sense."

"Not necessarily. They could have been children of tenants on the Scotford Estate who needed a helping hand. Perhaps they had a bad harvest one year and their fathers couldn't afford to pay for their sons' training. The Old Duke stepped up and helped out, the good man that he was. It's plausible," I said.

"Can't decide on one until you disprove the other theory," Maude advised.

"And how do we go about that?" Ewan asked.

"Gather together all the evidence you can. Go back to Scotford and ask Bertie for tenant leases and records, the Old Duke's diaries and journals, household staff information and anyone on record with the same surname as the boys."

"If a boy was illegitimate, there is no way the Old Duke would be on the christening record. Those secret children were kept very hush hush back in the day, mainly to prevent claims to the title and embarrassment in the aristocratic social circle," Gertie warned.

"Those aristocrats always have to avoid unpleasant dinner time chitter chatter, don't they," Ewan joked.

I gave him a stern look. "You and I both know that Bertie is not like that. He's a dear friend."

Ewan held up both his hands in defeat.

"What is the wavy line at the bottom of all these pages?" I asked. "Were they trying to be fancy?"

Maude smiled. It was a small, surreptitious smile, one that said 'I know something that you don't, but I'm happy to explain it to you'. "The wavy line was cut differently in each one of these six indentures. Did you notice that?" she asked.

We all looked over the six documents laid out on the counter and nodded.

"I don't understand," Ewan said.

"The wavy line separated two exact same copies. Each part contained at minimum the names of the master, apprentice and father, signatures and trade. The two-part format was there to ensure one could prove the right apprentice indenture was being referred to if there was ever a dispute in the future, or when the apprentice indenture was fully served. The father would bring the wavy lined paper back to the master and they would match up the documents to ensure that they were both talking apples to apples."

"No wayward sons," I observed. "Indenture complete."

"No wayward sons." Gertie gave me a hard stare. "Looks like we're going to need the GGRS van to trundle a bunch of us back to Scotford Castle."

Maude had a look of horror on her face. "I hope the records were not all kept on-site. With that fire, I would hate to think about centuries of precious paperwork and family records gone up in smoke."

"Oh, they've been digitized," Gertie said, "but digitization never replaces the original. Digitization is far too unreliable, considering all the poor quality scans, file errors, plus missed and overlapping pages. I've seen instances where key information is completely obscured by a stray page covering up the one underneath. Without the originals, vital information would be lost forever."

❊❊❊

Lunchroom. One Hour Later.

Candace enjoyed a cappuccino while the rest of us drank tea. I had nothing against coffee, just preferred tea. One thing about England, a warm beverage of choice was an extremely individual decision. Far be it for anyone, lower-class, middle-class or upper class, to impose their preference upon somebody else at the same table, or even in the same room. There were about nine thousand different ways to make a cup of tea, coffee, hot chocolate or cider and it was just one of those things that the British accepted as being unique to each individual. I supposed someone would look sideways at a person putting mango chutney into their chamomile tea, but apart from that, anything was fair game in a cuppa.

The cappuccino in Candace's grip was fairly standard. A bit of frothy milk foam on top and one sugar. She'd sipped it thoughtfully as she heard our banter about the indentures we'd found in a secret room behind Bertie's now deconstructed floor-to-ceiling hearth. It was a lot to take in for somebody here to get some pointers on how to help her mother write her memoir. I hadn't even asked about her own ancestry and that was shame on me. The fire at Scotford had just taken over our lives and in this case, rightly so. Bertie was always there for us as a community leader, and when his chips were down, of course we would all pitch in and help. Heck, even Candace stepped up to the plate and she didn't even know him. That's what I liked so much about GGRS. Everyone here was a good egg. Eccentric and researching some rather odd subjects? Yes. Would we help anyone down on their luck and in need? Of course. That's what GGRS was all about, and I intended to continue serving our founding principles.

"I hope you don't feel left out or brushed aside," I said to Candace. "It's just with the emergency at Scotford–"

She instantly brushed away any feelings of guilt that I might be harboring. "Please don't even give it a second thought. You had other far more important things on your mind than helping me write my mother's book."

"Please don't feel like your project is unimportant to us. It's of prime importance, but when Bertie's castle caught on fire, we all downed tools and rushed to help."

"I completely understand. Let's hope this is a once-in-a-lifetime event and Bertie can get his ancestral home back to the way it was in rapid time." Candace gave me a reassuring smile.

"We do have some really good resources on how to get started with writing a memoir," I said.

"Can I show you what I brought with me first?" she asked.

"Of course. We can go into another one of the offices where it's a bit quieter." I gestured for her to follow me. We left her empty mug in the dishwasher and then headed into a private meeting room.

Once inside, Candace hauled out her laptop and proceeded to show me a short video of her mother on a dig site in Canada, the Alberta Badlands, a place known for incredible dinosaur finds. Of course it was a protected site, not a place for the public to tramp all over due to the wonderful fossils that lay underneath the ground. I was taken aback by how the warm winds of the sandy landscape under a hot, summer sun really took one's breath away. One could describe it as a mixture of scrubland and tumble-weed, a place where the sun beat down and somehow coordinated with the rest of Mother Nature to preserve the bones of these massive animals that used to roam the planet. What I found really fascinating were the different layers of time seen when cutting away a slab of earth and literally viewing the different periods of time exposed sedimentary layer by layer, over millions of years. I remembered looking at this in school and being absolutely fascinated. Like most other topics in academia, one had to devote an entire lifetime to completely understand, else it just remained a burgeoning curiosity.

Interviews that Candace's mother gave were super informative and convincing. She was dressed in khaki shorts and a cotton, button-up shirt, sunglasses plus a bandanna covering her hair and the back of her neck. Her face was weathered by the sun and you could tell she just adored what she did for a living. Tessa Blightly had a PhD, was a world-renowned conference lecturer yet she much preferred dig sites to fancy hotel ballrooms. The fancy hotels welcomed her, as did all the top-level associations and organizations that studied paleontology, yet she preferred the real work 'out with her bones' as she referred to it on the video.

More of the Alberta Badlands landscape tracked across the screen. The video was shot by a drone and as it circled around the narrow area, I could see it focused on a new dinosaur dig below. It was one of those Tyrannosaurus Rex-like carnivores, with huge hip bones and hind limbs. It had a long stabilizing tail as well as ferocious-looking teeth. At public auction, the fossilized skeleton would likely go for millions. It was a shame when a private, anonymous buyer would hide the dinosaur skeleton inside a gated house, effectively preventing the rest of the world from seeing it. At the very least, I felt the buyer should have the moral fortitude to allow the scientists in to study the find.

Candace, her mother and I were on the same page.

I wondered what Ewan would think. We'd had this conversation multiple times before, but never about dinosaurs. Furniture, documents, wallpaper, photographs, yes. But never two-story tall dinosaurs. That was a matter for dinnertime conversation and handily we had one scheduled for tonight. Maude won our latest bet. Ewan and I were finally going on a formal dinner date. He'd booked a quiet table at my favorite restaurant and we'd both pledged to leave family history and antiques alone for the evening.

Or so we planned.

GGRS and its vast number of wonderful friends and visitors had a way of finagling their way into every hour of the day, so much so that it was just a part of one's life. I likened GGRS and the Greymore Hall estate to a warm, elegant shawl: it was always there for me, wrapping itself around me in coziness and utter comfort.

The dinosaur dig film ended the interview with Candace's mother, and the drone took off higher to film more of the striated landscape. There were dozens of little mountains everywhere. Larger than hills, they were comprised of dry, sandy-beige earth compacted down into a sandstone-like substance. Every now and then, there would be darker streaks of coal going through the rock and some of the hills were actually topped with dark brown and grey, almost a burnt orange look. Wind erosion had carved cylinders all joined together with flat mushroom head type tops, an unusual geological result of Mother Nature. It was a stunning, desolate landscape, one that hid secrets for millions of years until bright sparks like Candace's mother came along and dug them up for the world's education.

"You should put that all over social media. I'm sure lots of people would be interested," I said.

Candace nodded. "It's one of her most popular television interviews. I've got lots more, but this one shows her right before her accident, when she was at her peak."

"She's not too ill from her fall, I hope?" I asked.

"She's on the mend. The bed rest and limited mobility frustrate her; she's quite active, as you can see. Still, she's decided to make the best of it and get her memoir written because there's only so much television one can watch."

"That's very true. Despite the number of channels and streaming services, it's often a challenge to find a good new program to watch. One tends to go through the favorites and binge watch everything, leaving nothing for the next couple of months."

"Don't I know it," Candace said. "My mother is good at writing research papers and scientific facts but terrible at storytelling. We thought we could work together on this and come up with something decent."

"It certainly sounds like a plan," I said. "Do you know the difference between memoir and biography?"

"Not really. Could you explain?"

"Sure. Biography covers somebody's entire life. Memoir is basically a snapshot in time, an era or a limited number of months or years that you're going to describe. Both can be true or embellished, that is, saying 'based on the true story' or not. If it's for entertainment, then one has to decide where the facts are going to stop and dreamland begins."

"She wants the whole thing to be factual, making it unexpectedly hilarious. Apparently, there were a lot of hijinks at the dinosaur dig sites when she first started out."

"Those stories are likely the ones readers will most want to hear, especially in an audio book she can narrate herself. Is she perhaps writing a memoir of her early years as a woman in the field? That would be an interesting read."

Candace nodded. "And we don't want it to be just a recitation of facts. In 1980, I did this. In 1990, I did that. It needs to be an interesting story for people to read."

"We really should videoconference with your mother to get things moving," I suggested.

Candace's eyes lit up at my suggestion. "That would be perfect. Thank you so much."

❖❖❖

Italian Restaurant. That Night.

Ewan booked us the perfect table. At the back, near the veranda, away from the kitchen and behind four large potted palms. Red and white checkered table cloth. Plush booth seats. Tall candle melted into an empty, green Chianti bottle, long strands of hardened wax running down the sides.

And Ewan.

Here with me.

Just the two of us.

And then my cell phone chirped.

His face crumpled in disappointment.

I checked it, then looked up with a grin. "Apparently, I've just inherited £20 million from a person I don't know but who calls me an esteemed colleague. I'm to send them all my personal information right away so they can transfer the funds."

He gave me a quirky look. "Will those sorts ever give up?"

"Not so long as people are still falling for the scam." I blocked the sender then deleted the message from both my inbox and trash, just in case there was a virus attached.

"Can you turn that thing off for a few hours?" he asked.

It was the request of a lifetime. To disconnect from GGRS was like asking me to give up the crown jewels, chocolate and Greymore's miniature goats. It was unheard of in my little world.

"A few hours break would actually be good for you," Ewan counseled.

"I know. I just feel so, so ..."

Ewan put a hand over top of mine, the one that held the phone. "Relax. Enjoy our dinner together. Greymore can exist without you for tonight."

I looked into his eyes, kind, welcoming and sincere. "You're right. Maude and Dad are both there, and Jacques is working late." I switched the phone to silent and put it in my purse. "There."

"Good."

The waiter came over, took our order and the evening—hopefully a perfect one—got underway. It wasn't a super special occasion, but rather an attempt to rectify so many false starts in our burgeoning relationship. Every time we tried to grab a quick coffee, lunch or dinner together, we were interrupted by family history questions, escaped farm animals or got trapped inside a moving van that shipped us to Yorkshire by accident. It had been quite a ride so far, and I was surprised that Ewan still wanted to pursue me after all of these shenanigans. Looking back, it was rather amusing, but there was only so much a couple on the rise could take. One either had to make time and ensure it happened, or the flame would slowly fizzle. I didn't want to be a candle snuffed out by a small silver cone on a stick held by a stern butler. I wanted Ewan in my life and this was another chance.

"How is Bertie doing with the fire restoration?" Ewan asked.

"Right now, he's holding it together. But the insurance company won't confirm his payout until they make him jump through all these different hoops. It's really sad because this is a multimillion dollar castle restoration."

"What's the hangup?" Ewan asked.

"Making sure the fire wasn't deliberately set."

"As if an aristocrat would set his own ancestral home on fire,"

Ewan said. Then he gave me another weird look. "That is bizarre, isn't it? I mean–"

"Of course Bertie wouldn't do anything like that. It's just the insurance folks being difficult."

"Very sad," he said.

"It is, and it's also our local heritage. I already told Bertie that Fred was willing to get on the phone and play the nasty solicitor if they don't hurry up and confirm payment for the major castle restoration work. We can't let Scotford Castle become a ruin. That would be ridiculous."

We both thought on it for a bit. It truly was an awful, terrible tragedy.

"We're doing it again," Ewan said, giving me another kind look. "Heritage leads to family history which leads to genealogy discussions which leads to you picking up the phone just to check on Greymore for a minute or two which leads to a phone call to Jacques which leads to the miniature goats needing your attention which–"

"Okay." I rolled my eyes and pretended to be offended, but I couldn't last like that for very long around my guy. We laughed and settled back against the soft seating, pledging to each other that we would leave the trials of the week behind just for a few hours and enjoy ourselves here tonight.

When Ewan took me home, the kiss we shared was heartfelt and longing. He walked me safely up to my front door and then walked back to his car. Before he turned on the engine, I saw the blue light from his phone light up the vehicle's interior. My phone chimed a second later and I read:

Thank you for a wonderful evening. Here's to many more.
Love from Ewan.

My heart was filled with happiness.

Chapter 11

Stables, Scotford Castle. Next Morning.

Gertie, Maude and I were the ones relegated to this important family history, fact-finding trip. Specifically, we were on the hunt for more information about the indentured boys and their patron, one of the earlier Dukes of Conroy in Bertie's heritage.

Gertie and Maude had a stop to make first and said they'd meet me at the castle. I arrived early and had a quick chat with Bertie before the other two ladies arrived.

Bertie gave me a confident look. "I'm so glad to tell you this. I only keep the last seventy-five years of records or so here on hand at the castle. They're inside a fire-resistant, steel-enclosed cabinet. The rest of it's been put into storage at the Plumsden Archives. Only accessible by special request and permission granted by yours truly."

"I'm super relieved to hear that," I said. "Imagine if the collections were caught up in the fire."

"I shudder just thinking about it. All those centuries of history. All those valuable originals. Gone in a moment," Bertie said. "It's far too precious to me, to the estate and to our nation to be left rotting away in some damp room here in the castle. No, that was my father's doing; years ago before he passed, he got all the archives organized, catalogued and off into a secure, safe, climate-controlled location. He even funded a permanent archivist position to catalog and digitize them as a backup, plus consider various scholarly requests for access. I do have to personally approve each request, and while most are harmless, one has to watch out for the dirt diggers."

Bertie shot me a fleeting glance after his last remark. As if his castle burning hadn't caused enough heartache, in addition he now had to worry about a precious family secret getting blurted out to the latest tabloid.

It just wasn't right. My dear friend didn't deserve any of this.

He also didn't deserve Ozzie Boggs showing up, Timmy Hitchins in tow, looking for a free breakfast, snack and two pairs of wellies as they continued their metal detecting adventure. The intrepid pair had made themselves quite at home in the stables perched on two fancy-embroidered wingback chairs with polished Queen Anne feet.

"Do metal detectors work in the rain?" Bertie asked.

"I'm not sure," I replied.

Ozzie turned around and nodded. He answered, spraying out a light smattering of artisan apricot Danish as he spoke. "Of course, so long as you have the waterproof gear."

"Which, of course, I have for both of us," Timmy added with a reassuring grin.

A butler appeared with napkins on a silver tray. Bertie's staff were that good; they could anticipate every guest's need, including protection from apricot Danish crumbs. I noted how an underbutler was busy setting up two pairs of rubber boots at the side of the office on a thick mat.

"Sirs, your footwear is right over here," the butler said with a formal gesture of his open hand. He said 'footwear' with a slight bit of disdain in his voice, something Ozzie wouldn't have noticed.

I did.

Bertie did.

We exchanged a smile.

Butlers had to put up with a ton of chicanery, most of it due to their employer's eclectic taste in friends and business associates. After Bertie bailed Ozzie out of jail, I supposed one had to call them friends. There was no other word for it.

"Allow me to take those, please," the butler said, offering his now-empty tray for their crumpled napkins. When they placed them onto the tray, it looked like the butler was holding a rather sorry arrangement of amateur origami.

"I see that the Roman shards quest continues. Well, good luck to you both, gentlemen," Bertie said. "I have to meet with the insurance representative again. Today I believe he's after my grandmother's shoe size for the next form he has to submit in triplicate."

"Oh dear, that doesn't sound like too much fun," I said. I gave Bertie what I hoped was a supportive look.

He shrugged. "It must be done. Anything and everything to rebuild Scotford Castle."

Ozzie and Timmy headed out to the back fields, geared up again with their waterproof covers, rain suits and loaner rubber boots. I'd given up wondering about anything regarding Ozzie's lifestyle. He of the smoked mackerel sandwiches still surreptitiously brought his rubbish bin bags to GGRS for pickup because his rural area didn't have house-to-house service. Ozzie was entertaining yet infuriating, needy yet abrasive. He was certainly one of the most unusual people I knew, and that was saying a fair amount considering that I grew up around Aunt Edwina and her aristocratic set. Throw in Fred and his potbellied pig Barnaby, plus cousin Gertie known worldwide for her karaoke singing, and we had quite the troop of entertainers. A mere century or so past, and we could have gone on a successful tour as a vaudeville show.

But that was neither here nor there at the moment. Bertie and I walked from the stables to the castle's front room with its dismantled hearth, I noticed that there was a big gap where something rather important had once sat.

"Bertie, what did you do with the Old Duke's coffin?"

He issued me a terse look and a succinct answer to match. "Of course, the coroner had to come out and make his assessment. He brought two undertakers and somebody from the local university who studies heraldry. I never did figure out if he was a student or professor, but apparently his input was critical. They took the coffin back to the morgue to ascertain if there was a transmittable disease or mortal affliction associated with the body." Bertie spoke as if he found all of this pomp and circumstance rather overdrawn and overbearing.

"Bertie, surely it's necessary. I mean, you do have tourists going through the castle. You have no idea who is buried in there or what he died of. You have to be safe."

"To the outside eye, yes. But I happen to know that the Old Duke ran an alchemist laboratory. The most probable cause of death would be inhaling toxic fumes from some sort of experiment gone amok, something that probably put him into a long-term health condition, perhaps akin to the aftereffects of breathing mining or asbestos dust."

"The health and safety authorities would never let you get away with just plunking his coffin down into the family crypt. You and I both know that."

"It's just so undignified," Bertie said.

I could tell Bertie was actually quite miffed. I grinned. "I get it. You were hoping that Severs and a couple of other household staff could just hoist the coffin upon their shoulders and trot down to the local church, sweet talk the vicar, and do a quickie internment in the family mausoleum?"

"Something like that. My family name has to mean something," he said, morose.

"I think the Old Duke gave up that privilege when he died and somehow got himself buried inside the castle walls. Don't you even wonder how on earth that happened?"

"I hadn't really got that far. After the fire, seeing my entire life strewn out on the front lawn plus losing the contents of my safe … well, figuring out the mindset of my eccentric ancestor hasn't made it to the top of my priority list."

"Here's a thought. All of those things might be related," I said.

"My ancestors were all powerful people, every single Duke. A scathing glance from one of the Duchesses cut men off at the knees. However, I don't think even they were capable of creating a fire at Scotford Castle from beyond the grave."

"I don't mean the fire, silly. I'm talking about the indenture papers we found near the coffin. The collection of minerals? What if those apprentices had something to do with the Old Duke being buried inside the hearth?"

That made Bertie stand back on his heels for a moment. We took another careful look inside the cavernous area behind the crumbled hearth wall. It was definitely something to ponder, because whoever had bricked up the objects inside had obviously known about both. But just how involved were the apprentices that the Old Duke took under his wing? Was the Old Duke even still in firm grasp of all his senses? Reaching beyond seventy years in the early nineteenth century was quite an accomplishment, so one had to consider the question in the context of the time period.

Bertie cleared his throat. "This is obviously a last wish of the Old Duke and it brings two questions to mind. Number one, why did he want to be buried here? Number two, who ensured it happened?"

We saw Maude and Gertie approach. They both took a moment to look inside the now almost empty room. Maude spoke first. "This is where you found the coffin?"

"It was indeed," Bertie said. "And to think thousands of

unsuspecting tourists have filed through this room over the years, completely clueless at what lay behind the brick hearth."

"You would think the smell would have given it away," Gertie said.

"I think he dried up. He did pass away over a hundred years ago." I gave her a logical look.

"Right, he became a prune," Gertie said. "Well Bertie, there's only one way to get to the bottom of this mystery and that's to look at your family papers. What in the world of aristocratic archival happiness are you willing to share with us today?"

"I have current records here, however, I believe you'll need to visit the Plumsden Archives. The bulk of the records you need are going to be the older ones."

"What specifically are we looking for?" I asked. "If it were me, I would go directly to the archives and start with the oldest first, then work forward through time." I gave a plaintive look to Maude.

"We must begin with context," Maude explained. "The current records here should contain a complete family tree from ancient times up to today. They will also have any books that are continually being updated by the present household. I'm also interested in seeing what is provided to tourists from an historical perspective, because the general history will give us an idea how to specify record requests at the archives."

Gertie nodded in agreement. "It's always best to have general context before asking for specific items, especially when the collection's fonds are so deep and broad."

"Bertie had me at alchemy," I said.

"An alchemist in the family is good for historical perspective," Maude said.

"Up until now it made for good entertainment, but looking at these indentures and how the Old Duke was buried behind the hearth, it leads me to wonder if there's a lot more to it," Gertie added.

"What is that sticking out of the back wall?" I asked. Now my eyes were more adjusted to the light, and the room was emptier, I noticed something odd. The brick wall backing onto the wood paneling appeared to be less consistent than all the rest of the work. Right up high, just out of reach of arm's length, was one brick painted a bright, rustier orange than the rest. The paint had stayed true over time inside this hidden room. It was like looking, with absolute amazement, at an Egyptian Pharaoh's tomb, the kind at the bottom of a long, sloping shaft that suddenly reveals multiple panels of brilliantly colored hieroglyphics perfectly preserved for thousands of years, safe from the sun's harsh rays. It was an interesting juxta-position because the sun gave life yet it also sucked color out of everything in its path.

"What can you see?" Bertie asked.

I went over to touch the rusty orange brick. "Look," I said. "It's different than the others. This is a sign. It's something we've missed."

"How interesting," Bertie said, coming in after me. He put his hand up to the brick and started to wiggle it. With a teeny bit of effort—walls do settle over time and in this case we were talking over two centuries—the brick started to move. Soon enough, Bertie had it dislodged and he slowly pulled it back. He drew out the suspense by turning to look over his shoulder and saying to us, "I hope this isn't the only thing holding up the rest of the castle."

I shook my head, not fooled. "They have supporting beams, not supporting single bricks. Nice try, Bertie."

"It would be rather bittersweet, though, would it not? I pull out the one brick that may solve the mystery of the Old Duke's final resting place and the whole place comes crashing down around our ears?" He smiled.

"Go on, then," I said.

With one final, dramatic effort, Bertie pulled out the brick and then shook his head. "I should have known. The Old Duke was also very fond of practical jokes."

We all clustered around Bertie, eager to see what he found. With great dexterity, Bertie passed around the brick. "Feel how light that is?"

"It's much lighter than a brick should be," Gertie said.

"That's because it's hollow," Bertie said. He took it back and then with a little wiggle pulled the top part off the bottom base. It was like a hollow book where one would hide a weapon or stack of cash. This hollow brick had a little roll of paper inside plus a miniature portrait of the Old Duke's lovely wife, the Duchess.

Bertie had the roll of paper undone before I had a chance to say 'archival protocol'. It was part of his family's collection so I couldn't stop him, but unfortunately sometimes people were too fast to seek answers, and subsequently ruined archives and treasures in their haste. Fortunately the paper was intact and dry ... but it was blank. Whatever someone had taken such great care to preserve and hide was, in fact, a dead end.

"Blank? How can it be blank?" Gertie moaned with anguish. "Do we need heat applied to reveal writing made with lemon juice?"

Bertie chuckled. "It's just the cover page, likely to protect what's underneath. Here, take a look at this." He shuffled the first page behind a matching second and then we set eyes upon beautiful copperplate penmanship:

To my descendants. I lie here of my own accord, of my own wishes. My apprentices have done exactly my bidding and should I be discovered before their own deaths, do not punish them. They have completed my secret laboratory work and I am forever grateful. I have granted them each their own careers with funds to maintain their trades over the course of their lifetime. My experiments that remain on the estate are secret until somebody discovers them and learns the true meaning of alchemy.

"Wishful thinking is all those words are," Bertie said, checking to see that there was no third page and also that there was nothing written on the reverse of the second page. "If my ancestor had truly figured out how to make gold from basic rocks, the business wouldn't struggle to fund the castle's restoration."

Maude grinned. "You likely would own four Scotford Castles by now."

"Think of all the mango chutney you could produce at each estate," I teased.

"I want to know where the Old Duke's secret laboratory is here at Scotford," Gertie said. "Think of all the treasures you could find in there."

Bertie looked a little off kilter. "Think of all the chemical residues and what's left." He had a slightly alarmed look on his face. "Before this, all we had were jokes and unsubstantiated rumors about his laboratory work. Now we know for a fact that alchemy was actively practiced here and that a dedicated laboratory was—rather still is—on-site."

"Hence the need for the coroner to do some tests on the Old Duke's body," I said. "Let's just hope he wasn't using himself as a guinea pig for some newfangled experiment that's contagious."

"Can we please now get onto the genealogy?" Gertie pleaded. "I want to look up records, not talk about how to create gold from nothing."

Maude held up a finger. "Ah, but archival records do create family history gold. Never forget that."

Chapter 12

Plumsden Archives. Later.

We had to wear badges. And not the cheap, self-adhesive kind where the black marker goes through its base and bleeds through onto clothes. Nope. These were proper visitor badges made of hard plastic with one's photo laminated onto it. The badges had a rectangular hole punched through the top and a professional lanyard was attached. No more pins going through delicate silk blouses and tearing at strands of sweaters. This was the only way that visitor identification should be handled: first-class.

The routine was much the same as when one visited The National Archives at Kew in London. Of course, we had to put all of our belongings into lockers, and we were only allowed to bring in clear plastic bags containing pencils, notepaper, our wallets, cell phones turned to silent, and laptops. It was all in the name of protecting precious documents, keeping them clean and available, for multiple future generations. None of us had any problem with these regulations, and in fact we were glad to see them. Anyone working in the family history or genealogy arenas fully understood why Ozzie

Boggs's gooey chocolate bars and fountain pens were so dangerous in archival facilities.

What we weren't prepared for, however, was the colossal surprise we got after exiting the elevator on the second floor. I'd only ever been on the first floor of the Plumsden Archives, and it was a standard, government type office complex. There was an information desk with a pleasant, helpful assistant. Lockers were on the left-hand side and on the right were various instructional displays, toilets, and administration offices further down the hall. There were some seating areas in the lobby out front, including a few areas where one could access the building's free wireless internet. All of this was standard, modern day archives kit.

Second floor. The polite bell that signaled the doors opening was quiet compared to the gasps we emitted as we stepped out onto the shiny tiled floor. Of course, it was finished with an anti-slip coating, but the flooring did look awfully fancy. We looked up and saw four amazing, alabaster columns framing an entrance covered in gleaming brass fittings. Across the top of the entrance, spanning the full width of all four columns, were brass letters that boldly proclaimed, 'The Preswick Family Research Center.'

Wow. Bertie was gracious enough not to breathe a word of this incredible facility to anyone while we were setting up GGRS. That was a sign of a true friend. He had gobs more money than our family—we were aristocratic but not as high up the social rankings as a Duke—yet he never made one feel out of place. Bertie was always modest, giving and supportive. He was a wonderful art patron of mine as well as a decent friend to everybody who needed one.

It was apparent that we were about to walk in on something fabulous. We spoke in hushed voices as we approached the entrance. There was a touchless security booth to walk through as well as two stern security guards who stood at the other end, watching our every move. I looked up and saw discreet security cameras in multiple corners of ceilings, the black spherical kind that looked unobtrusive, yet followed everyone, everywhere. It wasn't spooky, just what had to be done to protect the collection. I didn't blame Bertie one bit.

We took another deep intake of breath once we were through security and stood in the front of the room. There, right in front of us, was an eight-foot tall globe on a stand, slowly rotating. It was an exact replica of earth, even including some topography and larger cities of the world. A posted sign invited visitors to give it a go.

"Look at that, look at what it can do," I said in an excited voice. I went over to one of the keyboards next to the globe and typed in 'Plumsden'. Immediately Plumsden lit up with a marker as the globe spun around and stopped right in front of me. Projected into the air was a small video screen that showed the population, commercial activities, weather and founding date of Plumsden.

"That's amazing," Gertie said. "What a smart thing to have. It gets you to focus on what you're researching right from the get-go."

"And there's even additional filters where you can add in the precise year that you're researching," Maude said, pointing at a few specialized buttons on the keyboard.

"This really is leading-edge technology," I said, typing in a random '1799'. I was pleased to see an immediate change to the Plumsden listing as I took it back a few centuries. The population was thousands lower but interestingly enough, many of the listed commercial activities were the same as today. It just proved that specialized trades prevailed in certain locations over time. Ewan had discovered that about pottery crafts when he'd researched his antiques shop's retail location on his Plumsden street.

"You must be the ladies from Greymore?" we heard behind us. Archivist Prunella Mayerthorpe rapidly introduced herself and immediately I could tell we would get along like a house on fire.

Okay, perhaps not the best analogy in these circumstances.

"His Grace said you are looking for help with indentured apprentices on the Scotford Estate?" Prunella asked.

"Yes, thank you. Specifically the nineteenth century and an elderly Duke who befriended six young boys to set them up in trade."

Maude bristled at the word 'elderly' and I knew I had to make a rapid correction.

"Of course, elderly being defined as over the age of fifty during the nineteenth century," I said.

Prunella and I exchanged a smile.

"Well, as someone who bicycled over that hill seven years ago, I certainly appreciate the clarification," Prunella said with a chuckle.

"I've already pulled some records for you. Let's get down to business."

"Is this entire floor dedicated to the Scotford Estate?" Gertie asked.

Prunella nodded. "With the exception of a very specialized set of bookshelves holding some medieval illuminated manuscripts."

"The books where monks actually hand-colored in multiple complicated drawings of people, flowers and other objects?" I asked.

She nodded. "Yes, they are amazing works of art. It's funny though, a few years ago, I was part of a massive queue lining up to see a world-renowned, illuminated manuscript at a famous library. Right in the middle of all of it, some tourists walked up the steps ahead of everybody else and told the guard they just wanted to see that one particular book, not the rest of the museum. He pointed at the line they weren't understanding, which was literally bent back on itself three times, packed with people. This one tourist yelled out to the rest of her friends, 'It's a forty minute wait, is it worth it?'"

Maude and Gertie looked shocked.

Prunella continued. "They'd only travelled thousands of miles to see some of Europe's greatest treasures, yet they were asking if it was worth a forty minute wait. I just didn't understand."

"What did they do?" I asked.

"I have no idea. I was getting close to the front of the line." She grinned. "Now, let's see how we can help you." Prunella got us settled at a large table where we could spread out the estate's ledger books from the nineteenth century. "There are three types of apprentice indentures: regular, charity and poor. Some apprenticeships required proof of minimum financial standing before a young man could set up in trade. Some locations even required the apprentices to be of English origin, born of married parents, and of sound mind and body. Often a formal set of indenture papers did not exist if a boy was taken into apprenticeship under his father or relative's wing. The Statute of Apprentices, in force 1563 through 1814, protected trades and related standards. Children needed to be between the ages of ten and eighteen, and serve as apprentices until at least twenty-one. A full seven years apprenticeship was required. Less well-off families could send their children courtesy of charity apprenticeships from various institutions, and benevolent donors provided funds for training."

Maude looked at us through her reading glasses, now firmly attached to a snazzy new chain. "Poor apprenticeships were for paupers, and this system was often rife with abuse including children being separated from their families and sent to other towns. Typical pauper apprenticeships were lower-level workers such as husbandry, aka agricultural workers, domestic servants or boy servants at sea. If exceptional aptitude was shown, then advancement to a more lucrative trade was indeed possible."

"The apprenticeship system sounds quite complex," I said. "We're wondering if the Old Duke was a benevolent donor," I said.

Prunella smiled. "It was well-organized training for young people. Definitely contained a lot of the class hierarchy norms, but at least there was a structure to life. And it wasn't just for society's apprentices; if a master refused to take a poor apprentice, then he had to pay a fine."

"I feel for those poor little ones who were unlucky enough to get a bad master," Gertie said.

"Indeed. Some masters were quite cruel to their apprentices, working them hard for twelve plus hours a day, six days a week and half a day on Sundays. Conditions were often damp, cold, dark and with unclean air. Have you ever seen the flour dust in an old bakery? Workers created baked goods inside a haze like a snow flurry. Terrible." Maude tut-tutted. "Some of the boys ran away, some died, and if a master died then the apprentice was 'turned over' to finished the seven-year term with another master."

All sobering facts, indeed.

"Shall we look at each apprentice indenture now?" Prunella asked.

"The more lucrative, exclusive trades required a higher premium paid to the master, correct?" I asked.

"Yes. Goldsmith, silversmith and cabinet maker are good examples of higher premium apprenticeships. The guilds and towns restricted the numbers of these apprentices. Trade guilds also kept good records of apprentices and masters," Prunella explained. "All apprenticeships required the father, widowed mother, or guardian to pay a premium to the master at the outset. If the boy was poor, then the Overseer of the Poor paid the master, and the boy would be put into the cheapest apprenticeship possible. One example would be husbandry aka agricultural laborer."

"And the higher premiums would be to help pay for more expensive stock and supplies?" Gertie asked.

"Yes. A goldsmith needs gold. A silversmith needs silver. A cabinet maker needs fine wood. They all need specialized tools. Not much sense in becoming an apprentice in a trade you can't afford," Prunella explained.

"I imagine many of them were burnt when the apprenticeship was served, much like burning a mortgage paper once it's paid off," I said.

"Correct. The temptation was strong. Horrifying for us archivists, but human nature is what it is," Prunella said.

"Does the paperwork tell us anything about the boys' families or stations in life?" I asked. "These indentures came completely out of the blue at Scotford Castle."

"We can get name, father's name and occupation, master's name and his trade plus the expectations of each party. All those are usually pretty standard," Maude explained. "Occasionally we'll get date and place of birth."

"And some of the restrictions were no gambling with cards or dice, plus no female followers, correct?" Gertie added.

I shifted position. Hours spent poring over old documents had ways of making a body feel quite stiff. "But there's nothing that would explain how or why these six boys were in the Duke's care as master?"

"Oh, the Old Duke himself wouldn't have trained them. One of his people would. He just took responsibility for their training, so it seems," Maude said.

"Remember what we told you about the crumbled hearth and what we found behind it?" Gertie asked.

Prunella nodded.

"Well, it appears the Old Duke was in on a big secret with his apprentices." Gertie said. "Figure out what the goal really was and his secrets are revealed."

"You think he was training six young men to service his rather unique scientific experiment needs?" I asked.

"Yes. And because his alchemy was so secretive, he likely had them keep quiet about it," Gertie said.

"The bricklayer apprentice makes sense. He'd be set to walling up the coffin, papers and rock collection inside Scotford Castle's hearth," I said.

"It does make sense. We can certainly confirm that the Old Duke was an eccentric type," Prunella said. "It's part of what keeps us here on this floor, that is, figuring out what his next experiment was."

"He kept records?" I asked. "Have you got the details?"

"We have multiple journals filled with his alchemy attempts to create gold. That's another use for the goldsmith apprentice."

"So we believe these apprentices were part of an elite crew? All we need to know is what, beyond alchemy and a mysterious wall inside a castle, they were asked to produce," Maude said.

The answer to her question would be fascinating, if we ever found out what it was.

❖❖❖

Meeting Room, GGRS. Next Morning.

Gertie, Maude, Candace and I faced a wall of small, plastic model dinosaurs on screen. Each one was quite detailed in terms of skin texture, crests, feathers, and toes. There must have been at least three hundred of them, all neatly organized on shelves inside Doctor Tessa Blightly's home.

"I hope your mother will make an appearance soon," Maude said, "I feel like I'm in another time period."

Candace laughed. "My mother insists on having all the dinosaur models as her screen background. She thinks it's entertaining for viewers."

"Why so many?" I asked.

"She's on a mission to correct the manufacturers with anything she can prove is not anatomically correct. In her eyes, the model had better match her fossil proof."

The audio came on. Introductions were made. The on-screen cameras worked like a charm.

"I'm the world's worst patient. I cannot stand being confined like this," Doctor Blightly said.

The three of us were immediately put at ease by the famous dinosaur researcher's honest admission.

"We're so sorry to hear of your accident," I offered.

"It was an unfortunate slip on the rocks in Alberta. We had to abandon the filming and I was rushed to hospital. It was such a shame because these particular geological formations are unique." She spoke with intense authority.

"Mum, the ladies here at GGRS are helping us with your memoir," Candace said.

Doctor Blightly clasped her hands together. "How lovely! We have so much information, yet it's hard to know where to start."

"Doctor Blightly–" I began.

"Tessa, please." She smiled. "I'm not much for all the formalities and besides, I can't expect you to call me doctor when I'm lounging about in a satin bed jacket."

Doctor Blightly—Tessa—was approachable. Better than that, she was an accomplished woman with excellent educational credentials who didn't have any airs about her. This was the absolute best kind of famous person to know: comfortable in their own skin, yet not forcing you to re-examine how you felt in your own.

"Now, we understand it's a memoir of your time as a dinosaur researcher that you are looking to write?" Gertie asked.

"Yes, that's by far the most media-friendly part of my life," Tessa said. "I don't think anyone would really be interested in my student life at pubs nor the time I hitchhiked across Nebraska."

"Both sound like interesting additions to your story," I said.

"You didn't, by chance, do any karaoke singing in pubs, did you?" Gertie asked. I was sure she still had a hankering to go back and try more of it for herself, but so far we'd managed to keep my effervescent cousin under wraps.

Tessa shook her head and chortled. "No, can't say that I did. Mind you, I've always been told my singing voice isn't the most melodic and–"

"I get that too!" Gertie exclaimed, leaning forward in her seat. "And after I won the prize for my efforts–"

"Er, let's get back to the memoir, please?" I said, putting a warning hand on Gertie's forearm.

"Right. Sorry," my cousin replied.

"What's that behind you?" Tessa asked.

"Oh that," I said, turning to look at the tray of minerals on loan from Bertie's place. "It's a minerals collection we found in a secret room at Scotford Castle."

"What does that have to do with family history?" Tessa asked, the curious academic emerging from within her mind. It didn't matter if she was in a satin bed jacket or not: her training took over.

"I'm helping them catalog things from the fire, Mum," Candace explained. "I was wondering if the rocks spelled anything out via initials, you know, the first letter of each rock is a code?"

"Is it a Victorian collection? Victorians adored riddles, anagrams and ciphers." Tessa stared at her daughter.

"So far, I have 'STOP'. S. T. O. P. Silver, tungsten, obsidian and pumice." Candace set out the rocks in order in front of her on the table.

"Have you considered all the minerals in the collection?"

"No, but these seemed the most likely candidates and–"

Tessa held up a hand. "What did I always teach you?"

Candace sighed. "That academic rigor must be present in all one does. Research. Life. And otherwise."

"I think you just came up with a title for your now slightly expanded memoir," I said. "Research. Life. And Otherwise. A Memoir by Doctor Tessa Blightly."

Both Tessa and Candace went silent.

The elder thought on it, pondered, and then spoke. "Brilliant. Now the cover's done and I just need the interior."

"Just?" Maude asked. "How many words have you got so far?"

"358. Exactly," Candace said. "An outline, with a long, long way to go."

"358 words. But boy, what a fantastic outline it is," Tessa said with a smile. "Candace says I'm to get at least half of it drafted during my convalescence."

"It's good for you," Candace replied with a firm glare. "It stops you from gallivanting around and disobeying doctor's orders."

"And I sense someone is very unwilling to take it slower in order to properly recuperate," I said, knowing full well my own father was like that too.

"I live that dream every single day," Candace moaned. "Mum's impossible."

"Well, ladies, all I can say is this: that memoir isn't going to write itself," Maude interjected. "You possess a wealth of information and the world deserves to hear your story."

Serious words that needed to be said.

I looked over at Maude with newfound appreciation. She was right. Everyone had a duty to share their knowledge with others. If one did not, then so much would be lost between generations, and that was a very sad thing indeed.

Chapter 13

Stables, Scotford Castle. Next Morning.

Bertie spread his manicured hands wide. "I refuse to let Scotford Castle fall into ruins on my watch," he said with a firm voice and furrow in his brow, "I'll use personal capital if I must."

I knew that the entire weight of his ancestors' long legacy now rested upon his bespoke, sport-jacketed shoulders. I gave him what I hoped was a sincerely reassuring look. "Bertie, Scotford will get rebuilt. The community as well as your friends wouldn't have it any other way."

"I appreciate your kind words. Unfortunately the insurers may decide otherwise."

"They're not still giving you trouble, are they?" That very thought struck terror into my heart.

He shrugged. "No insurer on the planet would eagerly step up to pay for intricate stained-glass windows, hand-carved wood paneling, eighteenth-century sculptures and original marble friezes."

"I suppose not."

We sat opposite each other and ruminated on it.

"It's a fate befallen many a grand manor house. All of the expensive, handcrafted fixtures, adornments, decorations, and fittings are stripped down before the structure itself is demolished. Valuable items such as these were sold all over the world for nouveau riche industrialists' mansions in the late nineteenth and early twentieth centuries."

"It's sad, isn't it, when heritage is auctioned off like that?"

"Indeed," Bertie replied. "Gutting houses strips them of their very souls. Hallways that once echoed with the lively laughter of boisterous children are rendered to mere shells, walls becoming patchy plaster, riddled with damp."

Ewan poked his head around the office door. "Good morning. You two look like you both just tasted some sour lemonade. Can I help?"

"The insurers are resisting paying the claim. That led Julie and I into a rather dour conversation about the downfall of many a great manor house," Bertie explained.

"Oh dear." Ewan looked genuinely sorry for the dark pallor that currently hung about the room.

"Well, I'm not sure what my news will do for the mood," Ewan said with a bit of trepidation.

Bertie perked up. "Do you have an update?"

"I do," Ewan said, coming in to sit beside me in a matching guest chair.

"And?" Bertie asked, leaning forward and clutching his fancy fountain pen as if his life depended upon it.

Ewan continued. "I've located your private stolen papers. They've turned up in an exclusive black-market sale another dealer alerted me to. Neither of us has any idea who is selling them, but the price tag is £5 million."

"£5 million? Are they online now? Public?" Bertie asked, taking a huge gulp of air.

Because of their secret contents, it was easy to understand his reaction.

Bertie seemed to read my mind and said, "Don't worry, Julie. I had Ewan sign a nondisclosure agreement. He's well aware of the secret I'm desperate to protect."

It was odd talking about somebody's child as a secret. But such was life of the aristocracy with large estates to hand down to the right person. In Bertie's case, it was also the case where the other parent of the child wanted her daughter to grow up free from the gilded trappings of Bertie's world. On one hand, I couldn't say that I blamed her.

Ewan shook his head. "All that's posted is a basic description of the papers' contents stating that they are owned by a modern-day aristorctica, but no names are given."

"Why haven't they contacted me directly for the ransom?" Bertie asked.

"It's much more anonymous this way. For all we know, they could be sitting watching the bids roll in from the comfort of their home in Antarctica. Black-market dealers are hard to trace, especially when online. They make big moves to cover their tracks," Ewan explained.

"Imagine that. My family papers in Antarctica–" Bertie started.

"I didn't actually confirm they were physically in Antarctica–" Ewan said.

"Of course not, no, no, it's just that … well, the chance of my secrets remaining secrets are pretty slim, aren't they?" Bertie asked. The lines on his face had deepened since his papers were stolen. I'd known him long enough to notice the subtle change.

"And that's where my news gets a bit better," Ewan said. "Has Constable Snowdrop dropped by this morning?"

Bertie checked his fancy gold watch. "He's got an appointment here at eleven o'clock."

Ewan nodded. "Good. He's bringing some enhanced video footage from the night of the fire. It may prove very useful indeed."

***

11:00 a.m.

Constable Bud Snowdrop arrived with Fred Todling, right on time. We saw the policeman bat Fred's hand away from the vehicle's dashboard, just as the siren started to wail and was promptly silenced. Fred got a chagrined little boy's look on his face.

"Oh lovely. Another solicitor having an early midlife crisis," Ewan said. "I had one in the antiques shop last week who wanted to purchase a Victorian parlor suite in red. Vivacious red."

"Present for the wife?" I asked.

"Er, for some sort of couples boudoir photography set decoration." Ewan shook his head. "I sent him on his merry way, quite glad I was unable to help him."

By now, Constable Snowdrop and Fred were headed over towards the three of us, both appearing officious and focused. We met just outside the stables.

"Good morning, gentlemen," Bertie said. "I hear you bring good news."

"Yes, we do," Constable Snowdrop said, hauling out his ever-present tablet. I noticed he'd obtained a new cover for it and it was littered with stickers of police dogs.

"Oh, are you working with the canine unit now?" I asked in all innocence.

Constable Snowdrop stood up straighter. "Yes. I'm helping train dogs to sniff out smuggled meat at airports."

Our local arm of the law was working to reduce the import of surreptitious salami.

"What kind of dogs?" Ewan asked.

"Beagles," Constable Snowdrop confirmed.

It dawned on me that we were in the midst of an aristocratic crisis yet talking about illegal salami.

"Right," Ewan said, stifling a grin.

Fred cleared his throat. "I think you'll be astounded at what we discovered," he said, putting his leather briefcase on top of double stacked hay bales. "We put our best videographer on it."

"Meaning the cinematographer for the film crew already on-site who was willing to moonlight on the cheap since he already had his gear unpacked?" I asked with a grin.

"It's wonderful what modern technology can do these days," Fred said in a smooth deflection.

"I thought it was rather a stroke of genius on our part," Constable Snowdrop said. "The thing is, when the film crew's camera was set up to capture some nocturnal wildlife images, it also collected some bonus footage. I'll show you on my phone ..."

"As in the thieves?" I asked, in slight disbelief.

"Thieves and ne'er-do-wells. Criminals, the lot of them," Constable Snowdrop sneered.

"Criminals who deserve to be locked up and watch the key get thrown away," Fred said with a matching sneer.

Both the policeman and solicitor looked particularly smug at this moment. Any more smugness in their grins and their uplifted cheeks would surely need more room on their faces. They were like two six-year-olds on Christmas morning, awake long before everyone else, and filled with glee at the prospect of finding such an unexpected gift. In our case, the gift was an exceptionally clear bit of film footage of ... a badger. Precisely, one large badger snuffling around the base of a tree trunk.

"And this is the dastardly culprit who stole my belongings?" Bertie teased. "How will I ever explain that to the insurance representatives?"

Constable Snowdrop fumbled with his phone, realizing that he wasn't exactly living up to the expectations of his policeman's uniform. "Apologies. It's the wrong file, er, Fred?" He looked to the solicitor for assistance.

Fred made a big show of unlocking his briefcase. Both of the brass locks flipped up, each emitting a large 'clack'. As he lifted the lid, we caught a glimpse of his impressive pen collection. On the very top of the stack of papers was a red file folder marked 'Top Secret' and 'Badger One'.

"You codenamed this investigation, 'Badger One'?" Ewan asked, incredulous.

Fred shrugged. "It seemed the right thing to do. Client confidentiality and all that."

"Riiight," was the in-unison response from Bertie, Ewan and I. One just couldn't make this stuff up.

Constable Snowdrop interrupted Fred's file folder reveal and triumphantly held up his phone. "Found it!" He shuffled his feet with glee, jabbed his arm up in the air with victory and then ... split open the back seam in his trousers exposing red-glitter-heart underpants. We all heard the stitches tear; it was the unmistakable sound of overly stressed material simply giving way to a much stronger force.

The pudgy policeman rapidly backed into a stack of straw bales and stood there.

We were kind, said nothing, and advanced upon the embarrassed policeman so he wouldn't have to move, thus making his trousers predicament even worse.

Bertie, ever the gentleman, picked up a groom's overcoat and silently handed it to our lawman in distress. It was donned lightning fast with a gracious look of thanks.

Next, we clustered around Constable Snowdrop's phone screen and watched two men in black stocking caps and masks hoof it out of the castle's front entrance. One robber carried the gilded framed portrait of Aunt Edwina—rest her dear soul—plus a diamond and emerald necklace slung around his wrist, swinging in the wind. The other thief carried a fancy silver coffee pot, likely circa eighteenth century. The pair raced out of the castle, apparently more concerned with their safe escape and loot than with the tower of flames behind them.

Fred coughed in a polite manner, his way of announcing he was about to say something important. "This was filmed approximately fifteen minutes after the fire started, once it really took hold in the back of the castle."

"It's a good start. Just recall we had staff, guests, plus a large film crew on-site so it would have been quite easy to stash things over the course of a few days inside a non-suspicious vehicle," Bertie said. "More than that painting, necklace and silver coffee pot was stolen."

Constable Snowdrop put on a most serious face, as serious as he could be while conducting himself inside a uniform we knew counted red-glitter-hearts at its very foundation.

Fred interjected. "And this is where Constable Snowdrop and I would like to interject a strong note of caution. Namely, in pursuit of a nefarious recalcitrance, we have devised a probable, statistically sound, responsible theory."

After that thesaurus-worthy sentence, our heads were reeling.

"Alright Fred, what's your best guess?" Ewan said, elegantly summarizing the conundrum.

Constable Snowdrop did the reveal. "We think it's an inside job."

A piece of straw could've floated through the air, landed on the stables' brick flooring, and shattered the silence.

"But my staff are all honest, hard-working people!" Bertie coughed out in disbelief. "Every single person on the Scotford team must pass a criminal background check. I just can't see–"

"Have you seen food prices lately? Interest rates on mortgages and car payments?" Ewan asked.

"Well of course, but surely that's not enough to drive my staff to steal … Is it?" Bertie looked flabbergasted.

Fred gave us a sobering thought. "Your Grace, the last sentence you uttered must be realistically amended to include the possibility that someone on your staff stole and set fire to an historic site of national importance."

We all took a deep gulp of air and contemplated the possibility: surely it wasn't true. Surely our friends and team members, volunteer museum guides and farm shop staff wouldn't be part of this. The fire and the robbery had to be masterminded by someone outside Bertie's circle of trusted team members … didn't it?

BOOM! BOOM!

Our thoughts of the unthinkable were rapidly overtaken by a short, sharp shower of dirt accompanied by a significant poof of pale yellow smoke in the far beyond.

"What was that?" I asked as small clods of earth showered down around us. Fred's glasses were covered in a film of semi-damp soil and everyone had tiny bits of turf stuck in their hair.

"It's coming from the back fields over there," Bertie said, already on the move. He took off at a jog, presumably wondering if another part of his estate was now under threat of a new type of disaster. Ewan, Constable Snowdrop, Fred and I all dutifully followed at a rapid trot. Fred grabbed a riding helmet on the way out and jammed it down over his perfectly smooth haircut. At all times, the legal mechanics of his splendiferous brain had to be protected.

The dirt clods finally stopped falling. We reached the edge of the field behind the castle. This was where Bertie grew cereal crops and tidy hedgerows to encourage wildlife, such as songbirds and hedgehogs, to nest. Today, however, was not a pristine countryside scene.

Today, as presented by Ozzie Boggs and Timmy Hitchins, showed them both in a rather unusual predicament. Both men sat on the ground, streaks of mud on their faces, their metal detectorist earphones askew. What hair they had was plastered to their heads. As we neared, I saw both of them had singed their eyebrows. Their camouflaged jackets and pants made them blend in with the ground. I also noticed two bent metal detectors laying in a twisted heap together, just off to the right.

"Good grief, what happened? Did you dig up the gas line?" Ewan asked, incredulous.

"We got a strong signal, so we dug," Ozzie said.

"Then this happened," Timmy said.

"There is no gas line running through my barley field," Bertie said. "I would have surely warned you about anything hazardous, gentlemen." Our host looked absolutely shocked.

"Assuming, Bertie, you knew it was there." I picked up a loose piece of fluttering paper caught between a stone in a plowed furlough. "Does this handwriting look familiar?"

Bertie took the paper from me and examined the old copperplate writing with all its fancy loops and squiggles courtesy of the quill pen's ink. "Well I never," he explained. "The Old Duke's been at it again."

"We need to evacuate. Pronto. Cordon off the site," Constable Snowdrop said, helping Ozzie and Timmy to their feet.

Fred peered over the edge of the hole in the ground. "Fascinating."

Ewan looked over at me, quizzical.

"I believe that some pent up gas was released. The firefighters will need to confirm it, but once the lid was blown, then the worst of it was over after the initial reaction," I said.

"Reaction to what?" Ozzie asked

"The disturbance caused by digging around an area that obviously had some type of chemical affected by the introduction of new air. It was an opportunity that simply presented itself. There is no way anyone could have known."

Everybody looked impressed at what I just revealed.

I shrugged. "I had to take a chemistry course as part of my art training. All about solvents and safety."

"Impressive," Fred said.

"Thanks to our two intrepid friends here," Bertie said, "we've now discovered the precise location of my ancestor's alchemic laboratory. This paper proves it." He waved it up in the air and at the very top everyone could see the headline that read 'Alchemy Laboratory Log, Scotford Castle 1809'.

"Think of all the history down there," Ewan joked, "if there's anything left."

"We might uncover the mystery surrounding his six apprentices," I said.

"Fascinating as this is, may we please leave the historical perambulations until later?" Fred asked in a hurried manner. "Remaining here on an open explosion site is not in our best interest."

He was right. The air around us was extremely warm and, despite my gut feeling, we didn't know what was going to happen next. Safety took over as the importance of the moment and we hustled out of the area. We were all safe. Ozzie and Timmy didn't appear any worse for wear, aside from their metal detecting equipment being rendered to sad bits of twisted metal destined for the recycler.

The last thing about this incident that would forever be buried in my mind was the sight of Constable Snowdrop trucking back over the plowed field, us following a beacon of glittery red hearts flashing from underneath the tails of his borrowed coat.

Chapter 14

————

Three Hours Later.

For the second time in a matter of weeks, fire and ambulance services dashed up to Scotford Castle. Fire trucks, medical personnel and long hoses were strewn across the property. The robotic bomb sniffer device was sent in, and its micro camera returned a video feed full of wonder.

We sat clustered around three firefighters looking at the contents of the Old Duke's underground laboratory. For all intents and purposes, it looked like one of those dusty, secret laboratories squirreled away, crammed full of glass beakers, vials, dried up concoctions plus rows of suspicious-looking ledgers. It had a long workbench, various cabinets with tiny drawers and a couple of well-used crucibles sitting next to a much blackened hearth. Somehow all this survived the explosion and the real damage was to the ceiling area and not what lay underground.

"Well, we finally proved it exists," Bertie said. "This is quite the historical experience."

"Once that picric acid reached the appropriate dryness level, you were quite fortunate not to be any closer," lead firefighter Stan said.

Stan was a tall, cool glass of water, muscular physique, kind eyes, confident and someone who wore his uniform extremely well.

Something resonated in the back of my mind. I recognized him from somewhere. Somewhere rather good, in fact. "Were you on the cover of–"

Stan grinned. "2023 calendar." He nodded. "We raised over £50,000 for the hospital's burn unit."

"Well done." I stared at him some more. Apparently, I wasn't alone, as most of the women in the vicinity suddenly had an urgent need to wander through the front courtyard near us.

Stan seemed used to it and focused on the task at hand. "Picric acid. Discovered in the eighteenth century, used as explosive when dried out. Also used with indigo to produce a yellow dye in the nineteenth and twentieth centuries."

"And the Old Duke was messing about with it in his secret laboratory?" Ewan asked.

"Appears that's the case. Stuff's like dynamite at the right dryness level. It should be kept inside a sealed container with a controlled moisture level," Stan explained. "My guess is the container degraded and perfect conditions were reached today. After all this time, I'm surprised it didn't go up sooner."

"How can you can determine the cause and exposure in three hours, but my castle fire takes weeks?" Bertie asked, slightly indignant.

By now two other firefighters had joined us and they looked at Stan. Stan was in charge. Stan would have the answer. Stan was the man. Stan spoke with the voice of experience. "It all depends upon the circumstance. A secret laboratory, untouched for years. An easily found explosive. The robotic microscopic camera. One contained location. Some cases are much more obvious than others. Having said that, we do go on the science too."

"Please tell that to my insurance adjuster," Bertie lamented.

Stan shrugged. "That's a tough one. At least the firefighting crew gave the all clear on this most recent incident so you can go back to exploring that tunnel once the structural engineer has signed off."

We all swiveled around to look at Stan in great detail.

Bertie spoke first. "What tunnel?"

"The long passage leading to the kitchen cellar," Stan said. "We had our robot travel the whole length of it and ended up seeing a pile of potatoes in front of a smashed wall. Must have come down in the explosion."

"Really?"

Fred stepped in. "Our honored battler of the blazes. In all sincerity, I hasten to add the present Duke had no idea about aforesaid unexplored passageway before our two metal detectorists enthusiastically and unassumingly dismantled a portion of His Grace's barley field," he said.

"Well, you have some fun ahead of you. Mind, AFTER the structural engineers have signed off. I don't want visits here to become a regular occurrence." Stan wagged his finger as he checked his phone. "Now, I'd better be off. Meeting at the fire hall in half an hour."

We waved the firefighters off and I sighed out loud, feeling Ewan's eyes on me.

"Muscles, big trucks and perfect, pearly white smiles. I can't compete with that," Ewan lamented.

I sidled up to him. "You don't have to." I adored Ewan for dropping everything to be here for his friends. Ewan Kilburn was the man for me: tall, good-looking, well-read, kind plus a huge fan of family history. He deferred to the experts, always offered to help and knew exactly when someone was pulling his leg. On top of that, he was playing a key role in saving the reputation of my dear friend, Bertie. In my books, stepping up when the chips were down out-muscled any calendar stud, any day of the year.

I leaned over and gave Ewan a big kiss.

He looked slightly surprised.

I smiled. "That's for being you."

❋❋❋

Stables. Later.

Ozzie and Timmy were released by the paramedics, having received the 'all clear' from their unexpectedly drama-filled, metal detectorist experience. The two adventurers, Bertie, Ewan and I sat clustered in Bertie's temporary office, awaiting direction from the aristocrat.

Bertie smiled and clasped his hands over the desk. "First things first. I am very relieved that neither of you were hurt today out in the field," Bertie said, looking straight at Ozzie and Timmy.

"We are, too," Ozzie replied. "When I saw what the explosion did to our gear, I knew we dodged a large one."

"Forgetting all that, we have some exciting finds to share," Timmy said, pulling out a leather pouch.

We all leaned forward in great anticipation.

"Roman coins?" Bertie asked, following up on their earlier assertion that a Roman Mint was located on the Scotford Castle lands.

"Not yet. But we did find these." Timmy proceeded to dump the contents on the desk. A small cloud of dry soil puffed up as the treasures settled in an untidy heap.

"Would you like to do the honors?" Timmy asked Ozzie.

"Right," Ozzie said, standing up as if he was ready to address the world congress of treasure hunters. "Here we have some startling finds. One gold ring."

"Roman?" I asked, intrigued.

"No. Shiny plastic toy, likely free in a cereal box for children over six," Ozzie explained. His answer fell flat as a deflated balloon. Then Ozzie continued. "We also have a wadded up old cloth, two squashed soda cans, three bent horseshoe nails, a tractor part and some broken pottery."

"Likely from the laboratory explosion," Ewan said.

"The tractor part?" Ozzie asked.

"No, the pottery." Ewan looked at Bertie. "Did they even have tractors at Scotford when your alchemist Duke lived here?"

"Hmmm. In the early 1800s? No, they would still be under horse power at that time."

"Hence, pottery is from the laboratory," Ewan said. "Or dropped at a later time."

"It could be Roman," Ozzie insisted. "We found bits of mosaic before."

"Which, gentlemen, turned out to be broken bits of a twentieth century crockery set made by a potter in Devon, I'm afraid," Bertie said.

Ozzie's and Timmy's faces both fell, tumbling down like an avalanche of sadness.

"I was going to tell you, I've just been so distracted with the fire and the robbery," Bertie admitted.

"You're absolutely, positively certain?" Ozzie asked.

Bertie nodded. "The words 'Made in Devon, 1989' confirmed it as a certainty, Ozzie. I'm sorry."

Ozzie scowled. "Worthless?" His question was rather plaintive.

Bertie nodded again. "Our 50/50 split amounts to zero compensation for each of us. Believe me, there is nothing more I would like to find than a huge gold hoard to help rebuild Scotford."

Ozzie and Timmy slumped in the chairs. Yet again, another get-rich-quick scheme had slipped through Ozzie's fingers.

"What's inside the cloth?" I asked.

Ozzie grumbled. "It's just an old shop rag. We brought it in so it wouldn't clog up Bertie's plow, you know keep the land clean, leave only footsteps."

"Footprints, Ozzie. Leave only footprints," Ewan said.

"Fine. Footprints." Ozzie glared at Ewan. This was obviously not his day.

Ever the diplomat, Bertie issued a quick thanks for their care. "That's very honorable of you both. That rag really could play up the works of a farming machine."

"May I?" I took the rag from Ozzie and then carefully started to unfold it. There was something I could feel inside, but I wasn't sure what it was. As the folds of the material came away, there was something inside taking shape. "It feels like links … a necklace?"

Ozzie's and Timmy's faces both lit up immediately. "We're rich! Rubies and gold! It's a Viking hoard!" Ozzie crowed. "I knew my hunch was right."

"You were looking for a Roman Mint. Now we've instantly changed centuries to the Scandinavians with helmets and long boats? Which is it to be?" Ewan asked.

"Doesn't matter. As long as it's gold," Ozzie said. He looked over at me, eager. "Unwrap it, show us what we've got!"

"Why didn't you just unfold the rag in the field?" Bertie asked.

"We only found it beside our collection pouch after the explosion," Timmy explained.

"Then Constable Snowdrop hustled us out of the area. No time," Ozzie said.

By now, all eyes were on me. With one last layer, I pulled open the rag and there, in my very hands on top of the oily rag, lay one incredibly used … bicycle chain.

"Arrgh!" was Ozzie's only comment as he buried his head in his hands.

***

GGRS. Two Days Later.

"We need our rock expert," I said to Candace Blightly.

"Here, at your command," she replied in a teasing voice.

I put a ten-pound rock on the table, one that was already split in half. Inside was a clump of gorgeous, grape-purple crystals. "The restoration crew found this near the laboratory explosion hole out in the barley field at Bertie's place."

Never thought I'd call a castle a 'place', but it suited this particular reference.

"Bertie is funding the laboratory's restoration?" she asked.

I nodded. "The insurers signed off on the restorations due to conclusive evidence that malice wasn't involved in the explosion."

"And the castle's fire insurance claim?"

"A continuing source of frustration, angst and handwringing," I confirmed.

"Oh dear."

"Oh dear, is right. I feel terrible for him," I said.

"Have they arrested anyone yet?" Candace asked.

"Negative on that angle, too."

"Constable Snowdrop has no leads?" Candace said his name with a bit of a smirk.

"He has leads, but I sense he's in over his head. Thankfully he's consulting with London now; there's some antiquities and art fraud division that should be able to help. We're hoping for some solid results soon."

"Well, best of luck with that. Bertie is such a good man. He certainly doesn't deserve all of this misfortune," she said.

"Quite correct. He's had such a run of bad luck lately. Things have to turn around soon."

Candace focused again on the purple crushed rock. "This is an amethyst geode."

"How old do you think it is?" I asked.

"Likely over a hundred million years. Give or take a few million either side." She spoke with extreme confidence.

I was stunned. "Really?"

"Yes. Forming stones takes time. There's no way Mother Nature could create something this beautiful in a few simple years or decades." Candace looked at it closer. "This is really a wonderful specimen. What will Scotford do with it?"

"Likely put it on display. Bertie is bringing the old laboratory into part of the castle tour. The film crew's coming back to do a documentary on the find, showing laboratory cleanup and reconstruction as it happens."

"Great fun!" Candace explained.

"Speaking of fun, how's the memoir coming along?" I asked.

Candace stood up straight and smiled. "My mother, I am very proud to announce, has written 4,893 words since our videoconference. She says GGRS inspired her no end."

"Wonderful," I said, "I shall have to tell Maude and Gertie."

There was a slight commotion out front. Candace and I both looked out the window to see the Major drive his vintage army jeep into a large plant pot. He paused, wore a horrified expression and watched the terracotta container wobble, crack, then fall apart into pieces. The small conifer it housed fell onto the car park surface like a rigid, dedicated soldier, doing his duty right up until the bitter end.

"That's not like him. I hope the Major's not ill," I said.

My question was answered a millisecond later when Abbyleigh got out of the passenger side, laughing hysterically.

"So much for my worry. Now I need to know who's going to pony up to fix this," I said.

"Watch," Candace said.

The Major got out of the driver's side and came over to survey the damage. He looked down, shook his head and seemed very upset with himself.

We watched Abbyleigh take his hand, pat it, and then say a few soothing words.

He smiled and all looked right in his world again.

But not so much for my fallen conifer.

We watched the couple enter the building. A few seconds later, we saw them at the GGRS entrance.

"Julie, I have a slightly unusual report," the Major started, in a faltering voice. Abbyleigh was behind him, ushering in the usually stoic man like an errant schoolboy found pelting rocks at the community center's windows.

"Yes?" I replied. "You look exactly like you did when you and Harvey drove the historic tank into the wrong meadow here at Greymore."

"I'm afraid so." The Major looked ever so sorry.

"I know that look too," Abbyleigh said, "I think it's devilishly cute!" Her Scottish accent was lovely. There was just something about her outlandish style and the way she looked at the Major. Well, it was hard to remain upset for any length of time, if any at all.

"What happened? I have to ask," I said.

"Well, you see, Abbyleigh was telling me a story about when she grew up and her father's sheep escaped in the Highlands and they had to round them up in a snowstorm and–"

I looked at him, trying hard to stifle a smile.

The Major shrugged. "How about I just leave it at 'her melodic voice distracted me and I wasn't paying attention'?"

"You're fortunate you weren't out on the motorway," Candace said.

"I realize I was foolish, and I should have paid better attention."

"What is it with you and errant vehicles, Major?" I asked.

Another shrug. "I was simply dazzled by my girlfriend's beauty."

Ah. Progress. We've moved on a few levels from 'scared to deliver roses' to 'my girlfriend'.

Well done, Major!

Still, it was early days in their relationship and I didn't want to embarrass the man in front of a women he was clearly smitten with here at GGRS. We encouraged people to be their best here, rather than tear them down for some minor foible or two. Still, there was one key thing that had to be put right.

"Major, I'm glad no one was hurt. However, my plant pot will need replacing and–"

"Of course. Think no more of the matter. It shall be done post-haste," he confirmed, earning a sunshiny smile from Abbyleigh.

"Good. Then all is right again in this world," I replied. "As you were."

The pair left hand in hand, and I noticed a definite spring in the Major's step.

"Who would have thought those two, a formal retired military man and a vivacious sheep farmer's daughter turned barista, would hit it off?" Candace observed.

I smiled. "Trust me. Families all over the world are comprised of the unlikeliest people who share a great love for each other."

Chapter 15

Scotford Castle. Afternoon. Two Weeks Later.

After much moaning and anticipation during the wait for the structural engineers, the tunnel from the barley field to Scotford Castle's kitchen was finally deemed safe for us to explore. A first-class engineering firm was employed to perform structural stability, soil, and construction material testing to ensure we could wander below without any fear of imminent tunnel collapse. Stan the firefighter was back to supervise the laboratory contents removal. Anything even remotely suspicious was dealt with by his hazardous materials removal crew. No one really knew what the Old Duke's secret laboratory contained, and we certainly weren't willing to take any chances. For the reconstruction of the laboratory for castle visitors, we would simply use prop bottles with fake chemicals, i.e. colored sand and clay contents, in order to eliminate all risk.

Bertie, Ewan, Fred, and I went downstairs to the castle's kitchen. It showcased the hum of culinary efficiency. The centuries-old space was now resplendent with every conceivable modern appliance.

Knowing Bertie's penchant to satisfy his guests' every need, he even had one frother for dairy as well as one for nondairy beverages.

We were faced by one stout cook at the end of her tether. "Your Grace, what about the dinner for our guests? You have the historical society committee here this evening. We were going to serve them in-"

"Yes, in the dining room that wasn't affected by the fire." He looked at us. "We're lucky to have a few dining areas to select from here at the castle."

"How handy," I replied.

"Er, quite," Bertie said, knowing he just inadvertently reminded us that he lived in a different stratosphere.

"Your Grace, what is the schedule for this kitchen now?" She likely was extremely tired of workmen tromping through her workspace. It was hard to produce fancy meals with everything covered in plastic sheeting and potatoes rolling everywhere on the cellar floor.

Bertie gave her a kind look. "The wall from the cellar to the tunnel has been reinforced. We've also added a new door to make access to the tunnel from the cellar much easier. There will be a separate visitor entrance for the castle tours."

"Glory be," the cook said. "When I saw that old wall collapsed on top of my potatoes, I thought, mercy me, the world is coming to an end. And all over my spuds!"

"Rest assured, we're taking care of everything so your kitchen is back to its usual normalcy," Bertie said.

"Thank you, Your Grace."

"And now if it's not too much of an intrusion—"

"Oh yes. Dear me, I've left the cheese cart in front of the cellar door. These renovations have got me all in a flap and fluster." The cook bustled about, working to clear the entranceway.

"That's all right, we understand." Bertie was giving us a master-class in how to treat staff: with respect, humility, kindness as well as an ear for their concerns. He was a much beloved leader of the estate, making a job here at Scotford Castle a plum piece of employment.

The four of us continued our quest below ground. Bertie pushed open the door to the cellar and we set eyes upon neatly arranged shelving units containing wooden pull-out trays of farm grown potatoes, beets, rutabagas and carrots. It was a cook's dream come true: somewhere cool and dry, perfect for long-term vegetable storage. There was a wicker basket hanging on a wall, a few metal scoops beside it, no doubt for gathering up smaller items here in season, such as shallots or cloves of garlic.

Bertie pulled a map out of his pocket. "Now, the engineers said that the tunnel runs a full half mile from the castle out to the field. The Old Duke likely thought he needed a fair distance to eliminate the risk to anyone nearby when he was concocting one of his experiments."

"He didn't count on Ozzie Boggs," I replied with a grin.

"I don't believe anyone can predict the Ozzie Boggs' effect," Ewan added.

Everyone laughed and the cellar reverberated with hilarity, including Fred's high pitched giggles that sounded like a train moving at high speed once he added in rapid breaths of air to keep up with himself.

"And so we walk," Bertie said. Temporary lamps lit our way down the length of the tunnel, as did fluorescent tape stuck to the walls. This was, after all, an incomplete restoration project. It was safe, yes, but far from ready to welcome the public.

The tunnel was colder than I expected and Ewan gallantly took off his jacket to put around my shoulders as we headed towards the laboratory. It was a fairly straight passage, heading to one destination ... or so we thought.

"Hold on, what's this fork?" Bertie asked. He shone his torch down over the engineer's blueprints he'd taken along with him. "It's on the map but no one told me anything about a second tunnel."

I came over and read the map over his shoulder. "It's the same tunnel, just a branch off the main one."

"Can't imagine where it leads."

"It's heading towards the village. Perhaps it's an old smugglers' route," Ewan suggested.

"Perhaps it's where lovers met, you know, like we found at Roycetonne house where Lady Adelaide, daughter of Lord Roycetonne, fell in love with a groom. They would have used a tunnel like this for their escape."

Bertie seemed oblivious to our commentary. "I believe this heads towards a few cottages on the estate, however I cannot be certain of which one. How fascinating." And before we knew it, our good friend the Duke of Conroy was off down the new tunnel branch, heading towards an unknown destination.

"Bertie! Is it safe?" I called out after him.

He turned with a grin. "Of course! It's on the engineer's map. Come on, finally a fun adventure this month."

We had to hurry to keep up with him.

This new part of the tunnel was a surprise to all of us. It went in a completely different direction from the route leading to the laboratory.

"Indeed," Bertie said. "Look at the workmanship. This tunnel was made a long time ago, likely over centuries. I can tell by the stone-work and toolmarks. I've read about this in my historic building restoration books."

We walked to the end of the tunnel and came to a dark brown door. There didn't appear to be any lock, so Ewan went up to Bertie and they both put their shoulders into it. With a groan, the door partly gave way, a wall crumbled, and we were coated in a shower of dust. We peered around the half-open door, and saw storage shelves of home-canned fruits, pickles and vegetables. I had never seen so many pickled cauliflowers in my entire life. There was also a white deep-freeze that hummed while it flashed a red light on its lid, a bevy of travel trunks, an old hobbyhorse plus a clothes rack of waxed jackets. We were peering into somebody's cellar.

"There's a set of stairs over there," Ewan pointed out.

"That might really frighten the homeowner," I observed. "Imagine you're just sitting watching television when all of a sudden three strangers pop their heads up from the basement. I'd call the police."

"And I'm sure Constable Snowdrop would come screaming up the drive wanting to help," Ewan teased.

"Please do not get me started on our local constabulary," Bertie moaned. "Thank goodness he's got London involved now." He looked around the cellar. "I'm sure it's one of my tenant's cottages. We haven't walked that far and I know the laboratory is only about another half a mile down the other tunnel."

"Do your tenants know about the barley field explosion?"

"Of course. The fire service went around and informed everybody. Black clouds of smoke in the air tend to make everybody a bit nervous."

Bertie decided to do the polite thing, went up the six steps and knocked on the cellar door. "Hello? Hello? It's the Duke of Conroy, Madam? Can you hear us?"

Silence.

Our aristocrat was used to having doors opened for him, so this was quite a novel experience.

Bertie tried again, this time with a louder knock.

This time he got a reply. Someone on the other side of the door knocked back and we heard a tentative female voice call out, "Who's there?"

"Madam, it's the Duke of Conroy. We just discovered a tunnel underneath your cottage leading to the Old Duke's laboratory. Do you perchance recall the black cloud of smoke in the sky from couple of weeks ago?"

"Goodness me!" The door opened a crack and we looked upon the kindly face of a gray-haired woman, her hair scraped back into a bun. She was of medium build, rosy-cheeked, and had the most surprised look on her face. "Your Grace? Whatever on earth? Do come in, do come in. I don't have anything prepared for you, Your Grace, but I could offer you some tea on short notice if that would suffice?"

Bertie smiled, relieved. "Mrs. Farmingham, you are a kind soul indeed. We invade your home, pop up like gophers and yet you still willingly invite us inside and offer us refreshment. You are the heart and soul of the Scotford Estate," Bertie said.

If I didn't know Bertie better, I would say he was laying it on pretty thick.

Rapid introductions were made as we brushed off the dust and were escorted up into her warm kitchen. The walls were covered in countryside-image porcelain plates. There were two antique Staffordshire porcelain dogs sitting on the mantelpiece beside a full set of miniature copper kitchen pots. We were invited to sit on chairs covered with chintz-patterned fabric.

Our surprised hostess gave us the most odd look. "Your Grace, this is rather unusual." She scuttled about in her kitchen trying to rustle up some tea and cakes for us. The woman was an angel.

"We apologize for the intrusion, Mrs. Farmingham. We were merely following a new tunnel from Scotford Castle and ended up at your cottage." At that moment, Bertie was a dusty aristocrat far removed from his coronets, ermine robes and heraldic crests.

"Well, of course you are most welcome. Oh Greg, there you are." A nervous looking boy of about six-years-old hovered by the door. Mrs. Farmingham leaned over and whispered to us, "My grandson. He's autistic and non-speaking, a bit shy around people."

We all gave warm smiles to Greg. The young boy wasn't quite sure about us; we were rather a lot of strangers all at once, plus he'd had no preparation time for our visit.

I noticed the Tyrannosaurus Rex on his T-shirt. "Do you like dinosaurs?"

He nodded, shyly.

"I know a lady who has over three hundred dinosaurs in her house."

Greg's eyes opened wide and he issued a small smile.

"Oh, if you're talking dinosaurs, you'll have his attention for the next half hour at least. Dinosaurs are his happy place. Greg, why don't you show our guests one of your dinosaur books?"

Greg vanished and quickly reappeared with a picture book showing some pretty ferocious meat-eating carnivores from millions of years ago. He hovered at the door.

I encouraged him over. "Greg, do please show us your favorite dinosaur."

He nodded but still stood by the door.

"Oh, sometimes he prefers to sit in the living room where there is more space," Mrs. Farmingham explained.

"We can accommodate, no problem," I said. I got up, took my cup of tea along and then sat crossed legged on the floor where Greg showed me. We proceeded to walk through his picture book, him pointing at various pictures of dinosaurs.

Half an hour later, I looked up and saw the three adults watching us at the kitchen doorway. Bertie pointed to his watch.

"Well, Greg, it looks like I have to leave. It was very nice spending time with you," I said.

He issued me another small smile.

Our visit was only short. We had to find a way to properly thank Mrs. Farmingham for her unexpected, last minute hospitality.

Chapter 16

Octopus Reach Pub. That Evening.

Ewan and I visited one of the pubs owned by now-GGRS regular Pamela Fulham. We'd recently helped her figure out a long-held World War Two genealogy secret concerning her ancestors and now she was eager to untangle more branches on her family tree.

Ewan leaned back against the padded booth. "Well, that was quite the day. Tunneling underneath a centuries-old castle, making new friends and dinosaurs."

"I told you that life with me is never dull," I said, toasting him with my cranberry juice.

Our waitress arrived and she was a vivacious young lady with sparkly eyes, heavy mascara and a light dusting of blush on her cheeks. She held a tablet in her hand. "Are we ready to order?"

Ewan gave me a kind smile. "Julie?"

"Yes, I'd like the chicken salad please, lemon meringue pie for dessert." I placed the menu at the end of the table and looked over at Ewan.

"Well, I'm not going to be that healthy. Coconut shrimp and French fries please."

I shook my head. "You have absolutely nothing green with that meal."

"It comes with pickles," he retorted.

The waitress laughed. She had a lovely laugh. "I can comp him a few bits of lettuce if that helps keep marital harmony in the house."

"Oh, we're not–" I started.

But our waitress had already flounced away, her eye caught by another couple at a nearby booth who held an empty ketchup bottle aloft.

"Saved by the ketchup," Ewan teased.

"If you want to live past the age of sixty-five, then you'd better take control of your eating habits," I said. "Salad is good for you."

"I know." He smiled.

"What is it?"

"Do you remember when we got locked inside that moving truck on the way up to Yorkshire and all I had in my pocket was a squashed, preservative-laden cake snack?"

"How can I forget? Not one of your most memorable moments." I took a sip of cranberry juice and then looked at him. Today, Ewan seemed a bit jumpy sitting in front of me. It wasn't like him to be this antsy. I wondered if something was bothering him. I tilted my head to the side. "Something wrong?"

"Not wrong so much as–"

"I forgot to ask. Did you want dressing with your salad? We have ranch, French, oil and vinegar …" Our waitress was back and looked at us with an expectant grin.

"Oh ranch is great, and on the side please," I said.

She flounced away again.

I look back at Ewan. "Sorry, you were saying nothing's wrong? You've just seemed a bit out of sorts today. Is it being in the tunnel? A confined space issue?"

Ewan gave an involuntary burst of laughter. "No, I'm not afraid of tunnels, nor the dark." He fiddled with his placemat and rearranged his cutlery a few times.

"Ewan, you're fussing. What is it?" I asked him. So far, we'd enjoyed our time together and become quite comfortable around each other. The only argument we'd ever had concerned the placement of the soup spoon and knife at a formal dinner service where multiple other pieces of cutlery were involved. It was a volunteer assignment we did for Bertie at short notice and I ended up winning based upon a hostess book I pulled out of the library to prove my point.

Ewan looked as though he was trying to get his thoughts together and tell me something but it was really hard. I reached over and took his hand in mine across the table. "You can tell me, you know. You've been there for me so many times when I was upset at losing my grandmother, through all our family history adventures. You even helped to set up the GGRS so it could become the success it is today."

He took a deep breath. Then exhaled. Then took a deep breath again.

"Would you like a paper bag?" I asked.

One more sigh and he was finally ready to talk. He pulled his hands away from mine, leaned forward and uttered words in a conspiratorial whisper. "I spoke with your father."

I smiled. "Oh, is he roping you in to move something else? Let me guess: it's either a piece of furniture he wants put in another room or a new piece of garden equipment he wants to keep in the shed."

"No, Julie. About us." Ewan gave me a serious stare. "I wanted to know if he approves."

I gulped. Men talking to fathers about their daughters usually only meant one thing. A big thing. The big thing. I supposed we had already danced around the topic multiple times, but now things were rapidly sounding far more serious.

We were in a pub called the 'Octopus Reach'. The last thing I wanted was a marriage proposal from Ewan down on bended knee at an eating establishment named after a reclusive sea creature known for squirting ink jets.

Ewan read my mind and put me at ease immediately. "Don't worry, there's not an impending large decision I'm asking you to make today."

Thank goodness!

"After tunnels and dinosaurs, I don't think I've got any more room in my brain left for anything else exciting, not today nor the entire month," I said.

"I want to explain myself. You see, it's something that's bothered me for an awfully long time, and we've never really talked about it. It has to do with my family."

"Family? The one you never talk about?" I asked.

He spread his hands wide and then gripped the edge of the table. His fingers turned white with the strength of his grip. He looked me in the eyes. "My dilemma is this. You come from an aristocratic family with a large estate and much love. My family is, well, the easiest way I can put it, utterly broken. To put it bluntly, I don't really consider myself as having a family."

"But your sister?"

"Ah. She's an old school chum who's a single mum needing a hand once in a while. We're not blood relations."

"Your aunt with the holiday cottage?"

"Same thing. A lovely friend who's old enough to be my grandmother."

"You have your own Aunt Edwina. That's nice," I said.

"I have a kind friend. But no real family," he said.

"What does your family have to do with us being together?" I asked.

"It's just that I don't feel that I'm good enough for you," he said. "You have family around you for stability. I have, well, old furniture."

"Nonsense. You are the nicest, friendliest, most knowledgeable man in my life. Your background means nothing to me."

"Which is why I went and spoke with your father. Before we take another major step, our first one being going away together–"

"Ewan, 'going away together' normally means a preplanned vacation or getaway, not getting trapped in the back of a moving van and then spending the night in a hotel packed full of weekend Vikings on holiday."

It was true. We had gotten stuck at a grand house in Yorkshire, arriving just in time for the annual Viking festival full of large platters of meat, hairy people and yellowed toenails hanging outside coarse leather sandals.

"You know what I mean. We've been together for quite a few months now, and I just thought it would be the right thing to do," he said.

"What's the right thing for us to do?" I wasn't exactly sure where Ewan was going with all of this, namely because he was so jumpy

"Well, the fact that you have a solid family background and I have crickets-all to show you with mine. Doesn't that make you wonder about our future?"

I grinned. "Ewan, my entire life now revolves around finding missing families and uncovering ancestors, some of whom are pretty well-hidden. Trust me, you being a blank slate doesn't bother me at all."

He looked absolutely shocked.

"Did you think I would say something different?" I asked.

"I wasn't sure. You know, it's all fun and games at the beginning of a relationship but when things start to get serious, it can all devolve into one big, hot, sticky mess."

"Ewan, slow down. I don't think we're a mess. In fact, I was actually really looking forward to a nice evening out with you. Did I give you any signal saying I was upset with you for not having family we could visit every Sunday afternoon for tea and cookies?"

"No."

"So why all the sudden anxiety?" I was having a hard time under-standing his fears, but it was in me to try. I had to try, for both our sakes.

"Dear, you don't understand how deep this pain runs," he said in a soft voice. He sounded slightly broken.

"Tell me," I urged him. "Tell me so I can help you—help us—overcome it."

His secrets came spilling out all at once, like a kid going down a slippery, wet piece of plastic on a hillside. "My younger brother died in a car accident at the age of eight. My mother was heartbro-ken, spiraled into a nervous breakdown and left us. My father had already died of alcoholism two years earlier. I was put into care and went through four different homes before I was eighteen."

And with that huge reveal, our waitress was back with our food. "Everything look alright?" she asked in her super-chirpy voice after setting down our plates.

I gave our food the once over and nodded. "Ewan, are you good?"

"All good." He picked up the ketchup bottle to prove it was full.

She smiled back and left us alone again.

"Our waitress has impeccable timing. What's that, the third time she's interrupted when I'm laying my heart bare?" he asked.

I shrugged. "Ewan, it wouldn't matter when or where you opened your heart to me. I would always listen. Given a choice, I would have picked a different venue, but a pub will do."

He reached for my hand and held it tight across the table. "Foster parents, you see ... no one ever wants the over-fives, and especially not the teenagers. Everyone wants the little babies that haven't picked up any bad habits or been traumatized by prior situations."

The things poor Ewan must have experienced. "Did you have any foster siblings?" I asked.

"There was one other boy, a year younger than me, Travis. We were at the same foster home for three years and were like brothers. He got adopted and I didn't, so that was the end of that."

"Yet you're such an adjusted, calm, kind human being. A businessman, so knowledgeable with antiques and history. How did you pull yourself up and out of your difficult start in life?" I asked.

"I had a couple of good teachers at school, one of whom recommended me for an art and furniture history program at university. I worked hard, got the grades and made that my main focus in life. I always knew I wanted my own business because that meant I had control over my future, control I'd sorely lacked growing up."

"What happened to your mother?" I could relate because my own had passed away when I was so young. I truly knew what it meant to live without a mother present. Luckily, my late Aunt Edwina stepped in to help my father raise me.

Ewan continued. "My mother was hospitalized for a few years so she could get over my younger brother's death. It was decided at the time that it was best for me not have any contact with her. I really couldn't tell you where she is today. I don't even know if she's still alive."

"Do you want to find her? Because I could help you look," I offered.

"That would be difficult because it was a different city, different country, and medical records are sealed for living people. Heck, there's even long wait times for medical records of the deceased. Just look at how long it takes for them to release the census," he said.

"It's largely due to the new privacy laws in effect. I can't say they're a bad thing, really. I certainly wouldn't want all my personal information made public."

"No, of course not. But to reunite families, it's a difficult one," he said. He gestured for me to eat. "How's your food?"

I looked down at my slightly started salad. "Perfect. Pamela's staff always do a good job. I've got tons of chicken and a variety of vegetables here, all fresh. My absolute favorite."

There was a lull in the conversation. We'd delved into some pretty deep, personal stuff and Ewan was really opening up to me. It just didn't seem like a pub was the right place to do it. Inside I chided myself, thinking I should have suggested a walk down a long, quiet, tree-lined lane where we could be alone. It would have made a far better choice than being surrounded by other people giddy with laughter, enjoying foamy beers over at the bar.

I fiddled with the straw in my drink. "So, what did my father say?" I asked.

"He didn't seem bothered by my past. I even showed him financial statements from the antiques shop and it didn't cause any majorly raised eyebrows, despite your wealth. His biggest question was whether I could handle how driven you are to make GGRS a success."

"My father knows me all too well." I grinned. "But I didn't earn my money. I inherited. So, in a way, you are far more successful than me. You created a business from nothing and turn a profit each month, enough for you to live comfortably. I, on the other hand, parse out gobs of money I had nothing to do with earning."

"Hmmm. That's an interesting perspective." Ewan thought on it.

"It's the one you and I need to follow if we're going to spend more time together," I advised.

My phone vibrated. I took a quick glance and saw who it was. "Text from Bertie."

"I would have put my money on GGRS," Ewan teased. "Is there a problem?"

"Does this make any sense to you?" I asked, handing him my phone. There in big, capital letters on screen were the words: 'BIG FIND IN LAB. NEED HELP NOW. PLEASE.' It was followed by a series of emojis that didn't make much sense: a painter's palette, a tool and a building.

Leave it to aristocrat Bertie to remember the 'please' at the end of his urgent message.

"I've never received a text from Bertie like this. I think we'd better get back there as soon as we can." I texted Bertie a quick reply: 'On our way'.

Both of us soon had empty plates. Ewan paid the bill and we left, heading for a familiar destination with a new, mysterious revelation.

Chapter 17

———

Underground Laboratory. Later That Night.

Ewan and I clustered around Bertie. The place had cleaned up really well, and now looked like a half-finished tourist attraction. Quite a few of the new props were obviously still on order, especially ones filled with colored sand mimicking the real chemicals used for alchemic experiments in centuries past. The workbench and stools were burnished to a shine from years of hard use and the ledgers filled an entire long shelf. I would bet that a museum production company had made fake ledgers while the real ones were now squirreled away in the Plumsden Archives, on the Preswick Family's special floor, and under a conservator's watchful eye. Real archives should never be left open to light and constant changes of humidity. Archives needed to be protected for future generations.

Ewan and I were still a bit unsure and looked to Bertie for an answer.

"Thank you so much both for scurrying back. I hope I didn't overly interrupt your plans for this evening," Bertie said. He looked at his watch and saw that it was just before midnight. "Oh dear. It is rather late. I got so caught up in this find ... I can't tell you how exciting it is. Well perhaps excited isn't the correct word, how about perplexed and shocked ..." His words drew into a faded ending and we were still no clearer on the reason for being summoned at such short notice.

"Bertie, did you want to show us something you found in the laboratory?" I asked in a tentative voice.

"Of course, of course. Here I am babbling on and you know nothing about what I mean. Come around to the workbench and I'll show you."

We walked around some piles of tools and a couple of sawhorses, and there, laid out on the top of the workbench, were parchment papers filled with brown-ink scribbles. There were also some intricate diagrams beside the scribbles, and it looked like some ancient plans for machinery.

"Now, please feast your eyes upon these papers. I'll specifically draw your attention to the name at the bottom of the page," Bertie said in a great, conspiratorial tone.

Ewan and I cast our eyes downwards and we both gasped at the same time. For there, right in front of us, was the last name 'da Vinci'.

"Looks pretty authentic, doesn't it?" Bertie asked.

"Yes, but I don't understand. All these pages are the same. It's the same machinery plans, the same explanation, and the same signature at the bottom. Why would someone need four copies of this?"

Bertie smiled. "I've now figured out how the Old Duke got himself out of rags and back into riches. You see, my friends, he was forging old da Vinci papers and selling them on as authentic."

This was something new.

This was something incredibly dastardly.

This was something that would set tongues wagging throughout the land, in every single museum across the United Kingdom as well as across the entire globe.

Forgeries were collectible in their own right, but every museum curator who proudly held da Vinci papers in their collection would now wonder if they were authentic or not. They would wonder how much they paid to acquire them and, most importantly, if they were acquired during the years the Old Duke was running his scam.

"Now, hang on a minute here," Ewan said. "I'm going to be the voice of reason. It's well known that Leonardo da Vinci wrote in mirror script, that is, writing backwards to conceal his ideas. It's pretty difficult to forge. He's also one of the most famous inventors and scientists in all of history. Why would the Old Duke choose him and call attention to such an illustrious group of papers for his forgeries? It would be much easier to pass off someone a lot less famous."

Bertie thought on it. "You make a good point."

"Even in the age long before telephones, computers and social media, da Vinci was incredibly famous. The risks of using his name for profit in your Old Duke's day and age ... well, it just doesn't make sense," I said.

"So my excitement was mislaid?" Bertie said.

"I don't think 'mislaid' is the correct term, perhaps a bit 'meandering'," I said, giving him a reassuring smile. "Perhaps they weren't for sale, rather were practice pieces for one of his apprentices. One of them was a scrivener, correct?"

Bertie and Ewan both nodded.

"But if these are his practice documents, then what was he actually forging and selling on?" Bertie asked.

"We don't even know if the Old Duke was selling forgeries," Ewan said.

Bertie shook his head. "Oh, my friend, I can prove you wrong on that count. Come with me to my office and I'll show you exactly how."

❋❋❋

Stables Office. Five Minutes Later.

"Take a look at this." Bertie pulled down an unusual-looking ledger book from a bookshelf laden with multiple tomes of Scotford Castle accounts, good horse-keeping books and silage harvesting magazines. As Bertie handed us the ledger, he said, "It's the only one I held back from the archivists. As soon as I started to read it, I knew there was something more to this family history mystery. I just haven't had the chance to fully peruse it."

I carefully placed the book on the desk in front of us and gently opened it. Inside, in the Old Duke's lovely copperplate handwriting, were lists of revenues. He sold everything including cattle, vegetables, machinery parts and papers.

"Go ahead. Turn to page 182," Bertie instructed.

We did, and read about halfway down the page until we stopped. I looked up at Bertie. "Your ancestor actually accounted for selling his forgeries?"

"The taxman cometh, no matter what the century," Bertie said with a smile. "It took me a while to figure out his code, but what else could he mean by 'historical items sold to museums'?"

"Just in England or–" Ewan started.

"No one knows," Bertie replied.

"It says here that he made thousands of pounds," I said. "That's a lot of money in the early 1800s."

"The only question now is what specific forgeries he was selling," Ewan said. "And once we find that out, I think you have a few telephone calls to make, Your Grace."

The look on Bertie's face was one of trepidation. They said that bad luck came in threes; Bertie now had the castle fire, the barley field laboratory explosion, and now his ancestor was proven to sell forgeries using inexperienced—perhaps naïve—apprentices as collaborators. It was quite the list. Yet, it was the clean-up and aftermath that were proving to be the most difficult things of all.

Chapter 18

——

GGRS. Next Morning.

Gertie and Maude set about making an accurate transcription from the recently located Scotford Castle ledger that listed all the 'historical items' sold during the Old Duke's tenure. There were eight sales in total, to vague museum buyers, with a grand monetary revenue of £236,865. In today's money that would translate into approximately £26 million, more than enough to set the Old Duke back on the field of prosperity. We also found dozens of entries where exceedingly vague payments were made to masters for 'apprentice services rendered on work articles'.

"Vague, indeed," Maude sniffed. "To think an aristocrat made all of this money selling forgeries to the good people at museums. It's just not cricket," she said.

"He must've been a pretty sneaky fellow," Gertie said, "and gutsy too, passing stuff off as real knowing full well that it was concocted in his laboratory and likely artificially aged in an oven tended by a sixteen-year-old apprentice. I wonder how he kept those young men silent."

"Indenture papers and withholding of food," Maude said. "Apprentices were under their masters' thumb, so it certainly made sense that they would keep silent."

"Perhaps he paid them extra," I said. "Think about it. The boys had already signed on with the Old Duke for their training. He was likely serving as the local Justice of the Peace or Magistrate who ensured the boys were well-placed. He also wanted something secretive done and my guess is that not all six masters, the ones who actually trained the boys, would have agreed to it willingly. So how about some after hours, extra pocket money for doing the Old Duke's work beyond their master's watchful eye? The masters had no choice but to allow the powerful Old Duke to meet with the boys he'd signed to indentures."

"And you want to sell that idea to Bertie?" Maude asked.

"At this point, I think he's accepted the fact that his ancestor was a scoundrel. Besides, it's not like he was the first aristocrat to live on the dark side," Gertie said.

"Speaking of the dark side," I said, admitting a small laugh, "here comes our chagrined plant maimer."

The Major strode up to the information desk looking a bit sheepish. Out of his wallet he produced a receipt for a new plant pot, new ornamental tree and a delivery work order. "I have made the purchase and arranged for it to arrive tomorrow, with your permission and approval of course." His bushy sideburns, as well trimmed as they were, quivered a bit as he awaited my approval.

I checked that all the paperwork was in order, then nodded.

The relief on the Major's face was palpable. "Once again, my sincere apologies."

"Just please take a little more care in our car park, Major. That's all I ask," I said.

"My apologies. My heart is aflutter with the warm, tingling feeling of romance these days and it has a tendency to distract."

I narrowed my eyes. "The next time you get that warm, tingling feeling, I have some weeding out in the back garden that needs doing."

"Right you are," the Major said in a formal voice. He gave me a stiff salute, turned on his heel and swiftly marched out of the GGRS.

"Honestly," I said, looking at the other two ladies who were slightly agog at how I handled it. The Major was one of our favorite guests here at the research center, but I had both Aunt Edwina's as well as Greymore Hall's reputations to uphold.

❅❅❅

Stables, Scotford Castle. Next Day.

"There's more?" Bertie asked Ewan.

My boyfriend nodded. Expertly. The look on his face said he was completely convinced. "The side chair in the Old Duke's laboratory? I looked it up. It's a copy, not a genuine piece from the Tudor Era. The super-even carving is a dead giveaway. Remember that set of silver vases? Also faked, likely hallmarks added well after the 1690s."

Bertie looked shocked. He had to sit down. "So, in other words, my aristocratic ancestor was running an emporium of forgeries, be it papers, furniture or luxury goods? Here, in the bowels of Scotford Castle?"

"I am truly sorry to say this but yes, he was," Ewan confirmed. "And that's where his team of apprentices were put to good use. He had all the skills he needed to produce the fakes he was selling on. Quite clever, actually."

I shot Ewan a look of doom.

"If one was of a criminal intent, that is," Ewan hastily added. "It's not appropriate, obviously." He glanced at me to see if I'd relaxed my horrified scowl.

"And what about the museums who bought these pieces? I somehow feel incredibly guilty," Bertie said.

"The only answer is to contact the museums and ask them to tell you about their holdings," Ewan advised. "I can help, if you wish."

"The hits just keep on coming," Bertie said with a disappointed sigh.

"Some museums do put their information online. Others may have disposed of them over the years. Can you just look up an auction site and see if anything is listed there?" I asked.

Bertie and I looked at Ewan.

"Reputable auction houses will list the provenance of all the items that they have for sale. And yes, if the museum already has a similar object, it is possible that they would sell one in order to release funds to acquire something different," Ewan explained.

"Run a search on 'Duke of Conroy Auction' and see what comes up," he suggested.

Bertie was at his keyboard and typed frantically. "Here's an auction house in Austria with an item listed. Duke of Conroy. Oh dear, sixteenth century. We need much later than that."

"It must feel odd, seeing your ancestors' belongings scattered around the world and being sold like assets," I said.

"Forgers aren't selling off the family silver. The Old Duke was a fraudster," Bertie said. "Which brings me to my next obvious question, Ewan."

Ewan shook his head. "No new leads yet, Bertie, I'm afraid."

There was a knock on the door and we all looked to see Severs there. Severs had a smile on his face, quite unusual for the normally stoic man. "Your Grace, may I have a word?"

Ewan and I beat a hasty retreat down to the stalls so Bertie could have some privacy with his right hand man.

I turned to Ewan as we reached the other end of the barn. We overlooked the smaller, grass turnout pastures the carriage horses were enjoying. "You do realize that what you told me about your family doesn't change the way I feel about you, right?"

He gave me a tender look. "I was worried you'd feel differently."

"Ewan, you need to move forward from your past. Certainly research and learn from it, but don't get stuck in it. You also need to look ahead in life."

He gave me one of his winning smiles, then bent down and kissed me. I fell into his arms and it felt so good, so right. I wanted this man in my life and no dark secret from his past could tear us apart.

There was a large clang further out in the fields. We hurriedly jumped apart and scanned the horizon. We saw the figures of two familiar men walking in the distance, heads down with earphones on.

"Looks like Ozzie and Timmy are back at it. Are they cleared for this?" Ewan asked.

"Knowing Ozzie, likely not. Then again, his logic will be that it's never been safer in that barley field because the Old Duke only had one alchemy laboratory. Now that it's discovered, there is nothing to cause concern," I said.

"Let's just hope there are no unexploded munitions from the prior two World Wars that we need to worry about," Ewan said.

"Bite your tongue, sir," I said with a grin. As I smiled, I caught a glimpse of Bertie down the barn aisle and he was frantically waving.

"Looks like the Scotford saga continues. Come on," I said, grabbing Ewan's hand.

We reached Bertie and saw a huge grin on his face. "Severs just told me the insurance claim has been approved! This means we can get going with full tilt restoration work here at Scotford Castle without bankrupting yours truly! It's such a relief."

I reached out and gave Bertie a hug. Not exactly formal aristocratic protocol, but it didn't matter. "That's wonderful, Bertie!"

Ewan shook Bertie's hand and offered similar congratulations.

"Do they know what started the fire?" I asked.

"A frayed wire used by the thieves' power tool to dismantle a component of my security system. They found no traces of accelerant. It proves I was definitely not at fault, neither were my staff, and all is bright in the world again." Bertie looked ever so pleased. "As I said to a reporter here right after the fire, I was worried Scotford would have to host a gargantuan bake sale to put the castle back together again."

"Forget bake sale," I said. "Think Fred and his ballet team doing a fundraiser. On Scotford's front lawn." Yes, Fred Todling was the lead sponsor for the local ballet studio and insisted on calling the dancers a 'team'. Heck, he even participated in the performances, green sparkly tights and all.

"Well, I suppose it would show community spirit and all that," Bertie said.

"Plus encouragement for youth to pursue their artistic talents," I added.

"Indeed."

"So, then, it wouldn't be an issue if such a charity performance still went ahead?" I asked, trying to keep my voice casual.

Bertie looked at me, perplexed. "But there's no need for it now that the insurance claim's been approved."

"But if it did?" I asked.

"Well, so long as it doesn't interrupt a visit from–"

"Another Duke or His Majesty?"

"Precisely." Bertie looked at me, curious. "You should let Fred know that we have a full time events coordinator here at the estate and she'd be glad to assist him."

"Already done."

"And we'd need the usual council permission."

"Granted."

"Then I suppose it would be full steam ahead." Bertie smiled. It was good to see my dear friend smile. A worry line or two also looked like they'd lightened up a bit, glory be.

He refocused on being excited about the castle's repairs. "I'll have to call in the stonemasons, the roofing contractors, the flooring people and ... Who's that out there?" Bertie asked. He shielded his eyes from the sun and stared out at his barley field.

"Just your friendly neighborhood metal detectorists," I explained.

"Well, let them have their fun. At least now I don't have to rely so heavily on Mr. Boggs digging up a gold hoard."

❈❈❈

Thirty Minutes Later.

With Ewan and I at his side helping, Bertie was ensconced in telephone calls, emails and draft castle restoration work orders. When Ozzie appeared at the door, Bertie looked up with a slightly complicated expression on his face. "Yes?"

"Duke, I've got something here you need to see," Ozzie said.

"Ozzie, I'm sure you have a fascinating set of historical treasures, but we're rather busy here right now–"

"You think I've got junk again, don't you?" Ozzie said, an accusing look in his eyes. He confidently strutted into the stables office carrying a bag that sounded like it was full of tin cans.

"Dear chap, I just find it highly unbelievable that you will locate a Roman Mint in my barley field. That rumor has existed for centuries and nobody's ever come through with anything."

"I agree with you on that," Ozzie said.

"So why the urgency?" Bertie said, clearly wanting to focus on the pressing matters of getting his castle put back together.

"This." Ozzie came into the room and proceeded to dump the contents of his finds pouch all over Bertie's desk. A cloud of dust rose up from the heap intermingled with various wafting smells of manure, seedpods and chaff. Ozzie produced a total of five squashed tin cans, all appearing about 1950s vintage.

"Take a look at that," Ozzie said with a knowing glance.

Bertie delicately parsed through the wreckage with the eraser end of a pencil. "I'm not quite following you."

Ozzie took a look at the heap and then looked at the ceiling. "Er, sorry, wrong pouch. I put the special find in a different area to keep it safe."

"So all of this debris is ...?"

"Interesting, but not relevant. But I'll show you something that is." With that, Ozzie swept all of the tin cans back into his pouch, leaving the silt covering Bertie's desk. What was an annoying mess quickly turned into a soft bed for something truly amazing. Ozzie reached deep into his camouflage pocket and pulled out not one, not two, but a total of nineteen hammered gold coins.

"Gold doesn't tarnish or rust, so these look exactly the same as when they were dropped in your field centuries ago," Ozzie said.

Bertie examined the coins closely, then sat bolt upright in his chair. "Good grief, these are King Charles the First vintage."

"Pleased?" Ozzie asked.

Timmy had now joined us at the doorway, stepped inside briefly and deposited twelve more of the same type of gold coins in front of our host.

"That should help pay for your new roof at least," Timmy offered.

"Gentlemen, gentlemen, what a find! Have you marked off the area?" Bertie asked.

"With fluorescent tape. We hurried back because we want to ask you to call in the archeology experts. We think there could be more down there because our machines are hard signaling all over the place."

"But your machines were all bent and twisted in the explosion," I said.

Ozzie smiled. "A good metal detectorist always travels with backup gear." He said it with the most officious smile, as if he really knew what he was doing. The fact of the matter was, Ozzie Boggs and his cohort had simply gotten a lucky break.

Still, no one could ignore this find.

Ewan was busy searching coin values on his phone.

"Well? Any idea what they're worth?" Ozzie asked.

"About £50,000 at auction," Ewan confirmed.

"For the pile of coins?" Timmy asked.

Ewan shook his head. "Each. It says here that each coin is worth approximately that much, in very good condition, for the same type and minting year as these." Ewan showed them the screen on his phone.

Some rapid calculations were performed and Ozzie's jaw sagged. "Nineteen plus twelve coins equals thirty-one. Thirty-one times £50,000 is £1,550,000." He looked up, shocked. "Timmy, we've done it. We're rich!"

I leaned forward and took one of the coins in my hand. Next, I started to scrape the edges with a fingernail.

Bertie looked at me, a puzzled expression on his face.

Satisfied, I placed the coins back on his desk. "Just checking to see if there was a foil wrapper that peeled off to reveal chocolate inside."

***

GGRS. Next Morning.

We had all the heavy hitters at the research center, ready to help.

I dove straight in. "Okay, Ewan's museum search came up empty, meaning the forgeries aren't on any current inventory disposal sales lists. As I learned in my Genealogy 101 course, if you hit a brick wall, then go sideways. I thought we could research the six apprentices and see if their families provided any clues to what they made and where the forgeries ended up."

Maude nodded. "An excellent idea. We can start with the Quarter Session records, then check the census for descendants."

"Too bad detailed census records weren't available until 1841," Gertie said. "They would help by showing the address, names of family members, ages, occupations ... all really helpful stuff to prove a line of research."

"How do the Quarter Sessions work?" I asked.

Maude took on that one. "The local magistrates, typically Lords of the Manors, ran the Quarter Sessions which were county courts that met four times a year, since medieval times. The magistrate had a list of boys that had been placed with masters and the Quarter Sessions show the boys' names, fathers' names and residence, plus master and his trade."

"All great information," I said, "but not enough to prove it beyond a reasonable doubt."

Maude was busy online. She brought up the local Quarter Sessions record for the Plumsden area and we watched as she waded through various case records of constables, bastardy, coroner's inquests, militia, roads, taxes and the inevitable few truly bizarre oddities.

I smiled. "A man was accused of stealing three chickens in retaliation towards the farmer he claimed sold him a milk cow gone dry?"

"Oh, plenty more where that came from," Maude said. "Here's one for a man accused of bigamy."

Gertie and I looked at Maude with great anticipation. Knowing Maude and her wry sense of humor, there had to be a joke's punchline close at hand.

"But?" I asked.

"But, when one delves further—and we see the clerk's notation in the margin—it isn't so. Turns out, the man was indeed accused of having two wives in two different counties. However, as the clerk notes, one wife was estranged and the husband simply married the second wife after they'd lived together for thirty years. She was called his 'housekeeper' until they could make things legal."

"They were essentially waiting for the first wife's demise?" Gertie asked.

Maude nodded. "It appears so."

"And the neighbors got curious. Fascinating. Unlike the afore-mentioned milk cow, the family history well never runs dry," Gertie said.

We watched Maude scroll some more. "Here, look at this. Here's our cabinet maker, Henry Dartnell. You see how it says 'cabinet maker app.' beside his name?"

"Yes, but how do we know it's the right Henry Dartnell? That's a pretty common name in Kent," Gertie said.

"Indeed. One cannot just pick the first likely-looking George when doing research. There are so many mistakes with amateur online family trees. I once found a woman who gave birth to chil-dren on two different continents, one each alternate year, and before overseas travel was available to the middle classes."

"Many people had the same name AND birthplace in earlier centuries," Gertie added.

"So we drill down for more details?" I asked.

"Yes," Maude said. "See on this record it lists the name of the master and the location where he worked? With this cabinet maker, it says he was in a cottage on the Scotford Estate so that's a really good sign. We can compare that to the information on the apprentice's indenture and see that the master's and apprentice's names plus trade are the same on both documents."

"That was very efficient."

Maude smiled. "We were fortunate in that all the records were digitized, our search targets were easily found on an index and double-checked with the original document, plus the census and Scotford Castle indentures were there to cross match. Genealogy isn't usually that easily done and dusted. I've had multiple times where the digitized version of the record is blurry, missing a page or simply gives you a 'file error' reply. That's why it's important to keep the original records."

"Only five more to go."

"I tried two of the others before our meeting today and came up with a few brick walls. One record's original clerk's entry was smudged, another on a torn page, and yet a different apprentice name was listed with two different masters. So, I'd recommend you get back to helping your dinosaur expert with her memoir, while Gertie and I dig further into these more obscure records," Maude suggested.

"Deal," I replied.

What we would ever do without Maude?

I don't even want to think about it.

❖❖❖

Stables Office, Scotford Castle Estate. That Afternoon.

Bertie had his head in his hands. Even though there was a hubbub of construction activity all around the estate, the look on Bertie's face said all he wanted to do was curl up into a ball and hide underneath his bedcovers.

"What's wrong?" I asked, immediately concerned for my dear friend.

Bertie handed me a printout of an email. I read:

Wire £5 million to us, then we shall return your family papers.

The message went on to list some bank account numbers and codes.

"Of course there will be no way of tracing this. It's obviously going to be some sort of private, online bank account with layers of security hidden in the dark web," he moaned.

"What do you plan on doing with this?" I asked, gently setting the paper back down on his desk.

He shrugged. "Police are on it. Severs is on it. Not much else I can do at the moment."

"Would you like to take a walk? We could revisit your new laboratory," I said.

Bertie looked at me, slightly deer-in-the-headlights. "What a marvelous idea. Thank you. I'm starting to feel much too sorry for myself in this cramped office."

Truth was, the office suited the head groom just fine. But add in an entire tableware setting for forty-eight plus a large number of silver tureens, vases and plaques and, well, the square footage did seem vastly reduced.

We headed for the tunnel, currently accessed via the kitchen. After walking the length of the tunnel, and without detours, we entered the ancient laboratory. It was taking even better shape as a new tourist attraction. Jars full of brightly colored powders and beads made for an attractive shelf display. The furniture and silverware Ewan had questioned were roped off to the side, kind of like naughty children being told to stand in the corner.

"I look around and wonder what else is a forgery," Bertie said.

"There's a reason I wanted to come here with you," I said.

"Oh?"

"Yes. I wanted to see if the apprentices left any graffiti in hidden places. That's another way we might be able to find out more about the forged antiquities racket." I started to check nooks and crannies for any telltale streaks and scratchings in the wood.

"You do know Ewan came up empty handed," Bertie advised.

"Yes. He couldn't find any museum selling off items with solid provenance from your ancestor, nor from Scotford Estate, for that matter. If he had found something, then that would have almost seemed too easy."

My fingers ran over the wooden counter and the lip underneath. I tried to think like a delinquent student. He would hide his graffiti, secretly satisfied it was there.

But where?

I looked around the laboratory and saw the obvious answer. A cabinet hung on the wall, fixed in place as if it were stone. Built strong as an ox out of a sturdy hardwood, it appeared to be the candidate I sought. I opened the doors and saw two empty shelves. The cabinet doors were firmly affixed on heavy hinges. I ran my hand underneath the shelf and sure enough, felt some rather thick indentations. I removed the shelf from the wooden support dowels, and turned over the piece of wood. Success was quickly apparent.

"Bertie, look at this," I said.

He was impressed. "I do believe you've found another clue to our forgery mystery."

What I'd located were some words crudely carved into the wood:

We help our dear Old Duke as thanks for lifting us from our poor stations.

Six Brothers. 1810.

Underneath the date were six sets of familiar initials, exact matches to the names of the apprentices Maude and Gertie were researching back at GGRS.

"It's them. The apprentices," I said.

Bertie looked at me, a small smile crossing his lips. "Well done, Julie. And our next steps are?"

I took out my phone. "Take a photo. Share it with our GGRS colleagues. We'll add this new clue to the genealogy mystery we're going to figure out for you, Bertie. Have faith that we will come through with answers."

"I suppose you'll tell me that every rogue Duke cannot be all bad?" he asked.

I gave him a sunny smile. "I believe that there is good in every person. Just like Scotford will rise from its ashes, something good will emerge from this forgery mystery. The apprentices liked the Old Duke and wanted to help. We just need the rest of their stories."

"You don't believe the apprentices were brothers, do you? Not all related by blood, that is?"

I shook my head. "No, that's too much of a coincidence. I'm sure GGRS researchers would call that too good to be true."

Bertie looked heavenward, yet all he saw were the bricks and stones used to round out the tunnel's ceiling. "Truth. After all that's happened to Scotford in recent weeks, the real truth would be most welcomed."

❈❈❈

Julie's Place, Scotford Castle Estate. That Night.

I cooked Ewan his favorite meal. After he finished his roast chicken, veggies then apple cobbler with ice cream for dessert, he pushed his chair back from the table and emitted a contented sigh, the kind of sound a man makes when his stomach is full of warm, comfort food.

"That was delicious, Julie. Thank you," he said. He got up to help with the dishes but I shook my head.

"Sit, please. I've got this. You've had a busy week helping Bertie."

He scoffed and got up anyways. "So have you. Besides, you cooked." He stole a kiss while I stood there, holding a drippy ice cream scoop.

"Er, Ewan, I'm going to get ice cream all over you."

We broke apart, but this time it wasn't awkward. In fact, it was cozy, right and all the good things I'd been craving.

The ice cream scoop clattered to the floor.

I'd clean it up later.

He'd clean it up later.

No one would clean it up later.

Ewan now had me in his arms and our lips were locked on each other's. He gently guided me towards the couch. "Dishes can wait."

I reveled in the strength of his arms. It must be his muscles gained from lifting old Welsh sideboards. His hands encircled my waist. Things were getting quite warm here in my cozy home.

A shrieking wail pierced the evening silence.

Ewan pulled back and grimaced. "Burglar alarm?"

I nodded. "Something must have tripped the sensor outside."

After turning off the alarm, we both went to the window and saw our mood killer. Ozzie Boggs stood in the bushes, bent over in half. Timmy Hitchins prowled around my front bay window, looking up at the nearest tree.

I opened the front door. "Gentlemen, there had better be an exceedingly plausible explanation for all this."

"There is!" Timmy yelped. "The rare owl was sighted over the barley field and we watched it fly towards your house."

"My house being the operative words. It's dark outside and I'm entertaining."

Ozzie stood up straight and peered inside the doorframe. "Oh, it's just Ewan."

I crossed my arms. "Exactly."

"Oh." Ozzie shrugged, then he got it. His eyes lit up. "Oooohh. Hey Timmy!" he shouted.

Ewan just shook his head. "Gentlemen, can we perhaps assist you to find the owl and then bid you good night?"

Ozzie dug his elbow into Timmy's side. "That would be convenient, hey?"

"There's a fifty pound bounty on that owl's head," Timmy called out.

I immediately switched into protector mode. "A bounty? On a rare owl? That's horrible. I will not allow killing on this property and I don't believe that Bertie would condone–"

Timmy held up his phone. "Photo bounty. Not shooting bounty."

"Oh, right." I should have remembered that no decent ornithologist would even consider for the remotest second culling a rare bird from the wild.

I looked over at Ewan, our chance at a romantic evening rapidly evaporating. I shot a plaintive look over in his direction. "GGRS strikes again?"

Ewan showed me two empty palms. "The mood is slightly shattered."

"I could put on some music ..." I said, heading back inside, my voice trailing off as Ozzie tripped over the front path's boot bristle brush.

It was obvious our two ornithology enthusiasts would be here a while searching for their precious, elusive bird.

"Oh, Ewan," I sighed.

He approached and beckoned me into a corner of the living room. "Never mind. I'm beginning to think a different approach is needed with you and I," he said.

"Stolen moments, no phones and a planned vacation on another continent?" I asked with a grin.

He grinned. "Something like that." He came closer and took me in his arms. "I want to be with you. Our tiny little snatches of time aren't enough."

I accepted his kiss. "Agreed."

Another crash outside. This time Ozzie had bumped into my birdfeeder and gotten his shirt caught in a nearby blackberry bush.

"Right." I gave Ewan a quick kiss. "That's me on duty again."

Ewan gave me a serious look. "I'd better be on my way. See you tomorrow?"

"Lunch?"

"Let's not plan it. Let's just take the day as it comes. If I catch you in a spare moment, I'll gallop in on my white horse and rescue you from oblivion."

"I wouldn't exactly call GGRS oblivion."

He kissed me, long and deep. "It is when you choose it over us." He gave me a sweet glance and then was gone, disappeared down my front path before I had time to reply.

Chapter 19

GGRS. Next Morning.

Maude and I were discussing the latest office supply order when Ewan strode up to the information desk.

"Good morning, ladies," he said.

My heart melted. He wore a muted tweed suit, the kind that screamed bespoke.

"Are we en route to a fancy meeting with an upper crust client?" Maude asked.

"Not a client, but an important lead on Bertie's forgery center."

"How so?" I asked.

"I received a hit on my antiques shop network. It turns out a business owner a few villages away heard of a similar chair on display at one of the big auction houses in London. So, I checked out more details and discovered it's offered for sale with a reserve bid of £35,000."

"For a fake chair?" I asked. "We're clearly in the wrong business."

"Hence the fancy suit," Maude observed. "Very dapper, Ewan."

"Thank you." He looked at us for direction.

"Oh, and I received a call from Prunella, the archivist we visited on Bertie's special floor at Plumsden Archives," Maude added.

"Yes?" I asked.

"She researched the cottage, the one with the cellar you accessed from the tunnel? Apparently, it used to be lived in by a goldsmith."

"Why would a prosperous goldsmith live in a modest cottage?" I asked. "Wouldn't he have taken lodgings in a large town, near the center of commerce?"

"Think like a forger, Julie," Ewan advised. "What better way to coordinate with your top client than via a secret tunnel connecting your house to his?"

"Got it."

"And on that note, would you like to accompany me to London?" he asked.

"When?"

"Now." He gave me a focused yet kind glance.

I thought on it. "Hmm. A day out with a handsome man in a fancy suit looking at mysterious forgeries. Sounds intriguing. But Maude–"

"Has everything here under control," she said, patting my hand, "you're free to go."

"But Bertie–"

"Is dealing with accountants and lawyers all day, solid meetings, back to back. I asked him this morning," Ewan said.

"I need to change first," I said, looking down at my all-too business casual outfit that would certainly not be suitable for an upscale

London auction house. I'd seen these places before in magazines. They were hushed places of reverence where the names of great craftspeople and artists easily tumbled from lips of people educated at world-renowned, brand-name schools. It was there that one got up close with the masters, yet only took them home if one could easily afford that third home in the sunny south of France.

I looked at Maude.

She nodded. "Go."

I looked at Ewan.

He smiled back. "Please?"

I took his arm and we left. Together.

✳✳✳

London Auction House. That Afternoon.

We walked in on near-pristine silence. It was a cavernous place, double height ceilings with a fancy dome in the center, reminding me of the one at Scotford Castle. Well, before the fire had blackened it so much with soot and ash.

The walls were grey-blue and stark white. The colors were a perfect backdrop for furniture and tapestries; the white made paintings really pop. A gleaming hardwood floor was a lovely complement to the soft potlights overhead. It was a place that oozed refinement, wealth and opportunity.

"May I help?" a pert, little man posed his question as he watched us make a beeline for a Tudor-era sideboard. Force of habit, I supposed.

Ewan dragged his attention away from the piece and extended his right hand. "Good afternoon." My boyfriend looked gorgeous and confident, my absolute favorite combination.

I'd personally tried to step it up a bit and wore a well-cut pantsuit and trendy loafers. With all the walking one did in the city, there was no sense teetering around on stilettos. It just wasn't practical.

"Earl Bovinks, Sir. Welcome to our house," the salesman said.

House. Interesting how they called the auction business a 'house'.

"Thank you. I'm Ewan Kilburn and this is Julie Fincher from GGRS. We're representing Scotford Castle. There's a particular chair you have listed in your catalogue that we're interested in." Ewan handed over his business card and I did the same.

"Yes?" Earl needed to be put into the loop.

"We recently found a chair made in the style of a famous eighteenth century furniture maker. It's a clear forgery and we understand you have one here of the same?"

Earl drew himself up to a stiffer stance. "One of them? Goodness man, there's only one in the entire world. I doubt you have a second to make a matching pair."

"Does it look like this?" Ewan asked, showing him a photo on his phone.

Earl put on his glasses and perched them on the end of his nose. "Good gracious! This really is quite extraordinary!" Earl looked up at us. "Do come with me."

We followed him down the length of the showroom, passing a hand-painted seventeenth century harpsichord, modern art and a lovely collection of silver candelabras. Around the corner and there it was, the object of our antiquing quest. The chair was protected from bumps and people by sitting on a riser. It was the exact color and design as the one in Bertie's alchemy laboratory.

"Do you know the secret of this chair? Of the forger himself?" Earl asked. "We call it our golden Easter Egg chair."

"It has a secret beyond being a forgery?" Ewan asked.

Earl nodded. "Yes. The front right leg unscrews and inside is a gold figurine of cupid. My take is that it's a bribe not to tell on the forger." He pointed to a framed picture of the winged cherub, hands outstretched and the other reaching for an arrow from his quiver.

I looked at Ewan. "We need to check that with Bertie's chair."

"What would a matched pair of these chairs bring?" Ewan asked.

"Well, considering the forgery is rarely found today and the maker's playfully hidden treasures are quite sought after, I'd say £100,000 for the pair." Earl gave us a focused glance. "That is, assuming yours still has the golden treasure within its frame."

"That's a lot of new drywall and carpet," I said, thinking back to Bertie's black hole called Scotford Castle.

"His Grace owns the chair?" Earl asked, astonished. "What a find."

"There are a few more pieces we're still investigating, but the chair's our focus at the moment," Ewan explained.

"Do you think he'd be willing to sell it together in a set with ours?" Earl asked.

"We'll check with Bertie," I said.

"It's amazing that forgeries are worth so much," Ewan said.

"Indeed," Earl said. "Collectors value quality, reputation and the unusual. This forger was particularly skilled at creating art within art, not achieved by many I would say. The fact that it's a forgery of such high quality makes his pieces famous amongst his quiet group of high end fans. It's the cabinet maker working with the goldsmith that puts these together in such an intriguing, desirable combination."

Ewan shook Earl's hand. "We'll let you know."

❀❀❀

Alchemy Laboratory, Scotford Castle. That Night.

We carefully took every piece of forgery-suspected furniture apart. The construction crew's spotlights gave a bright glow to the place. After all, alchemy laboratories were supposed to be places of learning and discovery, and it was pretty hard to do that in the dark. So far, we had a cabinet, two portrait frames, a small cabinet with twenty tiny drawers plus a lady's toiletry kit in pieces around the room. What a lady's hairbrush, comb and mirror, all backed with silver gilt, were doing in an alchemy laboratory was an everlasting question. The question was one that likely would remain unanswered. In these days of discovery and recuperation at Scotford Estate, one just had to roll with certain things.

There was a hollow area inside the small cabinet's lid. Empty. Nothing was found inside the portrait frames, despite my high hopes considering the previous secrets we'd found in old watercolors' frames bequeathed to me by my late Aunt Edwina. Ewan thought he had something in drawer number seventeen of the small cabinet, but it turned out to be a knot in the wood. The only item that remained was the chair, and we'd left the fabled object of our quest for last. The chair was perched up on a side table, its legs begging to be removed.

Ewan and I sized it up. "I wonder what we'll find inside our own Easter Egg furniture," he mused.

"Let's hope it's gold, and the mate to the chair we just viewed in London," I said. "Now, which leg was it?" We laid the chair on top of an old cloth on the main counter, gently unscrewed the right front leg from its base and saw the object of our search. One tiny glint of gold let us know the promise would be fulfilled. Ewan carefully reached in with a pair of tweezers and pulled on the extended hand of a golden figurine. Out came another cupid, this one in the exact reverse pose compared to the one we'd seen in London. A tiny scroll of parchment came out behind the figurine, attached to cupid's foot.

"Fascinating," Ewan murmured, taking a quick glance at the scroll to see if its condition was right to unroll it. "Camera ready?"

I got out my phone. We'd both handled enough old documents by now to know when things were fairly safe to proceed. Ewan unrolled the note and read: '2/6. H.D.'

"Two shillings and sixpence?" I asked. "Or two of six chairs?"

"Imagine what the full set would bring at auction," Ewan said. "Who is H.D.?"

"H.D. is Henry Dartnell, initials for the cabinet maker on the Old Duke's apprentice list," I said.

Our search for sketchy antiques was getting very interesting.

✽✽✽

Dining Room, Scotford Castle. Next Day.

Constable Snowdrop, Ewan and I sat around Bertie's large dining room table awaiting instruction from our host. The Duke appeared to be at a rather onerous impasse that tested the limits of his diplomacy skill set.

Bertie spoke in a clipped tone. "Really, I understand and appreciate how we must protect our wildlife corridors, but I simply cannot see what a badger has to do with my stolen items."

"We revisited the badger footage. Look how the headlight from the vehicle makes the badger cringe." Constable Snowdrop played it again for us.

"They make me cringe," Bertie said. "Honestly, Constable Snowdrop, if that's the best you and London can come up with then perhaps I'd be better off hiring a group of private detectives to figure this out."

"Wait, Bertie," I said. "Think about what he just said. Headlight. Singular."

"And?" Our favorite aristocrat was incredibly frustrated.

"And, that means we have a one-eyed monster out there. If we're lucky, the thieves haven't noticed yet. It is one of those particularly bright, newer ones, seen on SUVs. Perhaps we can do a scan of the parking lot and find the thieves."

There was silence in the room as everyone contemplated my suggestion.

"Do I hear stakeout?" Constable Snowdrop asked with great enthusiasm.

"Before you ask me to fire up Greymore's donut machine, let's be practical about this plan. Are the same film crew members coming back to shoot the laboratory documentary?" I asked.

All eyes went to our host.

Bertie shook his head. "I cannot be certain. Crews aren't hired as a full group. It depends upon the availability of the director, producer, cinematographer, sound engineer, makeup artist, hair-stylist, costume designer and many more. Just like casting, it's quite an art to assemble all the crew members on location at the same time."

"Even if you could, I don't think you'd want to alert them that we're checking vehicles," Constable Snowdrop said.

"Why do we assume film crew? It could be Scotford Castle staff," Ewan said. "And yes, I realize that's an incredibly unpopular suggestion."

Bertie sighed. "We cannot discount any possibility at this point. I say we go ahead with filming and plant some vanilla observers in the background to keep an eye out for anything suspicious."

"It won't be Groundhog Day, more like Badger Day," I said in a bright voice.

"Why, oh why, does this year keep bringing me such conundrums?" Bertie lamented. "The fact that they stole the portrait of Edwina makes it even more unpalatable."

I'd lent Bertie the portrait for his 'local aristocrats' exhibition and now she'd been stolen. Aunt Edwina would be shocked.

"Can we leave the arrangements with you? You're still working with London, correct?" Bertie asked Constable Snowdrop.

"Yes, we are a united team. I can assure you this will be done correctly, properly, and on time," our local lawman replied. "I'll keep Severs posted as well. He's already shared some insights that were quite helpful."

"Good."

Constable Snowdrop stood up straight and puffed out his chest. "London has granted me third-in-command position on this exercise. I have the say-so on when the takedown occurs."

It appeared that Constable Snowdrop was moving up in the world, far beyond beagles and smuggled salami.

✳✳✳

GGRS. Next Morning.

Gertie and Maude looked exceedingly pleased with themselves.

After I brought them up to speed on 'Badgergate' and Easter Egg chairs, we got down to more serious business.

"We've figured out more pieces to the puzzle," Maude said. "After a lot more research, including several calls and emails to longstanding trades guilds and associations, we've pieced together more of our apprentices' history. John Cooper, scrivener, was listed in the 1852 Official Directory for Medchester working as a Senior Clerk for the Navy. Keith Smythe, goldsmith, is in the 1835 Trade Directory for Medchester. Michael Munnie, bricklayer, is in the 1851 census for Plumsden, aged 61 with occupation listed as bricklayer. Charles Lyons, silversmith, is in the Oakhurst parish register for 1815 which records the burial of Charles Lyons, silversmith of Oakhurst, at the age of twenty-six. Daniel Yardley, bookbinder, is based in Carlingheath as a bookbinder in the 1841 census. Finally, Henry Dartnell, cabinet maker, shows up in the Plumsden parish register with a burial in 1842 at the age of fifty-two."

"That's impressive work, ladies. Thank you," I said.

"It means that they all continued with the trades they were apprenticed in, and stayed in the local area. That could be important to figuring out their connection to the Old Duke," Maude said.

Gertie put some pages down in front of us on the counter. "We already know that the goldsmith was working with the cabinet maker to hide small figurines of gold inside furniture. Why? Likely to bribe clients not to tell. They had the foresight to believe that their pieces would become valuable oddities in the antiques market." She referred us to an old newspaper beside copies of the goldsmith and cabinet maker indentures. "See here? This was found in the Old Duke's papers at Plumsden Archives. It's written by an antiques expert who predicts the craze in puzzles and hidden drawers in wood that was about to beset the nation in Queen Victoria's time."

"How could they have predicted that?"

"Aristocrats have long been fascinated with hidden pieces inside larger ones. This letter from the Old Duke to the master goldsmith mentions his own fascination and asks for his help in securing pieces for his own collection here at Scotford Castle."

"There's more?" I asked. "We'd need Ewan to go around the entire castle and unscrew chair legs to see which ones qualify. And good forgeries, well, they can be hard to spot."

"Maybe not so much," Maude said. "The Old Duke goes on to state his preference for Queen Anne style chairs in his collection."

"Bertie sold those off long ago," I said. "He needed room for the new catering kitchens and they'd sat, unused, for decades."

"So he possibly sold off golden Easter Egg chairs without even knowing?" Gertie asked.

"Perhaps," Maude said. "It is buyer beware in the antiques market."

"What about the other apprentices?" I asked. "The bricklayer?"

"He was likely there to brick up the Duke's eccentric resting place."

"There's the fake brick you found," Maude suggested.

"Yes, but bricks aren't antiques you'd sell at auction houses. What about the others?"

"Bookbinder, scrivener and silversmith."

"And what did the guilds say about those apprentices?"

Maude brought up a spreadsheet on her computer screen. "The guild said the silversmith was known to work on candelabras with intricate grape leaf designs. Also, the apprentice bookbinder's master was originally from Kent."

Gertie hauled out a color photocopy from beneath the pile of documents. "We found this in records from the bookbinders guild. Under the apprentice's and master's records was this note: 'Scotford Castle: Gosling Rebindings'. Do you think they're still here?"

"Bertie has over 12,000 books in his library collection," I said, my mind absolutely boggling at the proposed task ahead of us. "Location would be hard to determine at present, though." Bertie's library collection was scattered in multiple places at the moment.

"Any more clues on the silversmith?" I asked.

"Just that he also lived on the estate, like all the other apprentices, had a well-known master, and served his seven years. Nothing at all indicating what he specifically did for the Old Duke."

"Except he worked on candelabras."

"We just saw a bunch of fancy candelabras at the London auction house with our Easter Egg chair. I wonder if they came from the same seller," I mused.

"Can we bring the catalog up online?" Gertie asked.

"Sure." I led them over to a computer, brought up the auction house's website, then located the current catalog. "Here. It's the sale next week with items from fifty different private sellers and a couple of museums getting rid of excess inventory. Whoa."

"Did you find something?" Maude asked.

"Look at the seller number for the chair and the candelabras. It's the same for both."

Maude and Gertie exchanged a glance. "I think you now have good reason to ask Ewan to put on a fresh suit and take you back to London. Immediately."

I gathered up my things. I had a man to see about some antiques. I hesitated on an afterthought. "Anything else about the scrivener?"

Gertie waved her hand in the air, nonchalant. "Arrested for selling da Vinci forgeries on the historic streets of Plumsden."

"No?" My eyes opened wide.

"No, indeed." Gertie looked heavenward. "Goodness Julie, genealogy and family history research isn't that easy!"

We all had a good chuckle.

Half the fun of researching old records and family papers was the anticipation. With Bertie's unfortunate robbery, mysterious apprentices, antique forgeries and an alchemy laboratory, who knew what we were in for next. All I could say was that the ride was a fascinating one to date.

Chapter 20

Ewan's Van, En Route To London. Next Morning.

We had four panels of stained-glass plus the golden Easter Egg chair with us in Ewan's vehicle cargo hold. The stained-glass was from a decommissioned, derelict church being demolished due to subsistence of the building four inches below its original foundation. With fears of the ancient pews collapsing into the crypt below, the building was condemned and its contents sold off to the highest bidder. Proceeds were all earmarked for the local seniors' activity center. Ewan had attended a nearby village's auction and was pleased to obtain the four stained-glass windows that once sat up high behind the altar and choir stalls, filtering in tiny rays of light in every color of a prism's beam. The stained glass depicted scenes of peasants bringing in the harvest using oxen-led carts. Hard-working families used scythes and stooked bundles of wheat to dry in the sun.

I remembered Aunt Edwina telling me about this particular church and how her eyes lit up with delight when she described the stained-glass craftsmanship. It truly was breathtaking.

And now all four panels were with us.

I looked over at Ewan, busy navigating stop-and-go traffic. The London ring road was a bit like a car park at the moment; despite the city's congestion fee for vehicles, it had not stopped a massive, overwhelming, rush-hour melee.

"Who do you think will buy the stained-glass panels?" I asked.

"I'm hoping a kind donor who subsequently gives them to the seniors' center for a decent tax write off," he said.

"That would be the best of both worlds. Save the glass and install it somewhere that many people can still enjoy."

"We're on the same page with that one," Ewan said.

"I was sad to hear that the church was being demolished."

Ewan braked hard when a bubblegum pink hatchback zipped in front of us. "It had to be torn down," he muttered, gripping the steering wheel tight. Traffic started to flow again and he relaxed back in his seat. "So much of what I do is salvaging what's left behind of something beautiful. The church was crumbling down around itself. If they didn't act immediately even the precious stained-glass would have become broken, useless shards. I feel it's our duty to save what we can of our heritage."

"Like your family?" I asked, feeling he'd just given me a perfect segway.

"Yes and ... oh." He gave me a serious look. "You mean my lack of one?"

"Knowing what happened to them."

"I already explained. My father was dead, my mother was hospitalized, and my brother died. I even lost my foster buddy, Travis.

Understandably, when you grow up in care, most kids want to gain adulthood and independence as soon as they can."

I bit my lip, unsure of what to say next. Ewan was an easy-going guy, and I just hoped that I wasn't pushing him too far. In situations like this, my GGRS experience taught me the person in question would do one of two things: 1) embrace help to reconnect with their family; or 2) simply put up an imaginary steel wall and let no one disturb painful memories.

I tried again. "I just wanted to let you know that I can help. That is, if you want to pursue it."

It was a moment of truth.

Ewan smiled, reached for my hand, and kissed the back of it. "My dear, dear Julie. Your caring enthusiasm is why I adore you so."

"So, you'll let me help you find your family?"

"Yes, but only after Bertie's castle is well on its way to being put back together. Let's help him get that accomplished, plus help solve the robbery where our expertise is needed."

"Deal." I gave him a smile. "And make no mistake, I'm holding you to that promise, Mr. Ewan Kilburn."

❉❉❉

London Auction House.

Earl Bovinks practically tumbled out of the front door to greet us. He was all toothy grin as he took Ewan's hand, then mine, pumping our respective handshakes up and down with great enthusiasm. "Welcome, welcome, kind people," he said. "Did you bring it?"

"Nice weather today, Earl," Ewan joked.

Earl stopped for moment. "I do apologize. Our phone has rung incessantly, literally off the hook, since we posted our blog about the apprentice cabinet maker and his work with the goldsmith. It wasn't just the Victorians who were fascinated with the secrets one could hide inside everyday objects. The fact that this is a forgery of a well-known furniture maker plus has an added gold treasure inside, well, that's just the clotted cream and strawberry jam on top of the scone."

"Brilliant," Ewan said. "I do admit being a bit out of the loop on this particular forgery ruse."

"It's because there are so few pieces about. Much has been lost over time, I'm afraid," Earl said. "It's quite an exclusive club of collectors these days."

"The GGRS team thought the sale would be a wonderful way to share this unique history with the world. The current Duke also considers it his duty," I said.

"But to get the chair's sale approved so quickly. I must say, that's most impressive," Earl said.

"Bertie ensures Scotford Castle doesn't buckle under a ton of red tape. It's just him and a small senior management committee, all very practical people who pull in the same direction," I explained. "They get a lot accomplished that way."

"Excellent. Right. Now may we see the chair?" Earl was practically salivating at the thought, his prim suit clinging to his side amid his slightly perspired anticipation.

A small group of auction house staff had assembled to our right, trying to be both unobtrusive and interested. They moved as a pack towards the front window as we turned for Ewan's van parked at the curb.

I leaned over to Ewan. "I feel like they're ready to pounce on us."

"Good thing the chair's safely ensconced inside bubble wrap," Ewan replied.

We carefully lifted the chair out of the cargo space and Ewan asked me to stand guard while he brought in the four stained-glass panels.

Earl was kind and got three staff members to help carry the stained glass which was packed inside wooden frames and then inside crates filled with straw. Dropping stained-glass panels was definitely not an option.

Once the four crates were safely delivered, we could turn our full attention to the Easter Egg chair. We gently unwrapped the chair in front of our audience, one that was fixated on every single piece of bubble wrap up that fluttered to the floor. And there, after careful effort, sat our mysterious piece of furniture. It was a perfect match to the one already on display in the showroom. Ewan gave me a wink and laid it down on the bubble wrap. He unscrewed the right front chair leg and pulled out the gold cupid figurine, its rolled piece of parchment still attached.

Earl bent down to take a look, magnifying loop in his hand. "Incredible. To think for all these years, cupid's been a marvelous secret inside that chair."

"Chairs. Plural," I said. "And the mystery gets even better. Read what the parchment scroll says."

Earl unrolled it and read the '2/6' notation. He looked shocked, jaw dropping. "Two shillings and sixpence or," he said, jamming his glasses even tighter on at the end of his nose, "two of six chairs total."

"We'd like to contact your seller and get more information about the provenance of their chair and other items they are selling," Ewan said.

"Well, it is a private sale," Earl confirmed. "Still, matching all six chairs would be an auction house's dream lot on the sales floor, especially if they all came with their original golden figurines."

"Think of the publicity within the antiques trade, too," Ewan said, trying to sweeten the prospect.

"Let me make a phone call," Earl said, already scrolling through his mobile phone as we watched. "Lot number 15,243. Yes, the seller is usually at home when I call. Please give me a moment." Earl walked off so we didn't overhear his private conversation.

Ewan and I respected the seller's privacy. He or she had obviously entrusted the auction house to care for and get a good price for their goods. Part of that trust included keeping their identity concealed if it was so desired.

Earl was back in two minutes. "I'm going to text you the address of the seller. She is a dealer from East Sussex."

"Not Lorelei Stoneton?" I asked.

Earl looked quite surprised. "Why, yes. That's exactly who it is."

I smiled. "We know her. Ewan, remember the antiques fair in Waverly-on-Sea? The one where that male thief dressed as an elderly woman and pilfered your hat pins?"

"Clearly."

Earl smiled. "Lorelei would be very pleased to meet with you at her shop. Just give her a ring, she said, and she'll put the kettle on."

Chapter 21

Treemoreland Farm Antiques. Next Day.

The hand-carved wooden sign near the roadside made it clear we'd reached the correct place. We ended up going down a long, unpaved drive lined with mismatched trees spaced at irregular intervals. The farm boasted a set of stone-built farm structures: a house, barns plus a few small machine outbuildings.

Lorelei was a lovely lady, and still had the yardstick-straight, silvery-blond hair with a fringe we remembered from the antiques fair a while back. She was the kind person who'd given Gertie and I the idea that there might be something sandwiched between Aunt Edwina's watercolor artwork and its matting. As it turned out, she was right on the money. I therefore had high hopes for her sharing more wonderful details about our Easter Egg chair set and silver candelabras with their grape leaf design.

Lorelei and her daughter Stephanie treated us to a scrumptious lunch, and had obviously been busy in the kitchen prior to our arrival.

"This is really kind of you both," I said, sitting back after enjoying an amazing shrimp salad followed by a lemon tart dusted with icing sugar.

"We love to entertain, and rarely get the chance what with Stephanie away at university. You've caught us on a good week as Steph's home from uni to get caught up on her washing and ironing," Lorelei explained.

"What are you studying?" Ewan asked her daughter.

"Textile design through the centuries," Stephanie said. "It's truly amazing how much one can learn about history from the weave, material and color of a fabric."

"She's going to do some great work in the genealogy field once she gets her credentials," I said.

Stephanie smiled. "I'm keen to link families' historical clothing and jewelry collections with their actual lives. It really helps explain the social history of the time and place."

"Lovely. We need more family historians like you in the world," Ewan said.

There was a polite pause in our conversation.

"Now, would you like to see some antiques?" Lorelei asked.

Ewan and I both nodded, eager beavers that we were.

"Right. Please follow me to the warehouse," Lorelei said.

"Um, can we help with the dishes?" I asked.

Stephanie shook her head. "My job. I have to pay for laundry soap."

"Thank you," Ewan said. "Trust me, I remember those uni days. It does get better once you start earning a proper income."

"Quick, before my daughter starts passing around a collection plate, let's go out to the warehouse," Lorelei teased, earning a look of feigned offense from her daughter. She used the joystick on her electric wheelchair to head for the door.

As we went over to the warehouse, she looked up at us both. "Before you ask, it's progressive, chronic arthritis. My wheels make it much easier to get around and get on with daily life."

"I can't ever see you slowing down, Lorelei," I said.

"It's not in my nature," she said, grinning back. "They'll have to tie me down first."

She entered a six-digit code on an alarm keypad, a door slid open and we were granted access. The lights immediately came on and illuminated a half-acre of antiques wonders. There were dozens of rows of shelving in the center, ringed by larger furniture pieces around the perimeter of the room. The entire storage place was configured with accessible ramps and wide aisles. Shelves held smaller items such as medicine chests, silver tea services and multiple other mysterious objects wrapped in archival-safe materials.

"Wow," Ewan and I both exclaimed.

"You're looking at twenty-seven years of antiques trading. Twenty-seven years and thirty-eight days to be precise. The whole family's been involved for generations. I'm just a cog in the wheel of this enterprise."

"Those are the best kinds," I said. "I adore seeing founders' photos on the walls from past centuries."

"Oh, we have a few of those, but please don't expect to see me in the ones from 1890. I'm old but not that ancient."

We all had a good laugh.

Despite her massive inventory, Lorelei made quick work of finding the exact shelf we needed: a few fast keystrokes on the computer nearby and she brought up: 'Aisle 6, Shelf 2'.

She looked back at us. "Follow me."

We did a lot of that today. Once again, Ewan and I hustled to keep up with her. It made me so happy seeing her live life to the fullest, despite a debilitating disease. With today's living aids and technology, differently-abled people were valued, productive members of society. People needed to recognize and respect it as fact. Everyone at GGRS certainly did.

"Your apprentice silversmith was a busy man," she said. "I put the candelabras up for sale because I needed the room and didn't have much call for them here in this neck of the woods. I deal mainly in furniture and smaller household items. Those bulky candelabras, well, you could take one as your date to a formal ball."

She was right, they were over five feet tall and goodness knows how a footman would light the candles on top for dinner. Perhaps that was exactly the point. Centuries ago, the extremely wealthy often did not worry about those sorts of 'trivial' details. Their 'people' were expected to just make it happen.

"Your man also made amazing walking stick toppers," Lorelei advised.

There were about twenty in total, each one clearly labeled with an archival friendly paper tag and corresponding tie tape.

"May I?" I asked her.

"Be my guest," she said. "The one with the Bassett Hound is quite spectacular."

I picked up the one in question and examined it closely. The sturdy stick was indeed capped with artistry of the highest degree. Every single line in the silver dog's sorrowful face was present, right down to the long jowls that flapped and looked hilarious when this breed of dog ran. Somehow the silversmith had managed to incorporate all that emotion and animal charisma into the finished piece. It was truly a work of art.

"Candelabras and walking sticks. Did he work on anything else?" Ewan asked.

"We can check the ledger."

Music to a family historian's ears. "You have his original ledger?" I asked, thrilled at the thought.

Lorelei nodded. "Yes, we do. It starts at year one of his apprenticeship."

"That's got to be one of a kind," Ewan said.

"Would you like to see it?" she asked.

"Is the sun yellow?" I asked.

The ledger book and a related diary were stored together in a side office. We opened the ledger book first and saw tallies of stock for the master silversmith's shop. We read of silver ingots, silver wire, and semiprecious stones. There were records of tools purchased, candles for lighting and a new work desk for the apprentice, the one who had done the work for the Old Duke.

All looked normal until I stopped at one line entry. It read:

Miniature tea service for dollhouse.
Mrs. Brampton's daughter's birthday gift. £5.00.
Goods not picked up.

"Ewan, did you see this?" I asked.

He read the entry with great interest. "You're thinking Ozzie, right?"

"Ozzie?" Our hostess looked quizzical.

We rapidly explained our two metal detectorists' recent and supposedly glorious find.

Lorelei gave a hearty laugh. "From the looks of it, he's dug up an apprentice sampler tea set."

"Pardon me?" I asked.

"A sampler is a work assigned by the apprentice's master to determine his student's skill level. No hallmark would be on the silver. In this case, it appears a dollhouse tea set was the assignment."

"So much for Ozzie finding an offering to the pagan gods," Ewan chortled.

Lorelei chuckled. "Say, isn't Ozzie the man involved in a confectionery store scuffle a while back? I read something in the papers about a candied octopus ..."

I sighed. "Yes. That's one genealogy nightmare I never want to relive."

One Hour Later.

We turned our attention to the diary once we'd established the general contents of the apprentice silversmith's ledger book. The diary was written in lovely, artistic handwriting, something that didn't match the penmanship in the ledger.

"This is written in a different hand," I said, comparing the two bound books. "It looks nothing like the writing in the ledger."

Ewan perused it. "Yes, it is a different style, much more formal than this list of revenues and expenses. He's even signed the last page."

We set eyes on the initials 'J.C.' on the last page before the mauve marbled endpapers.

"That's our apprentice scrivener," I said. "And who wants to bet the diary was a sampler made by our apprentice bookbinder?"

"I do," Ewan said. "His name is right here." He pointed to another set of initials lower down on the page.

"Well, I never," Lorelei said. "And to think all I believed that I had here was a tentative link to the current Duke's family tree."

Ewan and I both exchanged a startled glance.

Lorelei continued. "I'll show you." She reached back into the cabinet and removed a scroll tied with archival safe tape. She unfurled it across the desk and once again we saw the scrivener's beautiful handwriting. There was a huge, colorful coat of arms at the top, leading all the way back to some medieval knight.

"It's quite the family tree," Lorelei said.

"Where did you get this?" I asked.

"A great uncle's estate. His family had no interest in genealogy, so they shifted all the paperwork on to me."

"That crest is splendid," Ewan said, looking over the red, royal blue and shiny gold embossing.

"As far as I know, it's to be believed. I'm a descendant of the apprentice silversmith. Our family goes back to, well, what King Arthur's time?"

"You need a lot of backup proof to say that with certainty," I advised. "Don't ever trust a twenty minute surname lookup that gives you supposedly dozens of generations back to the Bronze Age." I issued her a teasing smile.

She waved her hand in the air. "Don't I know it. I once saw a family tree service purporting to take gullible customers back on their genealogy lines, charging £100 per branch."

"They'd make no money if the research is done properly. It takes far more time than they were charging," I said.

Lorelei nodded. "Henceforth, the conclusion that all they were doing was selecting the likeliest-looking George, not triple checking via multiple sources like the census, parish registers and newspapers, before arriving at their grandiose conclusions."

"It's all smoke and mirrors," Ewan said, "likely enhanced with the cosmetics of a skilled artist's brush laced with gold paint."

We all refocused on the family tree before us.

I drew a finger through the air from Lorelei's eighth great-grandfather and noticed something else. "That woman's name is also on Bertie's family tree."

"I was hoping you'd notice that. That's where my daughter and I have our claim to fame. We're some sort of eighth cousins removed to the current Duke of Conroy."

"That possibly explains why you have the Old Duke's apprentice's diary. What's the exact connection?" Ewan asked.

"The silversmith apprentice was my ancestor. Sadly, he was killed in a carriage accident five years after completing his indenture. He left a wife and one small child behind."

We reflected on the sadness for a moment.

I pointed to a ledger page. "Our apprentice silversmith made dollhouse tea services and candelabras."

"And walking sticks," Lorelei added.

"Perhaps that's the lesson in all of this," I continued. "He worked hard, earned his way up in the world and left his legacy for us to read, courtesy of a fellow apprentice. Even though his life was short, he still is remembered."

❀❀❀

GGRS. Next Morning.

"30,401 words? Really?" I looked at Candace with amazement. "You have been busy."

Candace nodded. "Turns out my mother pilfered notes from her old dig journals, got busy on the keyboard and things just flew from there. She types lightning fast. Her goal is 80,000 words and then she says the world will tire of her story."

Gertie gave us a serious glance, looking up from her census record. "I don't think anyone will ever be bored hearing about your mother's adventures. As opposed to this census taker where he got a bit, er, distracted on the job shall we say?"

We all clustered around her computer screen. The digitized version of the original record contained a partly-visible doodle at the bottom of the page that read, 'Says she's twenty-three but looks thirty-nine. Am noting answer she gave as doubtful.'

"It's a shame digitization didn't scan the entire page properly," Gertie said.

"That's why having the originals to refer back to is so important," I added.

"At least the census taker didn't rate that woman out of ten," Gertie said.

"Were they allowed to do that?" Candace asked.

I stopped. "There are plenty of things they did back then that were not fit for polite conversation nor for today's more politically correct world. Some of the notes one sees in census records are beyond belief."

"As in?"

Gertie stepped up on this one. "Like the census taker who noted how one home appeared to be a house of ill repute i.e. a brothel.

The census taker who wrote his wife's shopping list in the margin of the page for rowhouse number fourteen. And then we have the one who listed the names of the dog and cats belonging to a certain family. Let's also not forget the man who noted the total number of pipes in the collection held by one eighty-nine-year-old man living with his daughter and family."

"It wasn't all super formal?" Candace asked. "I mean, governments take the census quite seriously."

"They tell you it's illegal not to fill them out, the modern-day census forms," I said.

"Heaven forbid," Candace said. "Can you imagine sitting incarcerated in some dank cell block, your only crime in life being not filling out the census?"

"They actually imprison you for that?" I asked.

"Why is everyone looking at me?" Gertie replied, indignant. "Just because I spent one night in jail after a misguided karaoke competition." Her voice petered out as Candace reached into her satchel and pulled out a canvas sack full of dinosaur models. "To celebrate the 30,000 word milestone, I convinced my mother to donate some of her collection to a very worthy cause," she said.

I knew exactly what she meant and was overwhelmed with joy.

Chapter 22

Mrs. Farmingham's Cottage, Scotford Estate. Later Afternoon.

Candace sat on the floor with Greg, her canvas bag right beside her. The young boy was super keen and quickly noticed a long, curved brontosaurus tail peeking out of the top.

"When I was a little girl, about your age, my mother gave me a set of dinosaurs to play with."

Greg issued her a tiny smile.

Candace continued. "And now, my mum would like to give you a set of your own dinosaurs. Would you like that?"

Greg's eyes opened wide. He gave a shy, half nod and looked towards the bag.

"I'll take that as a yes," Candace said, looking over towards Mrs. Farmingham and I.

"He's just waiting for the word go," Mrs. Farmingham said.

"Well then, no sense in delaying things any longer." Candace picked up her bag then handed it to Greg. The bag was plum full of plastic dinosaur models.

Greg delicately emptied the bag on the floor and started lining up the dinosaurs in a particular order.

"Is he going by size?" I asked.

Mrs. Farmingham shook her head. "No, Latin genus and species. He knows them all by heart. Greg has a photographic memory." She looked ever so proud.

"All the Latin names?" I asked, astonished.

"Yes. He's read every dinosaur book he can get his hands on, literally knows them inside out. I used to read some of them—the easier books—to him as bedtime stories, but the ones he reads now? Well, I can hardly pronounce some of those technical terms."

We looked at Greg, still busy sorting out his new collection. He was not a boy who would be distracted at the moment; he was far too intent on arranging his new models in a perfect order. Next, he left his neat row, got up and went to another room. The newly arrived dinosaurs now stood all attention, awaiting his return.

Mrs. Farmingham smiled. "Give him a moment."

Sure enough, Greg came back, carrying a thick university-level technical book on dinosaurs.

"Now he'll compare the models with the images in the books. All the information will be filed away in his memory," she said.

"He's brilliant," Candace said.

Greg's grandmother grinned. "Indeed he is. Now, may I offer you both some tea?"

Candace and I both nodded, so Mrs. Farmingham led us into the kitchen. We settled once again on the chairs covered with their delightful floral chintz pattern.

"Thank you so much for thinking of my grandson. He really is a delightful little chap," Mrs. Farmingham said she bustled about with delicate cups, saucers and a plate of lemon loaf.

"I'm happy to share our collective passion for dinosaurs with him," Candace said.

"Sugar?" Mrs. Farmingham asked me.

I was distracted, far too distracted to answer. The reason was I'd just spied something that meant a lot more to me now compared with the first time we'd visited this cottage. "May I ask where you obtained that gold cupid figurine?" I asked, gesturing to the top row of a knickknack shelving unit. It was filled with many other tiny objects including a thatched cottage made of porcelain, a bike made out of horseshoe nails plus a Welsh love spoon with intricate symbols carved into the wood.

Mrs. Farmingham looked up. "Oh, I'm sure it's not the real thing, but there's an unusual story behind it. We actually found it inside a wonky chair leg of all things."

"Here?" Candace asked.

Mrs. Farmingham nodded. "Yes, inside one of the four you're sitting on."

"You mean, you're using the set as kitchen chairs?" I asked, practically leaping out of my seat.

Mrs. Farmingham nodded. "The chairs were here when we moved in. I asked the estate manager at the time and he said no problem borrowing them while we lived here as tenants."

❊❊❊

Twenty Minutes Later.

Aristocrats always knew the right thing to say. That was, until they were speechless. This was Bertie's temporary affliction as he looked at the four chairs in Mrs. Farmingham's kitchen. By now, we had removed the chintz covers and found the chairs were perfect matches to the pair now sitting in the London auction house.

Bertie rushed over as soon as he heard the news of our find. He was giddy with excitement, unusual for our normally stoic and steady, upper crust friend. He held out his phone and panned the camera around the chairs in the humble kitchen. The furniture did look cozy, surrounded by older oak cupboards and mismatched sideboards. It looked like any shabby-chic kitchen in England with one exception: these kitchen chairs were worth a fortune.

Some garbled muffling squawked out from Bertie's phone. He adjusted the volume then spoke into the contraption. "Earl, you're on speakerphone. We're looking at the missing four chairs, sitting right here in Mrs. Farmingham's kitchen."

"I'm absolutely thunderstruck," Earl said. "Imagine finding the rest of the set. Is it really complete?"

Mrs. Farmingham frowned. "We've only ever had the four chairs."

"He means did you find any other gold figurines," I said.

"Oh, I see." She shook her head. "Only the one golden cupid, Your Grace." She handed the figurine to Bertie. "We never dreamed it was real gold."

"So all the other legs were empty?" Earl asked.

Mrs. Farmingham looked confused. "We didn't bother checking. Only one had the wobbly leg, you see. We thought someone had jammed the figurine inside to steady it."

Silence blanketed the room.

"<u>Each</u> chair contains its own gold figurine?" she asked. "We might've been sitting on all that gold for years?" Her face was a picture of disbelief.

"WAIT!" came a strangled, desperate cry from the man on the phone. "Please DO NOT try to take the chairs apart yourself. I will have an expert there first thing tomorrow morning to make sure it's done properly. Your Grace, I shall disconnect now and set about making the arrangements," Earl said.

"Thank you, Earl," Bertie said, ending the call.

"Can we stand the suspense?" I asked the group.

"We'll have to," Mrs. Farmingham said.

"Not a word of this breathed to a soul, please," Bertie said. "I'll have one of Scotford's security patrolmen stand guard tonight."

Mrs. Farmingham put a hand to her chest. "Mercy me, all this fuss over some old kitchen chairs." She leaned over towards Candace and I. "To be quite honest, I think they look much better with their chintz covers."

"You have hidden gems there, Mrs. Farmingham," Candace said.

I looked over at Bertie. "Where is Ozzie right now?"

"Where else? In the back barley field, with Timmy," Bertie said.

"You do realize there's a noninvasive way to figure out if there's metal inside those chairs," I said, a gleam in my eyes.

Bertie took a quick look around the small room. "Patience, Julie. Besides, I do believe that Mrs. Farmingham and Greg would prefer their hearth and walls to remain intact."

❋❋❋

Next Morning. 9:00 a.m.

True to his word, Earl's expert furniture craftsman, Karl Sommers, knocked on Mrs. Farmingham's front door right on time. He was a craftsman by trade, keenly revealed by his thickly calloused fingers and palms. His short fingernails were freshly scrubbed clean; he'd obviously been told that he would meet someone who lived in a castle. Karl's beard was neatly trimmed and from a few revealing tan lines around his ears, one could tell he also sported a new haircut. It was akin to a school picture day where every parent on the planet made sure their child looked their best.

Karl spied the chairs as soon as we led him to the kitchen. In Karl's hands, the chairs were revered, delicate objects of art. He whistled low, under his breath. "Just exquisite, these are. Forgeries or not, some say this workmanship is better than the authentic maker's pieces." Karl carefully unscrewed the front right leg of the first chair. A hint of gold and Karl carefully retrieved another gold cupid figurine from inside the hollow area.

"My, after all these years. We had no idea," Mrs. Farmingham said. "I feel a bit of a fool."

"Never mind," I said, "you weren't to know the chairs' full history."

"To think of all the family meals eaten at this table, all the time Greg's clambered up to play with his dinosaurs. It really makes one take a big step back," she said in awe.

"Step forward into the light, Mrs. Farmingham," Bertie said with great kindness. "It's because of your good housekeeping that these chairs were protected from damage."

"I bought the chintz covers to protect the wood. I found them at a clearance sale in my daughter's village years ago."

"Best bargain you ever made," Bertie said. "I shall, of course, ensure you get some of the proceeds from the sale of these chairs."

"Your Grace, that's very kind, but the chairs never actually belonged to me," Mrs. Farmingham said.

"Nevertheless, I insist. You shall have a new kitchen table and chair set, plus a bit extra for taking such good care of these special pieces." No one argued with Bertie when he was so sure of what to do.

In the corner, Karl was busy working away, Greg keenly watching over his shoulder. Karl had extracted two more cupids and, from the last chair, now pulled a tiny gold gosling figurine, quite young as it was tooled with a chick's downy feathers. "How unusual," Karl said. "Your Grace, does this particular bird hold any significance to your family?"

"A goose?" Bertie smiled. "Well, after the fire I was thinking my own goose was cooked."

We all laughed at that one.

"Joking aside, there is no goose on the family crest. We've always had swans and peacocks on the estate, but not geese," Bertie said.

"There was nothing about alchemy nor farming nursery rhymes containing geese in the old family papers?" I asked.

Bertie thought on it, then shook his head. "Not that I've ever seen. I could check with Prunella at the Scotford Archives, but that would be a bit of a longshot. Shire horses and cattle yes, but geese?" He pondered it some more.

"Earl said I'm to photograph all the figurines and email him right away," Karl announced. "Then I'm to put the gold figurines back inside the chairs and take them to London, well-packed inside bubble wrap."

"Of course," Bertie said. "And Mrs. Farmingham, I do sincerely apologize for all this inconvenience."

***

Stables Office, Scotford Castle. Next Morning.

Ewan and I visited Bertie. He was surrounded by piles of paper, architectural drawings and fabric samples.

"Looks like you need to open up an interior design firm," I teased.

Bertie sighed. "It's all for a good cause. Brace yourselves, here come our fearless metal detectorists."

Ozzie and Timmy sauntered across the courtyard towards Bertie's temporary office. The spring in their steps was obvious; the pair practically bounded across the path en route to see the Lord of this Manor.

"Let's hope it's more than old tins of beans today," Ewan said with a smile.

Bertie stiffened in his chair. "I'm girding my loins this time. The museum's report on the gold coins is back and–"

"And? How much is our gold coin hoard worth?" Ozzie demanded. He offered no 'good morning', no hint of deference to the affable aristocrat. The best Ozzie could do was a slight touch of two fingertips to the brim of his flat, slightly damp, tweed cap.

"Dear friends, I see you've put in some more hard work out in the Scotford barley field," Bertie said, sounding like he was trying to soften the blow.

"Yes, and we've got another fantastic find, beyond the Roman coins we already unearthed." Timmy held up a small, antique, locked metal chest.

"Er, about those gold coins," Bertie began.

"Is someone dragging their heels?" Ozzie asked as he focused narrowed eyes on Bertie.

"Not for the reason you think," Bertie said.

Ozzie straightened up and popped out his chest. "Well if it's not a red tape, then what's the problem?"

"Ozzie. Timmy. I'm afraid the coins are not authentic. The Old Duke has fooled us once again with another foray into alchemy," Bertie said.

Ozzie and Timmy both looked shocked.

It was Ozzie who tackled this one first. "But they're gold. They passed Julie's scratch test."

Bertie gave them a pained smile. "I'm afraid Julie's thumbnail test only goes so far. Upon full spectrum analysis in the laboratory, the coins turned out to have a lead center, surrounded by a layer of gold."

"So they're not authentic?" Timmy asked.

"No. The Old Duke probably cast them himself. Apparently, they already have five exact replica coins in the museum's collection."

"So what are they worth?" Ozzie asked.

"Not £50,000 each," Ewan said, leaping in to help Bertie.

"Ewan's correct. More like £300 each," Bertie confirmed.

I saw some rapid calculations being done inside our two metal detectorists' heads. Hopes and dreams of luxury vacations, motorhomes and champagne dinners were all quickly evaporating.

"Well, £300 isn't bad for a per coin price. Remember you started out with tin cans, a bicycle chain plus an apprentice's sampler dollhouse tea set," I said, hopefully with some encouragement in my voice.

"Talk about dashed hopes," Ozzie said.

I distinctly recalled being his least favorite person when I'd broken the news about the tea set's origins following our visit to Lorelei's farm.

"Why me? I always get stuck like this," Ozzie moaned, kicking the doorframe and stubbing his toe in the process. "Owww!"

"Chin up, Ozzers," Timmy said.

Ozzers?

I must remember that one.

Timmy continued. "Show them the chest."

Ozzie's face instantly brightened. "Right! They can't keep us down. Look at this!"

The metal chest had a strong hasp on the front and a handle on either side. Multiple parts of it looked quite rusted from sitting in whatever damp environment it was hidden. As Ozzie held it up, the rust finally took full hold and the bottom collapsed. As it fell to the floor, eight gold ingots tumbled out of the chest and scattered.

"Oh wonderful. We came to ask if you had the key, but now we don't need one. Now we have all of these!" Ozzie scrabbled down on the ground, collecting the treasures one by one. He handed the first gold ingot to our host.

"Look here," Bertie said. "It's stamped with a gosling."

We all crowded around to look at the image pressed into the gold. Each bar was the same.

"The gosling image matches the figurine inside the last kitchen chair at Mrs. Farmingham's," I said, holding out my phone to show everyone the image.

Timmy looked at the photo up close. "Your Old Duke sure liked his geese."

"Geese?" Bertie asked. "How do you mean?"

Timmy shrugged. "I was perusing Scotford's extensive ornithology book section in your library the night before the fire. I recall seeing several volumes on geese. One even had this exact gosling symbol in gold tooling on the spine."

We all looked at each other.

"We must find that book," I said. "It's the gosling rebinding."

Bertie's face crumpled in true archival agony. "How? Everything's out of order, in boxes, scattered everywhere due to the fire. There's over 12,000 books to sort through."

"Well, we can start by checking the volumes we're temporarily storing back at GGRS. Maybe we'll get lucky," I suggested.

"I don't have a lot of faith in quickly finding anything here," Bertie said. He cast his eyes around his office that seemed to grow smaller by the hour as more and more items were brought to him for an opinion or approval. "I recall seeing the Major trundling out random books in a wheelbarrow on the night of the fire."

"He wasn't the only one." I patted Bertie's shoulder. "Never doubt the organizational efforts of conservation specialists. They may know exactly where that book is after a mere few keyboard clicks inside their computer database."

Chapter 23

GGRS. Next Day.

"Is this what you're looking for?" our barista Abbyleigh said, handing over a book bound in navy blue leather with gold tooling on the spine. Part of that gold tooling included a gosling image.

"Yes. Where did you find it?" I asked, amazed we'd found the one key book in amongst thousands belonging to Bertie's collection.

Abbyleigh shrugged. "It was one of the books the Major stored in the spare room here after the Scotford fire. I started reading it on my break one day. But I did wear the white gloves, honest! I never brought in food nor a stick of gum, promise."

"Thank you. I'm glad it's safe and you followed proper library protocols."

In all honesty, Abbyleigh bringing us the gilded edged tome was a true lucky moment. For the past few hours, Maude, Gertie and I had parsed through the various boxes of books that GGRS was storing for Bertie during Scotford's rebuilding. Thank goodness it was saved and now retrieved because I had a feeling it held great secrets within its pages.

I tried to show my team but Abbyleigh had one more thing to tell me. "Just so you know," she said, "I wasn't the one marking up His Grace's book."

I frowned. "How so?"

"It's got random pencil marks underlining letters and words all over the place. I tried to form a word using the first six underlined letters but it was all gibberish to me. Here, take a look." She handed me a used envelope where it was obvious she'd been trying to work it out. Abbyleigh had given it a valid attempt, yet came up empty-handed. I thanked her and she went back to the café.

Such was often the case with family history riddles, especially those concocted by eccentric aristocrats with the needs and money to create the cleverest of anagrams, puzzles and trails of breadcrumbs. The repeated gosling symbol was trying to tell us something. But what?

We had gold ingots with a gosling symbol.

We had a gold gosling figurine from inside a chair's leg.

We had a book on geese with a gosling symbol tooled into the spine.

Geese all over, geese everywhere.

But where did the Old Duke want it to lead us?

I gestured at Maude and Gertie. They came over to see the book. I explained where it was found plus pointed out some mysterious underlining at random places throughout the book.

"Looks like a code of some sort," Gertie said. "Maybe the letters all add together to form a word."

I shook my head. "It's much more complicated than that."

"How about each letter of the alphabet corresponds to numbers one through twenty-six. Write down the numbers, add them together for some sort of bank account number?" Gertie suggested.

"Back in the Old Duke's day, I don't think things were that advanced yet. They had paper ledgers for bank accounts."

Maude cleared her throat. "Ladies, the best thing we can do is write down all the underlined letters on the whiteboard. Perhaps we'll see a pattern."

"We're not talking hundreds of entries, Jules, are we?" Gertie asked.

"I don't believe so." I quickly flipped through the book. "It's every few pages where one letter or one word is mentioned. The markings stop a few chapters in."

"Right. Let's get to work," Maude said.

✻✻✻

Meeting Room.

Gertie volunteered for whiteboard duties. As Maude and I flipped through the gosling book, my effervescent cousin started to sing a pop tune into the whiteboard marker she held like a microphone. A few moments of that and I was eager to get Gertie focused on something more serious. It wasn't that I begrudged her hobby; I just didn't want her doing it here within the confines of our research facility.

Too late.

Gertie closed her eyes and started to belt it out.

I cut off her high note with the letter 'K', quickly followed by the letter 'S'.

After writing down a few more letters, Gertie called out, 'Bingo!'

"Very funny. Keep going, here's another one," I said.

After an hour of this, the whiteboard looked like it had its fill. We read:

JC, KS, MM, CL, DY, HD

painting; brick; find; apprentices; behind; of; late; wall

"Let me check something from Plumsden," Maude said, opening a manila folder she'd brought into the room with her. She flipped through the photocopies in hand, speeded up by the use of the rubber fingertip that reminded me of an orangey-reddish, flexible thimble.

"Here we are," Maude said, triumphant. "Just as I thought. The letters match the initials of the apprentices."

"Looks like the Old Duke was still up to his games," Gertie said. "But why so much secrecy for his descendants? Surely he could have just told his son and then both agreed to keep quiet about it."

"I think he reveled in the eccentricity of it all," I said. "It was a game created by an aristocrat likely fiddling around in his alchemy laboratory in his slippers, muttering to himself as the latest concoction showed even more promise at turning into gold."

"So we are not to wonder why, just accept that's how he wanted things to be?" Gertie asked.

"Indeed. He did leave the estate in a much more solvent position," I said.

Maude frowned. "Yes, but he forged his way into regaining his fortune." She just didn't do the underhanded or criminal.

"Well, what's done is done," I said. "Now, the Old Duke left us a clue to seek out his last secret. Can we form a sentence with the underlined words?" After some intense verbal brainstorming, the three of us came up with this:

'find painting of apprentices behind late brick wall.'

"A late brick wall?" Gertie thought on it. "Ozzie already broke down the hearth at Scotford Castle."

"It could be a riddle. What else is late in the castle?" I asked.

"A death, the Old Duke?" Maude suggested. "However, it would be highly improper to encourage people to break into the family mausoleum."

"Late for dinner?" Gertie suggested. "Late to a fancy ball. Somebody of late acquaintance. Late to tea? Too late to care …"

The three of us thought on it some more.

I picked up my phone and dialed the only man who might have the answer. "Bertie, we've got a riddle for you."

❊❊❊

The Old Dairy, Scotford Castle. Half An Hour Later.

Gertie, Maude, Severs, Bertie and I stood outside the old dairy. Bertie had the key in hand. "You do realize you're asking me to do something quite unusual here? We just had this entire facility refurbished for the tourist trade a year ago."

"Did you tear any of the walls out?" I asked.

"No," he said, "we just refinished over top of the existing brick with smooth drywall."

"So how do you know what's behind the brick?" I persisted.

"Well, we don't." Bertie still looked a bit dubious as he led us inside and turned on the light. We were now in the midst of a mock dairy, filled with visitor information displays and even hands-on milking machines for the children.

I ran my fist along the inside wall, gently thumping every foot or so, listening for a hollow in the substrate. I stopped when heavy, deep sounds turned to light. "This is it," I said, turning to look at those with me.

"Your Grace, perhaps this will be of use?" Severs asked, handing Bertie a Scotford Castle architectural drawing open on his tablet screen. "It shows an empty cavity in the wall here, a place where something could possibly be hidden." Severs pointed at the location near, if not exactly right upon, the spot I had selected on the wall.

"Thank you, Severs. It's always good to have another piece of proof," Bertie said. The aristocrat then nodded at the carpenter from the estate who stood nearby, drywall saw at the ready. The carpenter put on his safety glasses and we all stood back.

Bertie grimaced as the saw's teeth dug into the pristine, smooth drywall; it was hard to witness the destruction of quality workmanship.

The carpenter soon had a large, square hole cut and pulled out the loose piece of drywall. He set it on the floor and looked over at Bertie. "Your Grace."

Bertie peered inside the wall cavity. All of us looked over his shoulders, eager. Bertie then reached inside and pulled out a simple yet dusty linen cloth. Seven pairs of eyes peered out at us. It was a bit unnerving to say the least.

"It's a painting." Bertie carefully reached in behind the drywall and, with Severs' help, they removed a portrait in a modest gilded frame. "It's the Old Duke with his six apprentices," Bertie said. "Their initials are painted on each of their sleeves."

It was indeed a solemn group of the aristocrat and his six young charges. The Old Duke, periwig, silk cravat and embroidered day suit, was in a formal pose and sat on one of the golden Easter Egg chairs. He held the book with the gosling tooled on its spine. The six apprentices surrounded him, five with a sampler in their hands demonstrating competency in their chosen trade. The goldsmith held a gold brooch, the silversmith an ornate tankard, the brick-layer held an ornamental brick, the scrivener a feather quill and the bookbinder a leather and gold bound tome. The cabinet maker leaned against the distinctive chairs that we now knew concealed a gold figurine.

The gosling symbol discretely appeared somewhere on each of their samplers. Behind the group was the shelving in the alchemy laboratory, a beaker of yellow liquid emitting some fierce steam on a counter rack.

"The secrets of Scotford Castle never end," I said, putting down my phone after filming the grand reveal. "This was likely painted when the six boys came out of their apprenticeships in 1810."

"Late. How do you get 'late brick wall' linking to a dairy?" Gertie asked.

Bertie grinned. "Something my family would find amusing, indeed. You see, the Old Duke was a polyglot, that is, a speaker of many languages. 'Late' somewhat garbled in French is 'lait', which is 'milk'. So, I thought the dairy would be a fine place to start. After all, the Old Duke's ancestral portrait in our castle gallery depicts him with a butter churn."

It was a stunning end to the mystery.

Or was it?

"Wait a minute," Gertie said, "there's something else here at the bottom." She reached inside the wall, down towards the base, and pulled out a small cloth sack tied with faded blue ribbon.

Bertie took it from her proffered hand and led us over to a counter in a corner of the dairy. He carefully undid the ribbon and spread apart the drawstring top. He carefully removed three gold ingots plus the six missing indenture paper matches, each cut with a different wavy line.

"This is quite the collection," Bertie said.

By now, a couple of expert conservationists were in the room, at the ready with archival-friendly file folders and boxes.

Bertie handed the objects over to them for cataloguing and safe-keeping, after the requisite photos were taken.

"There's one more thing," Bertie said, reaching down into the little sack one last time. He pulled out an envelope, sealed with red wax. It was addressed to, 'The Duke who figures it out'.

Bertie broke the seal and opened the envelope, removing a letter from inside. He read:

May, 1810
Scotford Castle

Your Grace,
I hope you enjoy discovering my little sojourn into the unknown. My apprentices and I were quite successful in our day, so successful, in fact, that Scotford likely still stands under your stewardship as a result.

Be a good chap and put what you've just found into a museum.

I have thoroughly enjoyed my life and know these young men will go far in theirs. Do not cast a disparaging eye upon them; I am the only one to blame for the false goods made for profit. I leave Scotford better than when I found it. Will you?
Duke of Conroy

PS: I left you a few gold ingots in case things are dire. Find the metal box in my laboratory.

"The rusty metal box that Ozzie and Timmy found out in the field," I said.

Bertie rocked back on his heels. "The Old Duke was eccentric all right." He grinned. "I suppose it's not really family history without a rogue thief here and there."

Chapter 24

—

Meeting Room, Police Station, Oakhurst. Next Morning.

Constable Snowdrop stood at the head of the table, quite officious. This was quite a feat in itself, namely because Oakhurst didn't exactly possess a ginormous law enforcement facility. It was much larger than a broom closet yet much smaller than a typical pub. Oakhurst's police building only hosted a small reception area with two visitor seats. It contained two offices, a meeting room, staff toilets plus three holding cells. Oh, there was also a small kitchenette with a counter that held a kettle, coffee pot, microwave and mugs ... but not all at the same time. Tea time appeared to be quite the scramble to get all the necessaries together. Constable Snowdrop usually worked alone, calling in resources from Plumsden and beyond if the need ever arose. Apart from Bertie's grand castle theft, the last time Constable Snowdrop raised the white flag was when three sheep were stolen from a farmer's field; they were apparently up and gone without a trace. Plumsden police were not amused when it turned out the sheep were merely on the lam a few pastures away, having escaped through a gap in a hedge that had seen better days.

Undaunted, Constable Snowdrop roped in the out-of-towners; they helped recapture the wandering livestock plus gave the farmer a hand in stopping up the hole in the hedge.

Detective Thomas Brondyn, a senior ranking detective from London, was here, dressed in plainclothes. The experienced look in his eyes marked him as someone to be reckoned with in any case. Detective Brondyn sat to Constable Snowdrop's right, Bertie directly opposite. Ewan and I were also present, but no one else. Frankly, they wouldn't have fit in the room.

"As you may recall, we have the badger footage," Constable Snowdrop stated.

Detective Brondyn winced, likely thinking it could not sound more country yokel than this. He gestured to Constable Snowdrop to move things along.

"And, with that footage, we know the thieves left Scotford Castle in a vehicle with only one headlight in working order." Constable Snowdrop made a big show of bringing up a detailed spreadsheet on the small room's wall screen. "With that clue, we did a search of all the repair shops in a fifty-mile radius. Since the fire at Scotford Castle, there were a total of 103 headlight repairs performed. This is a list of all of them."

Constable Snowdrop paused for dramatic effect and clicked forward to his next slide. "We eliminated the motorbikes from the data set because we know it was a four-wheeled vehicle based upon the footage. This brought our data set down to seventy-eight potential suspect vehicles." The spreadsheet lost some rows as he spoke.

"They would have needed a decent sized vehicle to carry off my papers, jewelry and paintings," Bertie said.

"Two micro, three-wheeled cars were also eliminated, bringing us to seventy-six," Constable Snowdrop said. "Much too small for the portrait of the late Aunt Edwina we all know and love." He rested his eyes on me, likely looking for some sort of praise.

I smiled. "Quite correct."

Constable Snowdrop continued his disappearing data chart show. "Now, from the remaining seventy-six repairs, we next eliminated all owners who could prove they had a solid alibi for the night of the fire. That brought us down to twenty-three vehicles." Once again, his rows of data reduced accordingly on screen.

"That's all fine and dandy, but what if they haven't got the head-light repaired yet?" Ewan asked.

"Well, that's a possibility, but hardly likely. Oakhurst, as you know, has very strict traffic policies in place."

I groaned. "No kidding. You ticket for everything. But Ewan's right. Say they were from out of town and didn't know how strict Oakhurst is with ticketing. That opens up a whole new set of nefar-ious characters."

Detective Brondyn saw an opening. "Excellent point, and that's why we ran a parallel data analysis of known thieves in the area, including those recently paroled or released."

"Any in the film crew?" Bertie asked. "I just don't see how some-one without local knowledge would know about my safe or my family papers."

"Another wise observation, Your Grace," Detective Brondyn said. "Here are some photos of dubious characters in the local area." He brought up a series of twenty pictures on screen, four per slide.

"There's definitely some hard luck cases here, but I don't recognize any of them," Bertie said.

"I don't expect you to know the local black market, Your Grace," Detective Brondyn said with a slight grin on his face, "you being in the high-end mango chutney market and all."

Bertie smiled.

It was so nice to be friends with an aristocrat who didn't take himself too seriously.

"Er, quite, but how will we find the right ne'er-do-well?" Bertie asked.

Constable Snowdrop took the cue from Detective Brondyn, an obviously kind man who was willing to share the credit. "Through the criminals' mistakes."

"How so?" I asked.

"Oh, they concealed themselves well, but they made two mistakes. The first was the missing headlight. The second was leaving this credit card receipt, laden with fingerprints, at the local café where they stopped in for lunch." Detective Brondyn brought a printed cash register receipt up on the screen.

"A ham panini and two cups of tea? How on earth does that prove who the thieves are?" I asked.

"And that's where the true detective work comes in," Detective Brondyn said, looking at Constable Snowdrop to bring this one home.

Constable Snowdrop cleared his throat just like a schoolboy ready to make his presentation at the science fair. "It is a rather brilliant piece of police work. Knowing that the thieves worked with someone on the dark web who wishes to remain anonymous yet also needs the help of locals ... what safer way than to infiltrate a local café?"

"Surely you've got more to go on than a ham sandwich," I said.

"Panini. It was a ham panini," Constable Snowdrop corrected.

"That's like saying, 'Oh, you're from Canada? I have a cousin who lives in Toronto. Do you know him?'" Ewan said.

"Except, dear people, when we also happen to know that this particular café was the one doing the film crew's catering at Scotford Castle during its recent filming."

The shoe literally dropped. We sat in stunned silence.

"But that café in Plumsden is run by two wonderful ladies!" I protested.

"They've been there for ages," Ewan added.

"Up until a month and a half ago when they sold up and retired to Spain." Constable Snowdrop said.

"You're kidding," Ewan said.

Our group in the tiny meeting room was obviously a bit out of the loop on recent café happenings.

"Yes, they left, a numbered corporation bought the business and we just discovered that it, along with the Plumsden snooker hall, were fronts for a money-laundering business."

"At least it wasn't the laundromat," Constable Snowdrop said with a snigger.

We all just stared at him.

"Laundering money? Laundromat?" He looked at us for any hint of a smile and received nothing for his painful attempt at a joke.

I ignored it and refocused on Detective Brondyn. "So, we now have the connection to Scotford."

"The café delivery van was one of the twenty-three vehicles that had a headlight repaired during the time period in question," Detective Brondyn confirmed. "We also just secured a laptop hidden behind a concealed wall panel in the staff lunch room at the café."

"My family papers?" Bertie asked, a hopeful gleam in his eye.

"A file containing scanned copies of your family papers is on that laptop and we can confirm the file was uploaded to the internet. Finding the recipient is proving to be quite the challenging task." Detective Brondyn looked at him in all seriousness.

"Do you know the locals who committed the robbery at Scotford?" I asked.

Constable Snowdrop nodded.

"Did you arrest them?"

"Not yet. We're gathering a bit more evidence first," Detective Brondyn said. "Don't worry. We've got them under round the clock surveillance. It's going well, thanks to help from United States law enforcement."

"How so?" Ewan asked.

"As it turns out, they've also been tracking the same two men for a string of big prize, big house robberies over in the Hamptons in New York. We shared information and got the win through teamwork."

"That's wonderful news," Bertie said. "Now about the confidentiality of my family papers–"

Detective Brondyn got super serious. "And that's where things get tricky."

"Who has seen my files?" Bertie asked.

"A US law enforcement official. Jason Raymond, out of Boston."

Bertie's face went white as a ghost. He clutched the edge of the table for support. "Jason Raymond?"

Detective Brondyn continued. "Jason's apparently been tracking these guys for a while. He leads the East Coast cybercrime unit. He took a real personal interest in the case."

"I would expect no less from him," Bertie said with a gulp. "What an amazing turn of events."

Chapter 25

Front Parlor, Scotford Castle. Two Days Later.

A tall, capable-looking man strode up the path alongside a twenty-ish blond woman. The man wore an elegant sports jacket and trousers; she was in a modest floral print dress. Smiles were on their faces, yet one noticed a little bit of trepidation with each step they took. The man reached the door first and poked his head inside. "Your Grace?"

Bertie saw them arrive the moment they stepped out of the Scotford estate sedan. My good friend stood up, and it was the first time I'd ever seen his diplomatic façade look a bit fragile.

Ewan and I hung back, giving Bertie space. He'd asked us to be present, in case things went slightly awry. Honestly, I didn't see how they could. Bertie was one of the nicest people on the planet and come what may, his natural charisma and good nature would win the day.

Bertie strode forward to the doorway. He extended his hand to the visitors. "Jason Raymond?"

The man responded and extended his right hand. "Yes, pleased to meet you." He moved aside to let the blond woman into the room with them. She stepped forward, offering a polite, yet slightly nervous smile. Bertie and she stared at each other for a moment, sizing each other up.

"I'm Melanie," she said, extending her right hand. Melanie, the daughter Bertie only ever knew through letters and school reports, had every right to be apprehensive.

Bertie brushed away her hand and embraced her in a gentle, somewhat stilted hug. "My dear, dear daughter." Bertie was misty eyed at their reunion. "I never thought this day would come. I was forbidden and–"

"Shush, I'm here now," Melanie said.

They pulled apart.

Bertie shook back to reality. "You're all grown up. The last time I saw you–"

"It's been a long time. My dad–" she halted, realizing her biological father and stepfather were both in the same room.

Bertie and Jason obviously had her best interests in mind, and didn't want awkwardness to spoil this moment.

Bertie continued in his kind tone. "I am so pleased to see you here as such an accomplished young lady. Your university studies, cello mastery and tennis trophies." He looked at her with great pride. "Please allow me to introduce my dear friends, Julie Fincher and Ewan Kilburn. Julie owns and operates Greymore Hall and Ewan has an antiques shop in Plumsden."

Ewan and I stepped forward to shake hands with Bertie's guests, offering them a warm welcome.

"Please join me for brunch in Scotford's dining room," Bertie said, leading us down the hall.

❋❋❋

Dining Room. One Minute Later.

We headed right back to where we started before the fire, wiser and perhaps even a little more jaded now that we'd experienced such devastation and thievery.

We sat down at the vast dining table, each of us with a thousand questions in our minds. Jason and Melanie's eyes roamed around the vast room, taking in the history of the family and all of the accoutrements that went with it.

Bertie, at the head of the table, seized the initiative. "Melanie, this must be a bit overwhelming for you."

Melanie grinned. "The story about you perishing in some horrific ocean surfing accident only rang true until I was about eight years old. I pestered Mom with questions until she finally relented and told me the truth when I was sixteen."

The closest thing to surfing Bertie would ever do was on the internet.

Bertie was surprised. "You've known about me for that long?"

"I knew you were alive and well, living in England. That's about it."

"Nothing about Scotford Castle then?" Bertie asked.

"Nada. Nothing about your being an aristocrat either. I only found out two days ago as we were making last-minute flight plans from Boston to London."

"And Lucy, your mother, how is she?"

"Doing well. Running her own business. She said this was to be my trip. Dad was already involved with the cybercrime work anyways." She reached out for Jason's hand and patted it. "It's a very unusual circumstance, beating crime and reuniting our family in one single trip."

"You do know that when you were a little girl, I flew to Boston and asked your mother to marry me?" Bertie asked.

Melanie nodded.

Bertie looked panicked. "But she said no and it was purely platonic after that, I assure you both," he said, shooting a rapid glance over at Jason.

"Lucy sends her best," Jason said. "And you'll have no worries whatsoever from me."

At this point, Ewan and I pretended to be incredibly interested in the hallmarks of a nearby silver teapot. It didn't really make sense to me why Bertie had either of us involved when he was delving into the dark recesses of his past, something that was so utterly private.

I supposed it was because he trusted Ewan and I, likely also because he wanted us there as a friendly safety net.

Melanie nodded. "Of course. It's sad that it didn't work out for you. However, a big part of me is glad that it didn't, because it means I have a wonderful stepdad in my life." She smiled at Jason, contented.

"Indeed," Bertie said. "Now about the family papers that affect all of us."

Jason broke in. "Bertie, I read over the file, and can assure you there was no exposure to the public. I spent a good many hours investigating the two local thieves and we finally got access to their boss' central data storage. Your files have now been wiped and deleted off every server. The original paperwork is on its way back from South America as we speak."

"South America?" Ewan and I both exclaimed.

"These guys operate from anywhere in the world, the farther away from their target the better. It's simply to preserve their identity and make it difficult to track them down and/or extradite them for legal proceedings," Jason explained. "We've worked long and hard to develop relationships with multiple law enforcement agencies across the world to try and bring these particular people to justice. It was a complete fluke that your local robbery provided us with the needed connection."

"I was shocked at their brazen attempt to sell our confidential information," Bertie said.

"For sure. From what we know, the local thieves set up with a fence in the next county to move the stolen goods. That fence knew someone who knew the guy in South America who wanted to ransom your—our—private family information." Jason smiled and pushed a box across the table towards Bertie. "Your stolen family jewelry, from the fence."

Bertie's eyes lit up with joy as he looked upon the missing gems from his family heirloom collection. No longer would he be shamed at having lost them on his watch. Collected over centuries, they were meant to be part of the family estate forever.

"Thank you so much. My title will always make me a target, I suppose." Bertie said.

"I'm afraid so, no two ways around it," Jason said. "We've recovered the rest of the stolen goods too, delivery scheduled soon, once we've got the fingerprint dust removed."

Bertie looked at Melanie. "My dear, what do you make of all this?"

She shrugged. "It's not what I expected. I thought maybe you were some mild-mannered accountant living in a rowhouse, commuting into Manchester each day for work. I had no idea my biological father lived in a castle and was a Duke."

Bertie scoffed. "A Duke who must keep the castle doors open to the public to fund new carpets and roofs–"

I grinned. "Plus someone who takes great pride in his mango chutney products."

"Mango chutney?" Melanie looked confused.

Bertie leaned back in his chair, much more relaxed now that we were on a subject near and dear to his heart. "You see, it all started when our kitchen garden had an overabundant tomato crop one year …"

✳✳✳

Scotford Castle Grounds. Late Afternoon.

After a delightful brunch—Scotford's chefs were true culinary experts—Bertie offered to give Melanie and Jason a personal tour of the estate. Ewan and I tagged along at Bertie's insistence. Everything was going swimmingly well until Melanie set eyes upon two lone figures trudging out in the back field. She watched as the pair worked, heads down, equipment scanning the ground.

"Who are those two people?" she asked me as Bertie, Ewan and Jason stood off to the side discussing robbery case logistics.

"Ah, yes. Ozzie and Timmy. Our local metal detectorists," I answered.

"Are they looking for old coins and brooches, things like that?"

"Yes, and they've done quite well so far," I said in a bright voice. "Gold ingots plus an alchemy laboratory."

Melanie's brow furrowed. "As in old chemistry?"

"Er, yes. Something like that," I said. "Those two are quite eccentric, so bear that in mind if you dare step into their purvey."

Melanie cocked an eyebrow at me. "My biological father's greatest passion is his mango chutney sales routine. I think I can handle a couple of metal detectorists."

I smiled back at her. "Fair enough."

"You're a good friend of Bertie's, thank you," she said. "Are you and he, you know ...?" She gave me a wink.

"Oh good grief, no. I'm his tenant and resident artist. Bertie and I are just good friends. We go way back to my beloved Aunt Edwina's time. I'm actually Ewan's girlfriend."

Melanie nodded. "I get it. Ewan's pretty easy on the eyes."

"Yes, and much more my age bracket," I said.

"Oh, there's something about an older man that's quite attractive," Melanie said.

I slung an arm around her. "Before you arrived, we were quite nervous at how this family reunion would affect you. Seeing as you're so confident here today, well, it lets us know that however this all turns out, you'll be just fine in life."

"It's all good," she said, starting to make tracks towards the barley field with me. "Now is that man the same Ozzie who has family connections to a candy store?"

"Oh, where to begin ..." I started as I waved over Ozzie and Timmy.

Chapter 26

———

Julie's Home. One Week Later. 7:00 p.m.

The Easter Egg chairs sold for £645,000, not bad for a set of forgeries. It astonished me that the forgeries were worth more than the pieces created by the original furniture maker.

"The forgeries are extra-valuable because of the expert craftsmanship employed, plus the fact that there is now a well-established, devious aristocrat behind the lineup," Ewan said as I brought him a cup of cocoa. We sat together on the sofa watching television. The news was full of the various bits of drama and negativity one expected on the television these days.

"It's the 'je ne sais quoi' factor," I said.

"The aristocratic mystique," he countered. "At least Bertie can afford his new carpets now," Ewan said.

"He's decided to hang the painting of the Old Duke and all his apprentices in front of the rebuilt hearth. The room is being turned into a gallery celebrating apprenticeships and skilled trades."

"That's a brilliant idea. There's lots of work for people who like using their hands to create beautiful things," Ewan said.

"I have a new watercolor I'm working on, but don't tell Bertie. It's of Melanie. I used a photo he took of her while we were touring Scotford."

"That sounds like a wonderful present. It'll remind him that he's not all alone in this world."

"Right now he's trying to convince her to stay a bit longer this side of the pond, extend their family reunion a bit. Bertie wants to be part of her life and she's game. They just need to take it day by day," I said.

Ewan nodded. "It's a lot to take in, all these new family discoveries and bonds."

"Speaking of which, are you going to let me help you trace your family?" I asked. "We have a lot of resources at GGRS to help you."

Ewan sighed. "Yes, I promised ... I'm just concerned about what we'll dig up."

"What's the worst that could happen? They say 'no' to a reunion?" I asked.

"They could be dead," he retorted.

"Possibly."

"They could have forgotten me."

"Unlikely."

"They might not want to dredge up the past," he said with a hard stare.

"Perhaps." I gave him a quick kiss. "But before we get all gloomy, let's also consider how well things might work out."

"As in they welcome me with open arms and we have pleasant

310

family meals with picnics in the park?" He scoffed. "My family is broken far more than you think."

I looked at him in all seriousness. "Ewan, you only get one chance at this life and each person should make the most of it. Can you at least agree to try?"

He looked at me with the steady eyes and kind expression that I adored. "I will. For you."

I shook my head. "For us."

We embraced and fell back against the sofa.

Two seconds later, a knock on the door interrupted us. We reluctantly broke apart.

Ewan growled. "If it's those two clowns looking for that owl again–"

"I'm sure it's not. They were going back to GGRS to do some research on their latest field find."

I got up to answer the door and found my landlord standing there, looking very apologetic. He held an extra-large gift basket, wrapped in clear cellophane, a bright blue bow on top.

"Bertie?" I said. "Do come in, we're just watching television."

"Thank you. I'll not stay long. Truth be told, I wanted to offer my sincere thanks for all you've done to help me with the rebuilding and getting to the bottom of the Old Duke's forgery business."

"You're very welcome. We were very glad to help," I said.

Bertie handed me the gift basket, chock full of wonderful jars, tins and packets from the Scotford Castle estate shop. It looked like something he'd tossed together quite rapidly on his own, with no mind for the expense. The fancy mango chutney, tinned salmon and caviar gave it away.

"The gift isn't really necessary," I said.

Bertie bristled. "Nonsense. You've been a lifesaver for me over these past few weeks. Both of you."

Ewan came up behind me, rubbing the back of his neck. "Oh, hello Bertie. Everything all right?"

Bertie was in my front hall and saw that Ewan and I were in the middle of a cozy, romantic evening. The red roses and open box of chocolates on the side table kind of gave it away. That, plus the fact that Ewan was hastily rebuttoning his shirt.

"Well, I can see you're both busy–" Bertie started.

Ewan laughed. He was now quite used to odd happenings around my place. "Those forged chairs did awfully well at auction," he said.

"Shockingly so. We're still figuring out what to do with the candelabra situation," Bertie replied.

"Sorry?" I asked.

"I forgot to tell you. I heard from an antiques dealer in Wales who thinks he might have one just like it," Ewan said.

"You lot and your matching sets of antiques!" I said.

"Hello, look at that," Bertie said, gesturing towards the television.

We all watched as our local news program showed the very public arrest of two local men, both ex-convicts, near Plumsden Town Center. Their suspected crime: the Scotford Castle robbery and fire. Constable Snowdrop looked very smug using his shiny new handcuffs on one of the suspects. It was doubtful the handcuffs had ever been used before in our hamlet. For his sake, I hoped Constable Snowdrop remembered where the keys were kept.

Detective Brondyn had the other suspect cuffed, and both law enforcement men walked their prisoners over to a waiting vehicle. Jason Raymond was in the background, watching the proceedings with practiced eyes.

"Isn't that near the Plumsden café?" I asked.

Bertie looked closer at the screen. "Yes, it seems that old habits die hard. And not to spill too much tea, but we figured out how Severs was rendered unconscious during the robbery."

Ewan and I both looked at Bertie with expectant eyes.

"Severs was offered a special coffee as thanks for his help during filming. Now, Severs doesn't drink coffee, so he politely refused."

And?" I prompted.

"Ten minutes passed and they tried again with tea."

"And?"

Bertie grinned. "At that point, Severs grew suspicious and started paying closer attention to the man running the mobile hot beverage truck."

"So what did they do, put a sleeping potion on a powdered donut?" Ewan asked, trying really hard not to laugh.

"They put a clear liquid sleeping draught into Severs' carrot and coriander soup. The laboratory results just came back today."

"That's outrageous," I said.

"Tell that to Severs' elderly mother. She made him a batch of twenty frozen portions a month or so ago, his absolute favorite.

He's crushed that one of them was wasted after only a few spoon-ful's." Bertie shook his head.

"Sounds exactly like what Severs would say. He's not someone usually caught unaware," I said.

"Oh, I'm to blame," Bertie continued, "the poor man was rushed off his feet trying to keep an eye on Scotford's treasures during film-ing. He recommended hiring more temporary security staff than I'd budgeted for and well, I ended up paying a heavy price for not heeding his advice."

"Without the fire, you never would have uncovered the Old Duke's mysterious past," I said.

"Nor gained auction proceeds out of £645,000 in sales," Ewan added.

Bertie sighed. "True, my friends, very true." He refocused on the opened, abandoned box of chocolates. "And on that note, I shall bid you good night."

As Bertie turned to leave, I put a soft hand on his forearm. "Good luck with Melanie. You have a lot of catching up to do."

❈❈❈

GGRS. Next Morning.

"It all came down to the gold dust we found in the laboratory's crucible," Gertie said.

"The gold ingots Ozzie found were part of an inventory used by the Old Duke to melt down and cast his cupid figurines," Maude added.

I looked outside the front window and saw a courier van approach the front entrance.

Maude saw it too. "Oh good. He's likely bringing the draft indenture layouts for Scotford's new visitors' exhibit," Maude said.

"Excellent."

"Bertie's got lots to work with," Maude replied. "The portrait of the Old Duke and all his apprentices, their indentures, their samplers and replicas of the–"

"Replicas?" Then I laughed. "We're making replicas of forgeries. There's something hilarious about that task."

Gertie snorted. "The gold cupids will all be made of pyrite."

"Fool's gold," Candace called out from computer carrell number two. She was in today for a bit of family history research while her mother continued adding pages to her memoir manuscript at home.

"At least we are assured that the exhibit will be precious and everlasting," Maude said. "It's commendable Bertie has created replicas of the fragile, original documents to share with the public. It's such a wonderful social history resource. Thousands will benefit from the education Bertie is offering."

"Fine craftsmanship deserves to be better understood and appreciated in the modern world," I said, "and GGRS is happy to support those efforts."

The courier was now at the information desk. He had not one but two delivery slips for me to sign. The draft exhibit pages package was easy to process. I put the envelope on the desk for Maude to look at later. The second item was a bit more complicated. I was asked to go outside and supervise the unloading of a large, flat, wooden crate. It had bumper pads on each side, then thick layers of bubble wrap over the top. There was a solitary gold envelope attached to the package, labeled with my name.

I removed it from the package and opened it. At the top, I saw the Scotford Castle estate logo. I read:

*Thank you for the loan. Now it's time for this grand lady
to come home.
Cheers, Bertie*

I knew exactly what the package contained and why it was wrapped so carefully.

Fifteen minutes later, we'd unpacked the portrait of dear Aunt Edwina and hung it back up in the blank space on our manor house's wall.

It was time for family to come home.

Chapter 27

Scotford Castle Grounds. Later That Summer.

Bertie did his family estate proud, hosting a fabulous outdoor event to thank the community for its help restoring Scotford Castle to her former glory. We were all in for a treat this afternoon as none other than Plumsden's own favorite solicitor Fred Todling had rallied his team for a musical/theatrical ballet performance.

And what a performance it promised to be: an upbeat, modern day production with a medley of pop hits playing as lithe dancers, costumed as apprentices and masters, moved about the stage. Gertie and Fred had put their heads together to come up with this unique musical interpretation of genealogy and social history. Regardless of whether the show was good or bad, smiles would be on the faces of our attendees. Our initial goal was to celebrate our community's generous spirit and ability to pitch in when the chips were down. Oakhurst and Plumsden responded beautifully with about four hundred people sitting on the lawn.

A plethora of tartan car blankets, collapsible beach chairs with cupholders and seat cushions intermingled with each other across the grass. Unsteady toddlers with thickly-padded, diapered bottoms cruised in and around their immediate family's vicinity, never straying too far from a parent's side. Local food trucks surrounded the area, making for a wide variety of meal and snack choices. The theater technicians had erected a portable raised stage, complete with curtains on all four sides, plus space for the live string quartet down in front. The performance was broadcast on the local TV channel to ensure those unable to attend, either due to hospitalization, immobility or scheduling, could also enjoy the performance.

Fred started us out with a full on, wide open mouth into the camera lens. He'd ruffled up his hair with gel to look like a hip pop star and wore a tight, shiny-copper buttoned shirt to complete the look. He was sure to either gain clients or lose them; there was likely no in-between. I made a mental note to refer him to Gertie who had experienced her own viral moment a while back when her pub karaoke singing made the global rounds on social media.

A set of spotlights came on overhead and we were ready to begin. I caught a glimpse of the Major and Abbyleigh at the front, near the stage. They looked cozy and comfortable together, just as it should be with loved ones. Ewan—dear Ewan—strode towards me, fleece blanket tucked under his arm and a paper sack of food in the opposite hand. He was a keeper.

A hush fell over the crowd as the narrator—this time it was Gertie—came out on stage. She was dressed as a bumblebee and had insisted on lurid yellow and black striped eyeshadow to complete the effect. Her transparent net wings bobbed up and down as she spoke. Gertie introduced the dancers and we were subsequently treated to a well-acted, enthusiastically danced story depicting the community coming to rescue Scotford Castle during the fire. The fire was depicted with strips of yellow, orange and red gauzy material blown upwards in ripples by a hidden wind machine. All the dancers acted as community members arriving to help carry treasures out of the castle in her time of need. Of course, they used props. There was no way dear Aunt Edwina's portrait would be subjected to a second unceremonious exit from its safe place on the wall.

Two of the dancers were dressed up as the thieves and selected members of the audience were pre-chosen to pelt them with prop soft toy tomatoes and cabbages. The dancers did look hilarious in their overdone cat burglar costumes. As they tiptoed across the stage, one of them held a huge paste emerald and diamond necklace and the other a reproduction portrait of Aunt Edwina. I could only imagine what she would think of all the shenanigans here at Scotford Castle today.

And the bumblebee costume's meaning? Well, it was the performance's tribute to Mother Nature, thanking her for not raining as we got the antiques, books and other treasures sorted outside, into barns, vehicles and underneath the disaster response firm's waterproof tents. All in all, the amateur production was an absolute triumph.

"This is truly wonderful to see," Bertie said, standing over Ewan and I at the back of the crowd.

I reached up for my friend's hand. "Everyone is here to support you, Bertie. Their rapid downing of tools when the fire broke out is testament to that fact. Everything you've done for the community over the decades: the sports team sponsorships, the school tours, hosting seniors' knitting bees and teas ... it all counts. It's all recognized here today."

"I'm quite chuffed," Bertie said, a pleased look on his face.

"And now we come to the sketchy part," I said, issuing a slightly uncomfortable grin.

"Sketchy?" Melanie asked as she walked up to us and sat down beside me.

"Watch," I said.

Ewan and Bertie both held their breath.

Gertie the bumblebee and Fred, our slightly sweaty pop star, were now on stage together.

"Oh no. She's actually going to sing," I said in a worried voice as my effervescent cousin approached the microphone.

"Can't bet against you on that one," Ewan said.

Gertie leaned in and started her vocals. It began all right, actually not bad at all. Her cover of a current pop single resounded with the crowd. People actually started to get up and dance on the vast lawn.

"Is she professionally trained?" Melanie asked.

"Church choir," I responded, amazed at what I was hearing. "I do recall her saying that she and Fred did a lot of rehearsing."

Gone were the high-pitched shrieks and unsteady high notes.

Gone were the creaky melodies and humming to cover the spots where she forgot the lyrics.

In essence, Gertie was doing a fabulous job.

Fred joined her at the microphone and they turned it into a duet, the kind that reminded the audience of times where two pop stars got together and created a beautiful love song.

Not that Gertie had designs on Fred.

Not that Fred had designs on Gertie.

No, this was just two performers lost in their on-stage moment and doing one heck of an impressive job. They didn't do it for the applause. They were simply sharing their talents for the sheer delight of bringing joy to the community. And when their duet was over, it took three standing ovations before the audience allowed them to leave the stage.

I caught up with Gertie backstage in her small dressing room inside a hefty trailer on wheels. Once again, her eyeshadow had run into the creases of her eyelids. Her bumblebee costume wings were limp after all her strutting about onstage. None of it mattered. What mattered was that Gertie had tried. She'd made people smile. She'd demonstrated how lots of practice led to a great performance.

After all we'd been through with recent events and family history surprises, this unforgettable, special day was a welcome moment of celebration. It was everything our hard-working, kind community members deserved to enjoy … together.

Epilogue

———

It was a coffee table book to end all coffee table books. It was also an instant bestseller in the estate's gift shop and at various online retailers. Much more than a glorious recollection of Scotford Castle history and current treasures collection, it actually showed all the lumps, bumps, warts and stains that were part of running a large country estate owned by a member of the peerage. It was usual to have the glamor shots of the estate, both inside the stately castle and outside on the grounds. There would be a couple of mandatory photos of the current peer, leaning against a wood-paneled wall, looking ever so relaxed and posh as he went about his daily business of running the estate. Normally, readers would then delve into chapters about the library, dining room, china collection, furniture history, car collection ... and end with a few sporty pictures of a loyal golden Labrador walking along a forested path with its owner.

Bertie's coffee table book was different, and radically so. He was bound and determined to show life as it really was for him and included photographic proof. Sure, he included the requisite beauty shots. Yet, he started with the not-so-glamorous new boiler installed seven years ago. We saw photos of window washing, carpet cleaning, wood floor replacements, the broken hearth ... and unplugging the stables drain that got plugged with manure one crisp Boxing Day morning. The film crew was there, along with all us locals dressed in fancy costumes. Fred's warm up vocals, accentuated by his singing a pop song with seemingly elastic lips, were captured in a vivacious photo that would be talked about until the cows came home. The solicitor's embarrassment was sufficiently mitigated, however, by the photo on the opposite page showing him onstage, looking out at a standing ovation while he was presented with the community spirit award from the Mayor of Plumsden.

The charred embers after the fire were on full display, showing the devastation inside Scotford Castle. There was even a half page of the coroner's report showing the line where it was solemnly declared that the Old Duke's coffin was full of stones and gravel, thus making his final resting place an unsolved mystery. The last page of the book was a nighttime photo of Timmy's rare owl perched on a lamppost right near the front entrance to the estate. The dusky light focused the lens on the magnificent owl's wide, yellow eyes, giving the book an incredible concluding image.

All these unique details were part of the book because from the embers rose a rebuilt castle. The bedrock was the wonderful community surrounding it. Scotford Castle welcomed tourists, locals and visiting dignitaries with ease. Ancestors, genealogy, families and social history were all celebrated. My dear friend Bertie made it so and that sincerely warmed the cockles of my heart.

THE END

Thank you for reading!
Please leave an online review and/or
rating at your retailer and book club of choice.

ACKNOWLEDGMENTS

Sincere thanks to beta readers extraordinaire Penny, Brenda and Val. You are always so willing and can be counted upon for wonderful suggestions. Thank you so much for your time, patience and enthusiasm.

Thanks also to Gwyn Flowers at GKS Creative for design work. You are a very talented lady.

Wolf Wenzel: once again, you created a fabulous cover. After all these years, I'll bet you never expected to draw a castle on fire, two thieves on the run plus an unlikely metal detectorist. Well done.

Finally, to all the lovely readers who are fans of the Aunt Edwina series. Thank you for your support, kind comments and reviews. Thank you for being on this writing journey with me.

About the Author

Lynne Christensen is a world traveler who enjoys visiting museums and archives. She grew up roaming around graveyards in Europe with her genealogy-loving parents in search of elusive ancestors. A lifelong learner, she earned both Master of Business Administration and Bachelor of Commerce degrees plus has multiple years of experience in marketing and corporate communications. Her writing is published in numerous magazine articles, case studies, advertisements and technical manuals. She lives on the West Coast of Canada in a house full of fascinating books.

Northleo
WRITING INC.

www.lynnechristensen.com